Bheja Fry

Praise for the Book

'Sharp as a scalpel and warm as a bedside conversation, *Bheja Fry* is a rare book – one that peers into the human brain while gently exposing the human heart.' – *Boman Irani*

'Reading Mazda Turel makes you feel that one should have 2B (brain and back) issues so that not only can he cure you but also make you laugh even while he is doing so.' – *Sunil Gavaskar*

'Mazda Turel is the latest entrant to the brilliant Indian doctor-writer pantheon. A master storyteller, his writing is as incisive as his knife. A fascinating look inside the human brain that is also entertaining and funny as only a "mad bawaji" can be. I highly recommend this book to anyone who has a brain.' – *Sooni Taraporevala*

Bheja Fry

Heartfelt Stories From a Neurosurgeon's Clinic

Dr Mazda Turel

juggernaut

JUGGERNAUT BOOKS
C-I-128, First Floor, Sangam Vihar, Near Holi Chowk,
New Delhi 110080, India

First published by Juggernaut Books 2026

10 9 8 7 6 5 4 3 2

P-ISBN: 9789353458812
E-ISBN: 9789353455453

Typeset in Adobe Caslon Pro

Printed at Thomson Press India Ltd

To all my patients, who survived in spite of me.
To all my family and friends, who keep masquerading as patients.

Contents

Introduction

VEGAS ⟶ VELLORE

A neurosurgeon lives at the intersection of precision and unpredictability. We work in millimetres and live in uncertainties. We approach the body through the scalp, skull, spine, nerves and blood vessels – but what we really trespass upon is identity, memory, language, fear and hope.

People often ask what we do. The simplest answer is that we operate on the nervous system. The more dramatic answer is that we are entrusted with the wiring of human existence. We remove tumours that threaten memory; clip aneurysms that could erase a lifetime in a heartbeat; drain blood that steals speech, balance or the self; fix fractures that paralyse; sit with families who are about to lose someone they love and occasionally, against biology, odds and common sense, we bring people back to life – however pompous that may sound.

The nervous system does not merely control movement or sensation. It governs breath and beat, love and longing, gladness and grief, appetite and addiction, faith and fear. It is the conductor, archivist, tyrant, poet and saboteur. It can heal, deceive, improvise, rebel and surrender – sometimes all within a single hour.

To work in neuroscience is to watch biology exemplify philosophy in real time. A man awakens after surgery and remembers every detail of his childhood but not his daughter's wedding.

A woman, paralysed from the neck down, laughs before she cries. A tumour distorts a personality and, when removed, restores a marriage. A haemorrhage turns a professor into a child who must learn to walk again.

In the clinic, in the operating room and in the corridors outside ICUs, we see the entire spectrum of human emotions play out at close range: terror, denial, doubt, courage, fury, tenderness, numbness. The brain has a way of revealing people to themselves and to others. Neurosurgery is not merely a speciality; it is also a vantage point from which one can see what it means to be human.

Medicine is full of stories. And like all good stories, it contains dichotomies: triumph and loss, humour and tragedy, absurdity and awe. There are days when the heart sinks, days when it soars and days when both happen before breakfast. You learn that no scan captures the battle inside a waiting room. That no monitor records a mother's prayer. That healing is not only anatomical but relational, emotional, spiritual, occasionally chaotic and frequently mysterious.

My lifelong tryst with my vocation began when I was a kid, watching my father, also a neurosurgeon, operate with an artist's patience. I would sit beside him while he watched his surgical videos at night, sipping a single malt and explaining anatomy with the reverence of a man analysing constellations. By the time I was eight, I had decided that I too wanted to work on the brain and the spine, though I would later discover that it was not always as glamorous as childhood imagination suggested.

My sojourn in medical school began at Grant Medical College in Mumbai. Since I had secured admission without us needing to sell any family jewellery or property, my parents allowed a friend and I to backpack across the US. They felt that this small act of independence deserved an act of indulgence. So there we were. Caesars Palace, Las Vegas. Three in the morning. Two medical students in a city that has all kinds of gambling devices: dice, roulette, slot machines and wedding chapels. The casino's age limit was 21 and we were 18, but we had come prepared. We had fake identity cards from the Rutgers University in New Jersey, had grown out our freshly sprouted facial hair and walked as if we had boils in our armpits. Nobody doubted us. It was an advantage that my friend was 130 kg at the time, which is considered average American size.

As I said, I had wanted to become a neurosurgeon since childhood, but that night in Vegas, between neon lights and naughty nightclubs, I realized that the brain may only be my second favourite organ. After six weeks of whirlwind travel, we returned home with a mild refractive error from staring too long at things one does not speak about in polite company.

Grant was legendary. It seemed every doctor of repute had either studied there or, at the very least, passed through the building. Pioneering malaria research had been conducted within those walls. The Bombay blood group had been discovered here. Waldemar Haffkine had worked on the plague vaccine in the very pharmacology hall in which generations of students slept dutifully through lectures, unaware that history had once sat upright in their seats. Robert Koch had conducted research on cholera in our labs. Vandyke Carter, spirochetes, relapsing fever – the list went on. Even the dean of our rival college had trained at Grant. We were a modest institution, except when it came to boasting.

In my five years there, this tradition of significant discoveries continued. The canteen acquired more items than the menu could accommodate. The boys' common room stayed open longer than officially permitted. Couples discovered and colonized new architectural spaces. The college festival was stretched from four days to one glorious week. Attendance remained theoretical, but patient care was sacred. We might have skipped classes, but we never skipped a ward round. Our shoes may have appeared worn out, but our conscience was polished.

We tossed our caps at the oath ceremony inside the 150-year-old anatomy hall, every wooden bench holding not just students but also memory and lineage. Our teachers taught us lessons beyond anatomy and physiology: do more than care, help; do more than belong, participate; do more than forgive, forget. They shaped our moral vertebrae before we ever touched a spine.

And then I got the opportunity to enrol at the Christian Medical College (CMC) in Vellore. I arrived on 15 August 2005 with the confidence of a man who thought independence was a constitutional right and not a refundable deposit. Before I even entered the city, my freedom was quietly taken away.

I was a pre-resident. That meant a year of working, proving yourself and studying for the entrance exam that would decide whether you would be accepted into or discarded from the residency programme like expired medication. It was also, as I was gently informed, one of the ways the system prevented suicides in young surgeons. Neurosurgery does not merely test intelligence; it also tests stamina, faith, insomnia, bone marrow and, occasionally, sanity.

The hostel room I was assigned that afternoon looked like the aftermath of a failed revolution. Beer bottles strewn like fallen soldiers. Cigarette packets formed archaeological layers. The bathroom was a sociological study in neglect. The toothbrush and toilet brush looked interchangeable except for philosophical differences. The smell suggested that something had died, been resurrected and died again. I shut the door, said a quiet prayer for whoever had lived there and went looking for a safer habitat.

Which is how I ended up at a modest lodge across the hospital. From my third-floor window, I could see the hospital standing tall with a cross on its chest, stoic and eternal. My room had granite tiles pretending to be marble, a bed with ironed white sheets, a ceiling of odd angles and a television with only Tamil channels. The toilet did have provision for hot and cold water but only in terms of colour coding. I bought a cream-coloured plastic chair and an olive-green study table and declared it my penthouse. The terrace outside served both as a party space and a laundry museum. A massive water tank presided over my life like a benevolent deity, from where the entire city of Vellore spread itself out like a patient waiting to be examined.

Saajan, the manager, was a man of deep hospitality and questionable toasting skills. I learnt that every shade of brown bread represents a philosophical evolution of burnt toast. My *dhobi* [laundryman] was efficient in ways I did not anticipate: black underwear turned grey, jeans became pyjamas, full sleeves became half sleeves and pants were retired as capris. With two pairs of clothes, I lived an unexpectedly varied and adventurous life. A busy, noisy street with numerous autorickshaws – whose drivers either looked like Rajinikanth or proudly displayed his photo on their vehicle – separated my heritage structure from the hospital. Everything was available in an instant, though it took me a lifetime to convey my needs.

Gandhi Road was the Las Vegas Strip of Vellore. If Vegas offered temptation, Gandhi Road offered survival. Shops blared Tamil rock music regardless of whether they sold electronics, vegetables or divine salvation. Coconut vendors stood against posters of voluptuous heroines, as if hydration itself required motivation. Sweets glittered under silver foil and flies, guaranteeing a steady hospital inflow. Armani shirts could be purchased for ₹60, and I dutifully bought souvenirs for my friends, because love must be economical.

Work was relentless. Residency, someone told me, is a dog's life. Divorces matured like complication rates. One registrar looked like he had been born tired. Another prescribed antidepressants to his patients and took some himself in solidarity. We all walked fast and looked worried in order to appear indispensable.

Unfortunately, despite all my hard work, I failed my entrance exam the first time around, but quickly learnt to cremate disappointment instead of embalming it. I stayed back another year. I studied harder. 'Better is always possible,' says bestselling author, American surgeon and public health researcher Atul Gawande. 'It does not take genius. It takes diligence. It takes moral clarity. It takes ingenuity. And above all, it takes a willingness to try.' I passed the second time and, for the first and perhaps only time in my life, came first. I wonder if patients ever consider that half the doctors in the world graduate from the bottom half of their class.

Dr Jacob Chandy's presence lingered in Vellore like a quiet benediction. The father of neurosurgery in India, he had passed away earlier that year at the age of 97, and soon after I joined, the hospital decided to honour his memory with the Jacob Chandy Oration – a day-long meeting where people travelled from across the country to celebrate the man and his legacy. He founded the first department of neurological sciences in India at CMC, Vellore, in 1949, and went on to become the founding president of the Neurological Society of India. What began as a unit of neurology and neurosurgery eventually grew to include neurophysiology, neurochemistry, neuropathology and neuroradiology – like an orchestra slowly gathering its sections until the music felt complete.

Chandy had many offers when he returned from Montreal and Chicago, where he studied, but he chose Vellore for its values: institutional work, shared purpose and service to those who could not afford care. It was not glamorous and it was certainly not lucrative, but it was meaningful. For his contributions to the neurological sciences in patient care, education and research, he was awarded the Padma Bhushan in 1964.

A multitude of his students were present at the oration that day, telling stories about him, because none of his contemporaries were alive anymore. His son spoke about how he first saw his father when he was five, because Chandy had left for training in America while his wife was pregnant. It was a reminder of a generation that had built institutions with grit, sacrifice and very little technology, at a time when the craft was closer to faith than science. For over 12 hours, speakers shared memories while we were served breakfast, lunch, snacks, high tea and dinner in sequence. I was deeply inspired, and a little overwhelmed. I promised myself that one day I too would be celebrated, but with a fame modest enough that people could wind up their tributes by lunchtime.

Until that happened, I had a residency to complete. Sleep was a rumour. One night, around three in the morning, I drilled my first burr hole. The skull powdered softly, the dura turned a poetic shade of blue from the underlying blood and when the clot was released, the brain rose like a relieved sigh. It was like watching the air return to the lungs of someone who had been underwater for a while. And right away, the patient promptly woke up and abused us with astonishing linguistic range – which in my culture, and, as I later learnt, even in Tamil Nadu, is a reassuring sign of neurological recovery.

The time had come to shift from my modest penthouse into MIQ, the Men's Intern Quarters at CMC. After bribing the superintendent with a box of sweets, I secured a room on the top floor, the only level where we could install our own window air conditioners. Without one, the Vellore heat could melt bone; though, to be fair, the volcano within us was always active anyway.

The room itself was a familiar 12-ft by 12-ft hovel: cracked walls, a stone floor that had lived several lives, broken furniture and a toilet that looked like it had seen combat. But this time, there was no retreating. I realized that creativity, combined with my parents' bank balance, could work miracles. I had the toilet scrubbed with acid, whitewashed the walls, polished the furniture and then slowly populated the space with hope – a fridge, an AC, a television and a geyser to begin with.

Cool rugs covered stained floors, a giant collage of a hundred beloved faces masked the cracks on the wall and the old wooden windows were replaced with glass panes through which I could watch the mountains stretch awake each morning. A bamboo plant sat in a corner, doing double duty as greenery and feng shui. A foam mattress was placed on the bed, a comforter was brought in from Mumbai and tiny plastic jars of cashews, chocolates and other dry fruits started filling the corners like small emotional investments. Cheese and energy drinks rotated briskly through the fridge. And just like that, I created my own little luxury apartment – only, this time, I had earned it with equal parts effort, humour and stubborn survival instinct.

Training in neurosurgery in India means working 20, even 24, hours a day in suboptimal conditions, sacrificing family, friends and a four-letter word that also starts with 'F': food. A residency in the field also serves as the best contraceptive. Years passed in exhaustion and grace. We were constantly between 12 and 14 on the Glasgow Coma Scale, which was appropriate because most of us functioned in moderate confusion; for reference, a completely coherent person has a score of 15. But hardship has a strange alchemy. It chisels judgement. It sharpens instinct. It replaces arrogance with humility. It teaches you to ask every day, 'Am I doing the right thing for this patient?'

Life became a blend of sterility and chaos, of prayers whispered under masks, of midnight coffee and early morning despair, of triumphs that felt like grace and losses that lingered like scars. I trained for five years, taught as an assistant professor for two and received a medal named after the man who had pioneered the field in India with courage and faith. I then travelled to Toronto, Chicago and Shanghai over the next three years for advanced fellowships, finally returning home to Mumbai to begin again.

Along the way, I began to encounter not just patients but also stories – stories that stayed with me even after the patients were discharged. A tumour that rewrote a family. A fracture that repaired a marriage. A child with epilepsy who taught us resilience. A man who returned from the brink and changed the way we thought about faith. A woman who laughed her way through tragedy because she did not know any other way to live. Neurosurgery became the language through which I learnt to read the world. And eventually, almost accidentally, it became the language through which I began to write.

I did not set out to write a book. I set out to survive Sundays.

Seven years ago, Tinaz Nooshian, the then editor-in-chief of *Mid-Day*, decided it might be a good idea for me to write a newspaper column to humanize doctors and enthuse the common man with medical stories of grit, gumption and grace. Somewhere along the way, people began reading them. Worse, they began remembering them and urging for me to publish them, and Juggernaut obliged.

I wrote them in between surgeries, on planes, in airport lounges and at home after I put my daughters to bed. I wrote them after rewarding days in the operating room and after days that refused to leave me alone at night. I wrote them because neurosurgery is full of stories, and in stories, endings matter.

I have written about tumours and tenderness, aneurysms and affection, fractures and forgiveness, inflammation and intimacy. I have written about the people we save and the people who save us. I have written about victories that felt undeserved and failures that taught me more than success ever could.

The brain, for all its brilliance, is a poorly behaved organ. It forgets, it lies, it panics, it dreams and, occasionally, it sabotages its owner. We celebrate it as the seat of intelligence and consciousness but spend most of our lives trying to manage its moods. As a neurosurgeon, I get to look at it up close. As a writer, I get to look at what it does to us.

These essays are not about being clever. They are about being human in places where humanity is often overwhelmed by machines, monitors and numbers. They are about the moments that do not make it into medical textbooks: the jokes cracked before administering anaesthesia, the silences after bad news, the families who wait, the patients who surprise you and the ones who never leave you even after they are gone. They are about how medicine can be both funny and tragic at the same time.

In all these stories, I've honoured the indestructible force of the human spirit, but we've also learnt that nature has the final word. In an attempt to provide the reader with a glimpse into the life of a surgeon, I've shared some deeply personal experiences – the highs, the lows, the resilience of families, the determination of doctors and the dissonance of nature. I've laid bare what it means to lose patients you care for with savage tenacity and the exuberance of saving lives that were deemed impossible to survive. I believe these narratives have allowed people an honest entry into a world of medicine about which they often have so many preposterous presumptions.

Diseases have a way of lacerating families and pulverizing dreams. The ongoing challenge in life as a surgeon is how to maintain outward confidence and stoicism in the face of internal cataclysm and upheaval. How to achieve an inner stillness amidst extraneous cacophony. How to make loss a reason to live more deeply.

There is one truth that neurosurgery teaches you over and over again: medicine is not a linear science but a landscape of uncertainties. We work with scans, algorithms, experience and reason, yet so much of what unfolds on the operating table lies beyond prediction. Two patients may have the same diagnosis, the same anatomy, the same surgery – one walks out of the hospital, the other never wakes up. A minor procedure spirals into catastrophe, while a hopeless case returns from the brink and asks for tea. You begin your career believing that outcomes are earned, that success is a reward for skill and diligence; you grow older and realize that biology has its own moral code. Standing so close to life and death has not made me arrogant about understanding science, it has made me reverent towards the unknown. Neurosurgery humbles you into accepting that we are not masters of fate, only its participants. And somewhere in these mysteries – in the inexplicable recoveries, in the unanswerable losses – lies the deeper reason I write, which is that the brain does not merely challenge our knowledge; it also deepens our awe.

If this book has a philosophy, it is a simple one: medicine is an art and a science practised by people on people. No algorithm can replace presence of the doctor. No machine can measure hope. And no surgeon, however skilled, operates alone. You do not need to understand anatomy to read this book. You only need to have lived in a body, worried about your health, loved someone who was unwell or sat in a waiting room pretending not to be afraid. In other words, you need to be alive.

Somewhere between Vegas and Vellore, I realized that the nervous system is not only an organ system but a way of looking at life. It governs every movement and memory, and it governs longing, imagination, pain, love, grief, ego and meaning. To work with it is to witness the fragility and magnificence of being alive. To write about it is to attempt, however imperfectly, to honour that privilege.

This book is called *Bheja Fry* because that is what life does to us eventually. It heats us up, stirs us around and leaves us a little scrambled. But if you cook it long enough with care, and with the right amount of spice, it can still taste surprisingly good.

Section 1

CONSULTING ROOM CONFESSIONS

These are stories from the small rectangular room where patients walk in with illnesses – and unpack entire lives instead. Here, fear comes wrapped in humour, grief arrives with bravado and medicine becomes equal parts diagnosis, listening and gentle negotiation. These are encounters had across the table, where conversation heals as much as surgery ever can. These essays explore the art of listening to symptoms, to silences and to the quivering space between what a patient says and what they mean – reminding us that sometimes the hardest surgery is the one performed on pride.

Food for Thought

'Good evening, Doctor *Saab*!' Jayesh Bhai walked in with his wife to meet me. The couple were in their mid-fifties and seemed pretty jovial. He had a round face that sat atop an even rounder torso. The buttons of his bright yellow shirt were struggling to keep its two halves together. Through two of those buttons, his navel looked like his third eye, staring me in the face. Sensing my unwavering gaze at his centre of mystical enlightenment, his wife remarked, 'He loves to eat,' which I acknowledged because I do too. 'And I love to cook for him,' she continued dotingly.

It was of little concern to them that Jayesh Bhai had a brain tumour. 'I was having headaches and my GP asked me to do an MRI. He said he had heard a lecture of yours where you mentioned that people with persistent headaches should get an MRI,' he explained. I peered through the scan to note it was a benign tumour arising from the pituitary stalk and pressing against his hypothalamus – the control centre for hunger and satiety, besides a myriad of other functions such as regulating hormones, body temperature, heart rate, blood pressure, thirst, mood, sleep and sex drive. He had no issues with any of the other functions, he clarified, and his wife confirmed. The weight he was putting on had simply been attributed to his love for food. I explained to them that not everyone who lives to eat has a brain tumour, but subtle shifts of patterns should not be neglected. He had put on over 20 kg in the past six months.

'Can I continue to eat *dhokla*, *khandvi* and *undhiyu* before surgery?' he questioned, listing out his favourite food items.

'Of course,' I said without hesitation, 'but we will need to check your hormone and sugar levels,' I cautioned. I detailed a battery of blood investigations and booked an appointment with our endocrinologist, who helped manage such patients perioperatively.

Before leaving, he asked, 'Is it true that you become hot-tempered if you consume too much spicy food?' He smiled at his wife, who shook her head, denying the allegation.

'It's possible,' I said, having read this in a publication.

'I'm telling her to eat more sweets but she's just not listening,' he said, as both of them left the room laughing.

He came back really upset a few days later. 'The endo doctor you sent me to has stopped all my desserts! No chocolate, no cake, no jalebi, no gulab jamun, not even *aam ras* [sweetened mango puree]! Season is coming to an end. What does one eat?' He questioned, disapproving of medical nutrition. 'One day, science will show that sugar is really good for us and the whole medical community will have to eat its words,' he muttered, disgruntled.

'As long as we are eating only words, we won't put on any physical weight,' I punned, only later realizing that the emotional burden of eating one's own words is even heavier.

'Let us quickly get this surgery over with, so that I don't have to deal with all these dietary restrictions,' he told me.

I agreed, adding, 'It's also possible that you might not want to eat as much after the surgery relieves the pressure on your hypothalamus,' and watched his face shrink with dismay.

Patients often ask what foods to avoid after brain or spine surgery, and unless they have a specific medical condition, my answer is always peppered with the sagacity of ancient wisdom:

everything in moderation is okay. I advise them to eat fresh fruits and vegetables, go easy on the carbs and avoid red meat. People wonder if certain foods will affect wound healing or cause a tumour to grow back. They wonder even more if eating too many pizzas, dosas or spring rolls might have caused the tumour in the first place. I also often get asked what foods are good for the brain, and the answer is berries, nuts, green leafy vegetables, avocado, fish and eggs. And, if you're Parsi, eggs on top of eggs. The foods we eat should bring us both health and happiness.

We operated on Jayesh Bhai a few days later. The tumour had a large cyst with golden fluid within it, resembling the crystalline oil his jalebis were fried in. We peeled it off the hypothalamus and the pituitary stalk in the hope of restoring his internal balance.

'Your hospital food is very tasty,' he later proclaimed, sipping on cream of tomato soup, but with his eyes fixated on the pudding next to it.

'Can I eat *pav bhaji* at home?' he asked, before getting discharged. I nodded. 'And a small drink once in a while is okay?' he winked. I granted permission with a big smile.

According to a lot of data, research and science, we are what we eat. But we are also the five people we spend most of our time with. We are the culmination of the experiences of our several lifetimes. We are the ratio of the suffering we caused to the suffering we endured. We are the failures we were unable to fathom and the successes we were able to surpass. We are the hopes we racked up and the sorrows we shared. We are the strings we pulled and the ropes we hung on to. We are how stoically we portray ourselves and also how vulnerable we might choose to be. We are the questions that quench and the answers that ask more questions. We are the ships we sailed in and we are also the ships we saluted from the shore. We are our insight and intuition. We are our hunger and our cravings, our weight gain and our weight loss. We are the stories we tell ourselves. We are all. We are one.

Jayesh Bhai came back three months after surgery for a follow up. He had lost 10 kg. Now he was Jayesh Bhai Jordar. His shirt fit well. The third eye had closed.

'Doctor *Saab*!' he greeted me in his trademark fashion, handing me a box of chocolates. 'Can I eat sweet and sour pickles that may sometimes be spicy also?' I don't know if there was any item on the menu that he hadn't cross-checked with me in our time together.

'Besides human beings, you can eat whatever you want,' I proclaimed with folded hands.

The Real Therapist

Zane walked into the office holding Sanjana's hand, who shuffled in with a bit of a limp. They were a young couple in their forties, but they helped each other settle into their chairs like 80-year-olds do – slowly, gingerly, tenderly. As I directed my gaze towards Sanjana to ask about her problem, she shook her head sideways, pointing her thumb at her husband. 'Don't look at me; he's the patient,' she said, articulately lifting the veil of bias we subconsciously carry within us.

I asked him what the issue was.

'I had an aneurysm that ruptured in June 2020,' he said, a little saliva drooling from the corner of his mouth. His speech was slightly slurred and garbled, with the intonation of someone who was intoxicated. 'They did an operation in Singapore to treat it, but now we've moved back to Mumbai and I need someone to fix back the skull, which they had removed at the time of the operation because of brain swelling,' he explained, taking off his monkey cap to show me the defect over the right side of his head, which caved in like a saucer.

'They tried to place it back nine months after surgery, but it got infected twice and they had to discard it,' Sanjana chipped in, pointing to the scarred areas on his scalp that now looked like a battlefield after the war was over.

I explained how we would have to treat the skin with tissue expanders before we could design a customized titanium plate to refashion his skull, and that that process would take a few months.

'While you're at it, perhaps you could also help me get his life back. He's just not the same person anymore. It's like he's completely checked out. He's physically in the same room, but emotionally or mentally, I don't know what he's thinking or feeling any more. He's not willing to get a job; he sits at home all day long and goes through intense bouts of anger.' She gave me the emotional side of clinical medicine, which we, as doctors, often don't have time to indulge in.

'Tell me more about him.' I wanted to help.

'He worked at BusinessTech, in the travel domain, and was head of management consulting for Asia, Africa and the Middle East – the blue-eyed boy at work until this happened and turned our life around completely,' she said, her eyes glassy. Before I could reach out, she got up and walked across the office to grab a tissue from above the washbasin. Zane looked at her with concern.

'And why are you limping?' I asked curiously.

'I was run over by a drunk driver when I was eight,' she said with unparalleled stoicism. 'I needed three surgeries where my leg was amputated at the hip. I contracted Hepatitis B during the first blood transfusion, and was in the hospital for 60 days, my parents were told to wait for me to die from the hepatitis. I have somehow programmed myself to overcompensate so that people can see me before my disability,' she said, mentioning that the gait was due to her prosthesis, which goes up the hip and needs to be disarticulated every time she needs to use the washroom.

She told me she had met Zane through common friends, and surprisingly, he never saw her differently like most other people did. 'Till date, I am amazed by his ability to love and accept people as they are,' she said with glee. She had the best kind of marriage anyone could wish for. 'For my entire pregnancy, I was on crutches and a wheelchair because I couldn't use my prosthesis, as it covered my abdomen,' she told me. 'He would religiously take me for a walk every day, wheeling me along non-existent sidewalks in the city,' she looked at him fondly, and he looked back as if it was no big deal.

They had moved to Singapore in 2016 when their daughter was a year old. He had taken care of them financially, emotionally and physically. He'd been the most involved dad and a true son to her parents. 'He was as good as it gets,' she declared.

'But now, it's not good anymore,' she confessed. She believed she had underestimated the impact of this rupture. 'After hoping and praying for a few long years, I have accepted that he may never be the same person again.'

'And that's okay,' I completed the sentence. 'Most people will have three or four marriages in their lifetime, albeit to the same person,' I explained. No two people remain the same. No situation is constant. All circumstances are beyond our control. 'Life is more random than you think,' Nassim Nicholas Taleb once wrote, 'and your ability to navigate it rationally is more limited than you think.'

We discussed the various options through which we would get Zane back to speed and how he could be gainfully employed again. He promised he would try his best – for himself, for them.

I imagined how most people in their circle would enquire about Zane while seeming to not acknowledge Sanjana's disability. Even if she voiced how she was feeling, she would be fed with toxic positivity. I figured how they'd be unintentionally excluded from social functions because Zane didn't interact much anymore. I realized how no one understands the caretaker's burden. I speculated about how we wait for people to fall ill to be nice to them, to understand them, to go back to loving them – but sometimes even that is not enough. 'And that's okay, too,' I told myself. I thought of how patients come to doctors for help and how doctors take on the role of being their therapists while, in reality, it is the doctor who is in therapy.

P.S.: We operated on Zane a year ago and the outside of his head is as good as new. The inside too has helped him get a job and renew his relationship.

Another Kind of Love

'I'm so sorry I haven't come back to see you in months,' Fionna told me with a weary look on her face. 'My back is doing much better with the physiotherapy, but the pain going down the leg is worse.' She drew a line with her little finger to explain where her sciatica spread.

'What have you been doing recently that's aggravating it?' I asked to identify some triggers.

'I've had the most physically and emotionally draining 12 weeks of my life,' her eyes welled up. I handed her a tissue and asked if she'd like to talk about it. After all, I'm always in search of a good story.

'It's my daughter Zoey,' she began. 'She's six years old and the love of my life. She's curious, intelligent, kind and has the gentlest heart,' she described. When someone starts with a description like that, it immediately tells me that Zoey's facing something she doesn't deserve. 'I noticed a little discoloration on her belly and also found a small lump, measuring around 2 cm,' Fionna said, holding up her index finger and thumb in an estimate of the size. They'd waited a week, but as it hadn't gone, they'd taken her to a skin doctor.

'This will have to come out, but we'll have to do it under general anaesthesia,' he'd told them, concerned that it could be a malignancy. 'It's rough and firm and doesn't look like something we can ignore,' he cautioned. He asked for a bunch of tests that are routinely performed before an operation and scheduled surgery within a few days.

'The ECG and 2D echo showed a cardiac anomaly in Zoey,' she continued. 'She was diagnosed with a degenerative mitral valve, where the heart valve thickens and prolapses and doesn't close properly, causing it to leak,' she explained.

'But this doesn't happen in kids,' I stated.

'That's what I thought, too,' Fionna retorted, 'but the doctors say there is a variety that affects the young; it's super rare and it needs to be fixed at the earliest.' The family was shocked that their happy-go-lucky, always ready for an adventure, full of energy, merrily running up and down the stairs five times a day child, could have heart disease requiring major surgery. 'She had absolutely no symptoms,' Fionna said in utter disbelief.

A consultation with the cardiologist ascertained that, without surgery, there would be a certain decline in her heart health, affecting quality and longevity of life. The procedure involved fitting a custom-made clip device on the apex of the heart. 'However, the surgeon had only performed this procedure aboard, as the technology was just a year old and hadn't come to India yet,' she explained, adding layers to her story to which I was completely glued.

'And in all this drama of getting tests and consultations, the lump on her belly completely disappeared!' she exclaimed. 'I don't know if this was providence or the devil in disguise, to be honest,' she confided.

'But you couldn't escape the heart condition?' I asked, eager to know if they had decided to go ahead with surgery for the little one.

'She was put on oral heart medication until the doctor ordered the custom-made clip from Shanghai, as they planned to operate in this way in India for the first time,' she continued with a story that was getting more complex. While waiting for the four weeks it took for the clip to arrive, Fionna told me that her heart and mind were riddled with a multitude of thoughts about whether they were doing the right thing for Zoey, whereas Zoey was blissfully unaware of what was going on. The entire family was sombre and anxious. 'I held her closer as she slept, woke up several times at night to just watch her, putting my hand on her little heart, and kissed her and cuddled her even more than usual. We took her for late-night car drives and let her eat her favourite ice cream more often. And I prayed … prayed hard and from my heart,' she gestured with hands folded. I was beginning to guess that the story was going to have a happy ending.

'On the day of the operation, with all our hearts weighing a tonne, Zoey was wheeled into the operating room,' she told me. 'The surgeon said it would take three hours and smiled to reassure us, saying that it would be perfect. "Get out of here, have some breakfast and come back," he told us. But I stayed glued to the chair outside the OR.

'Two hours passed, three hours passed, then four hours, and my heart was beginning to tremble. Just then, the doctor burst into the waiting area,' she said with a quiver in her voice. 'He pulled down his surgical mask and I could see his lips pursed tightly into a frown. Softly, he said, "We were about to implant the clip when Zoey's blood pressure plummeted to dangerous levels. Her oxygen saturation also dropped to 64. We tried to stabilize her as best we could, and the levels would rise only to crash once again. We decided that under the circumstances, to continue with the procedure would mean putting her life in jeopardy. We aborted the procedure and have closed her up. We are doing all we can to stabilize her, but she is critical."'

Fionna said she sat outside with her sister and children, their hands entwined in each other's, saying the Lord's prayer like a litany. 'He came out again after what seemed like an eternity to tell us that Zoey was stable. She was to be put on a ventilator overnight, and they hoped to remove the breathing tube the next morning. When she came out of the operating theatre and was wheeled into the ICU, she had pipes and wires sticking out of her everywhere,' she spoke of the experience. 'However, with the grace of God, over the next few days she was discharged from the hospital, alive and well,' she breathed.

Fionna acknowledged that while the surgery would have set a record since it would have been the first of its kind to be performed in India, the doctors showed courage and compassion in taking the call to abort it.

'What about her heart now?' I was curious.

'She has to be on cardiac medication for life. If she develops symptoms, we might have to try out the procedure again, later, the doctors told us.'

The things parents have to go through for their children, I thought.

'Perhaps now that everything's well, you guys can take a short summer vacation before she starts school again,' I suggested.

'School? What school?' she looked at me perplexed. 'Zoey's my beloved six-year-old black and tan dachshund!' she exclaimed.

This time, it felt like my mitral valve had suddenly prolapsed.

Competence or Empathy?

I am on a WhatsApp group that found itself seething because one of its members died trying to seek a consultation with a famous doctor. It was probably something that required early attention, but no appointments were available, and the patient insisted they wanted to see only him. They were furious that some doctors had now become stuck up and pompous and were misusing the gift of healing that has been bestowed upon them. 'I feel ashamed that such rude and non-compassionate doctors exist in our country,' an exasperated member lamented. 'It's our fault alone that we have relegated doctors to divinity,' someone else ranted.

The discussion reminded of the time a patient of mine, Rakesh, who had a brain tumour, once candidly told me, 'Sir, *hum bade bade* doctor *chhod ke aap ke paas aaye* [I ditched some prominent doctors to come and be treated by you].' I was perplexed for a second about whether to treat it as a compliment or criticism. Should I be elated or offended? It got me thinking about what makes a doctor *bada* [a big shot] and, more importantly, what a patient expects from their doctor. So, I put out the question to the same people and a few others with the intent to help make us better doctors.

'Tender loving care,' was the promptest reply. 'We want our doctors to give us time, undivided attention, answer all our queries and allay our fears,' was another reasonable request. 'We know you are short on time, but we are also worried,' interjected someone else. 'Patience for his patients,' was typed by another in all caps. I thought about it and realized that every patient wants more time with the doctor, except the patient that's waiting to be seen next.

'I've been waiting for an hour and a half to see you, Doctor, and I can't sit for long,' an elderly man once told me.

'I deeply apologize, but the lady before you had a typed-out list of 73 questions I needed to answer,' I explained.

'It's always the ladies,' he shook his head.

'Listening with an open mind, empowering patients through education and allowing them to explore other options and second opinions not only fosters trust and collaboration but can also be a transformative experience,' was someone else's two cents, as they themselves called it. But an invaluable two cents, I felt. Empathy and kindness were a given.

'How do I become a *bada* doctor?' I once asked a friend.

'Don't give appointments very early unless it's an emergency,' was the blunt advice I received early in my career. 'If you're easily available, people will think you're *faltoo* [useless],' I was told. 'That's how misplaced we are as a society,' he added. '*Bade doctor ka appointment jaldi nahi milta* [It's not easy to get an appointment with a big shot doctor]!' To date, I give appointments at the earliest.

Also on the list were the famous Four A's that good doctors are meant to have: accessibility, affability, accountability and affordability. 'I *toh* want to be able to talk to my doctor on WhatsApp any time I want,' someone else demanded. This was a popular interpretation of accessibility in today's highly connected world.

Speaking of affability, I once asked a friend about a visit to a new endocrinologist she had been recommended.

'I didn't like him at all,' she said condescendingly.

'Why, what was the matter?' I asked, intrigued, because I had heard such good things about him.

'He's too short,' said the 5'8" lady with zero irony.

'You don't have to slow dance with him to bring your sugar down,' I said, challenging her absurdity. Even if he was vertically challenged, he was still not going to be 'looking up' to her.

Another complaint was that some doctors keep sending you from one specialist to another. 'The buck just doesn't stop with the first consultation,' I am told. 'We want our doctors to partner with us all along in our healing journey,' someone added, which I agree is good accountability. 'Also, what are these crazy charges? Some doctors charge ₹5,000 for a five-minute consultation and scribble something on some paper that only the chemist understands,' was another viewpoint. 'Do they think they are God, or what?'

That brought to mind Alec Baldwin's speech in the 1993 film *Malice*, during a deposition he gives in the film for having removed a seemingly healthy ovary. The prosecuting attorney asks him if he has a God complex, and Baldwin's character replies, 'If you're looking for God, he was in operating room number two on November 17, and he doesn't like to be second-guessed. You ask me if I have a God complex. Let me tell you something: I am God'. The movie was ludicrous, of course, but also lots of fun.

I was a little surprised that no one had yet spoken about what I thought was the most important A, the Fifth A: ability. Doctors study for over a decade in medical school and residency to enhance their expertise and sharpen their skills, yet that requirement doesn't come across as a top priority. I think it's because most people agree that doctors are good at what they do. A few people might clear their throat or raise an eyebrow at that statement, but I also know without a doubt that most individuals have had positive interactions with their doctors and proudly recommend them to others. Especially those on disgruntled WhatsApp groups.

To further expand my research on this subject, I asked my tennis buddies the following question: 'If you had to pick only one of the two qualities your doctor could have, competence or compassion, which would you prefer?'

The response was immediate. 'I don't care if my doctor is a sociopath – all I want is that he's knowledgeable, sound, can communicate clearly what needs to be done and do it,' was the reply from a practical mind. 'If I'm having a heart attack, I don't want TLC; I want the freaking clot unblocked ASAP!' he rationalized.

'Compassion without competence is a friend,' another buddy said.

'And competence without compassion?' I asked.

'That's a transaction,' he said, without a thought.

The relationship between doctors and patients is built on a delicate balance of expectations and understanding. For doctors, it is essential to remember that while competence is the cornerstone of medicine, compassion is what turns a good doctor into a great one. As patients, we must realize that doctors are human too, with limited time and countless responsibilities; yet, as doctors, we are all committed to your well-being. When we understand this, healing becomes a partnership. As Hippocrates, the Father of Medicine, once said, 'Cure sometimes, treat often, comfort always.' But if he were alive today and had a long day in the clinic, I'm sure he would have resorted to 'We can't cure everyone, but hey, we can at least try not losing our minds in the process!'

P.S.: Hippocrates was really short too.

The Flirt

'Come quickly, I'm alone in the room with the doctor,' 40-year-old Radha spoke to her husband on the phone, who happened to visit the washroom just when it was their turn to be seen by me. This was a follow-up appointment to remove sutures after we had extricated a tumour from inside her spinal cord two weeks ago. She was a roundish mother of two with her long thick hair plaited in a single braid, not the image of someone who typifies amorous mischief, but I've long given up on stereotypes. Her husband of 12 years sat beside her in a bright yellow T-shirt, immune to her disposition, as she leaned forward to tell me a secret.

'The first time I saw you was when I decided that you'd do my operation,' she said with a beaming, impish smile.

'And why is that?' I asked curiously.

'Because you are so handsome!' she whispered with a straight face, while I couldn't contain my blush.

I remember what a detailed conversation we had had with her entire family regarding all the complications that could arise out of opening up a spinal cord, removing a 6 cm tumour from within it and putting everything back together. It was a pretty intense discussion that had included the slight possibility of paralysis and loss of bowel and bladder function.

'I have two little children,' she reminded me every time I spoke of something that might go wrong.

'You also have a husband,' I reminded her.

'As long as you are there, I don't have any worry,' she said, looking at him playfully from the corner of her eye. Why is it that most women worry about their children more than their spouses, while most men prioritize their wives over their kids?

'All the other surgeons I went to were very old ... white hair, thick glasses; *mazaa nahin aaya* [I wasn't filled with joy],' she confessed. This was the first time my youth had worked in my favour. Most often, people who require brain or spine surgery want someone significantly experienced, and that is unfortunately a surrogate marker for being slightly aged. I often keep a salt and pepper stubble so that patients might assume I'm a little older than I actually am; if it starts getting uncomfortable, I get rid of it.

'When you held my hands to examine me, I knew that I wanted those hands to operate on me,' she toyed with me.

'Thank you for not giving me all this information before the surgery, or else I would have been very nervous!' I acknowledged in jest, playing along. 'Also, because your surgery was extremely complex and difficult,' I added.

Her tumour grew from within the centre of the spinal cord in her neck and had pushed the cord to its edge, flattening out the fibres responsible for hand and leg function. She realized something was wrong when she noticed a slight weakness in her right hand and an inability to write, eat or comb her hair. When we opened the spinal cord, it looked like a rugby ball, bulging in the centre and tapering off at its ends. The tumour was dirty grey, clearly demarcating itself from the angelic snowy whiteness of the normal spinal cord. We were able to remove it meticulously, preserving motor and sensory function.

'But there is one problem I've been having after surgery,' she went on to elucidate. By now, I was convinced that it was going to be unrelated to the actual operation. 'I'm not getting any bad thoughts in my mind,' she left me to figure out what she meant, while her husband sat with his head in his palms. I simply had a big smile on my face and encouraged her to elaborate. '*Kya bataye sir, sirf bhagwan ki yaad aati hai.* [What to tell you sir. I'm only having spiritual thoughts.] No gossiping, no bitching, no sex. *Kuch toh life mein excitement honi chahiye!* [There should be some excitement in life at least!]'

'I can't help you with the gossiping and bitching, but I can give you permission to have sex after two weeks!' I stated, smiling at the twinkle in her eyes. 'With your husband!' I added, and her face dropped for effect.

Patients seldom flirt with doctors, and when they do, it is often harmless – at least in my limited experience. They do it to breed familiarity and often to create a distraction from the looming threat of a serious illness. For some, it is unlacing the corset of a coping mechanism, while for others, it is holding up a dagger of defence. 'There is no terror like the terror of being known,' Emerson anguished in his journal while trying to navigate a deep and complicated relationship. For most people, flirting is just a personality trait reminding the doctor to keep things light and easy. It's important for a surgeon to not feel flattered or get carried away because that could hinder decision-making. And if someone were to go down (from a complication, not in the way you're imagining!) the fun would be instantly replaced by fear. Delicate and difficult.

The women who most often flirt with me are mostly above 70 and single, so I'm just a little surprised when someone my age does *masti* [flirt]. I recollect an octogenarian whose hand grip I was once examining. I asked her to hold two of my fingers in the palm of her hand and squeeze. When I was done and told her to let go, she shook her head and said, 'I don't want to,' with such sweetness and longing. We held hands for five minutes, me thinking of my long-gone grandmother and her ... God knows who. There is so much tenderness, warmth and grace in the vulnerability of the elderly as they express their longing. As physicians and surgeons, all we are really doing is walking our patients home, fathoming our own lives as we deepen their living.

Before Radha and her husband walked out of the consulting room, she requested that I always be available to answer all her queries, and I, in return, dramatically promised, 'I will be with you for the rest of your life!' She clasped my hands with love, entwined my fingers with hers and amusingly bid her husband goodbye.

Animal Instinct

'He kept sniffing my right breast for a whole five days,' a 62-year-old lawyer friend of mine was speaking to me about her Labrador, Oscar, as she narrated the story of how she discovered she had cancer. 'He even on occasion dug his snout into my bosom to tell me something was amiss.'

Oscar had lived with her for the past eight years after the unexpected passing of her husband. She had no children and he was given priority over everything, including her high-profile clients who came to consult her at the home office she worked out of. Oscar was always around – attending the meetings, briefings and mediations that took place in the office – and if anyone had a problem with him, they were explicitly asked to leave. 'My dog knows more law than you do,' she had once told a client who requested for the hound to be taken to another room while discussing a sensitive matter.

'So, for the first few days, I simply passed it off as him being horny,' she said in her usual unruffled style. 'But he would not let people get close to me and suddenly became very clingy. I could not understand what was going on!'

'This can happen with pets if you change their routine or they are unwell themselves, if they can't see or hear properly,' I interjected, having heard a few such stories. 'But did you check for a lump, could you feel one in your breast at all?'

'No, I couldn't feel one!' she exclaimed, gesturing animatedly. 'I could only confirm that there was something after I went to my doctor and he pointed it out.' The mammogram showed it was the size of a pea, and she went ahead and got it removed in its infancy. This only required her to be on oral chemotherapy, which she has been tolerating without any side effects, and she is currently in remission.

'He really deserves an Oscar for all the drama he created in making you aware of this and prodding you to get diagnosed,' I told her.

'Best male actor in a supporting role!' she acceded with a gratified laugh, now that this was all behind her.

Dogs have a sense of smell that is several hundred thousand times stronger than that of humans. It helps them detect various chemicals that the body emits when a person is ill, imagine what bad body odour must do to them! With astounding accuracy, a canine can smell lung cancer on someone's breath, pinpoint a mammary tumour or detect bladder or prostate cancer in someone's urine. If your pet is paying special attention to certain parts of your anatomy, it's time you do the same.

Some dogs can detect epileptic seizures 30–40 minutes before they occur. They can sniff out the odour of a seizure or may be picking up an energy frequency or vibration that the human emits prior to a seizure. Science can only prove what it knows, but animals know so much more. There are organizations that provide service dogs for people with epilepsy and, in several cases, this has been lifesaving: the reactions exhibited by these dogs before the onset of a seizure has given epileptics valuable time – time to take their medication, which prevents or reduces the severity of the seizure, and time to move somewhere safer, where an injury is less likely to occur.

Based on this research, scientists are trying to build electronic noses that are as powerful as their canine counterparts. As of now, however, e-noses are nearly half as effective. Dogs were able to diagnose the coronavirus with an accuracy greater than 95 per cent, and in some countries they were used to screen patients at airports and railway stations. In our country, they were trained to bite those carrying fake RT-PCR test results for travel.

As part of Zoroastrian funeral rituals, a dog is brought near the dead body to confirm that the individual is truly dead before they are carried away. It also could be that we Parsis don't trust our doctors fully and need to wait for one final 'lab' result. It is also believed that a dog's gaze is purifying and drives off demons. The bridge to heaven, our scriptures say, is guarded by dogs.

I recently went for a trek with a bunch of friends. The moment we got out of our car, a handsome German Shepherd appeared at the foot of the hill, the kind whose shaggy neck you can't help but jiggle in your palms. He was black, brown and golden, and had decided to hike with us as if he was instructed to by some higher power. Sometimes he led the way and other times he walked behind us, but he never left my side. He growled at others at the edge of the cliff to secure our path. I wondered if he was sent to protect and guide us, and I felt a deep connect with him. We fell in love instantly. It felt as if a part of my soul was awakened.

But this dog kept doing something strange. He kept sniffing my backside intermittently. After these recent stories I had come across, I wondered if he was detecting a rectal cancer, and I freaked out, my mind's eye imagining myself post-surgey and radiation, sitting with a colostomy jutting out of my abdomen – until it dawned on me that the dog was really only after the scrumptious chicken sandwiches in my backpack. The moment we reached the top, he wolfed them all down, instantly demystifying all the spiritual significance I had given him so far. In his language, I guess I was barking up the wrong tree.

Animals speak to us all the time. It's we who need to evolve to understand what they are telling us.

Caregivers

What would happen were your life to completely turn around in a day? The unexpected and heartbreaking loss of a loved one, the impulsive conception of a baby, a fortuitous reunion with an adopted twin, an unanticipated life-imprisonment for a crime you did not commit, the prodigious inheritance of an undeserved fortune or the startling loss of all your material possessions, an acid attack or an awakening, the loss of sight or deeper insight … would you be ready if any of these were to happen to you?

Many years ago, my cousin delivered a gorgeous cherubic baby boy. Ours is a family of over a hundred people, so there is no such thing as a contained celebration; the hospital security found it hard to regulate visitors. Soon, though, we were given unnerving news. On Day four, just as they were to return home, the baby was observed having some unusually brief jerky movements in his limbs. He began blinking his eyes unconventionally. His mother instantly knew that something was amiss, and an astute neurologist recognized these to be seizures or, as we understand them, epileptic fits. An electroencephalogram (EEG) confirmed the diagnosis and an MRI done at one week of life showed an abnormality over the right half of his brain.

'We have to start him on anticonvulsants, and if the seizures cannot be controlled, we might even have to operate to disconnect the abnormal focus from firing,' the neurologist proclaimed. We brought him home on a plethora of medication.

'We can't operate until the child weighs at least 5 kg and

is about three months old,' I cautioned. 'It's too risky, as this surgery involves some blood loss, and if we can't replace it, we might lose him,' I concluded, seeing him twitch in front of our eyes. It happened 40–50 times a day, each time damaging a little more of his precious brain.

My cousin gave up a flourishing career to focus on him. She overdosed him on her breast milk so he would put on the weight required to withstand surgery. She fed him his medication like clockwork. While the phones of other parents are filled with giggling kids, hers was brimming with records of variations in seizure activity to send to the neurologist so as to adjust his medication. We went ahead with surgery at four months of age.

'It was overwhelming to see this baby of mine come out of the operating room with a huge scar across his head, and drains and pipes sticking out from every orifice of his body, but the greatest blessing has been that he's been seizure-free since surgery,' she says with a smile that never left her through her stoicism.

They brought him home a month later, but the real work of paddling her canoe upstream had just begun. It was time to get him up to speed with the cognitive development that the seizure activity had taken away thus far. Every single day for the past several years, it has been a routine. She sleeps past midnight and wakes up at 6.00 a.m., cooks his food herself, then wakes him up, brushes his teeth, gives him a shower with a loofah to provide adequate tactile sensory input, gives him towel compressions and then does a series of vestibular exercises to zone him in. After some breakfast, they go to the terrace to get some sun and indulge in physical play, which, after a few years of diligent work, now includes football, learning how to cycle, running and crossing obstacles.

Before the pandemic she used to take him to the physiotherapist and occupational therapist five days a week, to the speech therapist once a week and do a follow-up of all the therapies at home after the sessions. However, thanks to the lockdown, she had to turn into all the therapists herself, learning the dos and don'ts from each of them and then teaching them to her son. There are daily vision, oro-motor and sensory exercises to be done. And, in all of this, she still has to ensure he gets his medication on time.

Evenings are usually sibling play with actions, song and dance. 'I cook, clean and take care of all my other stuff whenever he's napping,' she says without sounding exasperated. 'And I couldn't do any of this without the support of my husband and everyone else at home,' she smiles, giving him a huge whack on his back while talking to me. 'I'm filled with joy to see our son do the things we always wondered how he'd ever do … and he completes our family in the most unique way.'

While the centre of every illness is the patient, we often tend to neglect the immediate caregiver. We ignore their struggles, make assumptions about their resilience and never pause to ask them how they are doing. We have no idea what they think about in their quiet moments, what their fears and insecurities are. It's unfair to believe that they don't need to be fortified no matter how tough they may appear. We need to ensure that their cup is always full; only then can it overflow. There is a caregiver in almost every other home of every street in every corner of the world who is looking after a child or an adult, resolute in helping them get better. We need to recognize, celebrate and salute them.

After three years of nursing him without a break, the pandemic arrived. 'Madzu,' as she fondly calls me, 'I've been having fever and a sore throat for two days, what do I do?'

'Get tested for Covid,' I reflexively retorted. 'But who'll take care of my son? I can't afford to fall sick for a single day.'

'This is your chance to get a vacation. Take some time off, get some rest; you really need it. There are four others in the house and they'll manage at least half of what you do; it'll be okay. Go, put your feet up!'

The test result came back positive and she gleefully retreated into her room for a two-week break after being on duty for three straight years. We talked about the music she would listen to, the movies she'd watch, the yoga and meditation she'd indulge in, how she could light some incense candles and order gourmet food.

On day two of quarantine, she called again. 'Madzu, everyone else in the house including my son also has fever – and everyone's tested positive. Vacation over!' she hung up playfully. She was back to tending to her husband, schooling her daughter, caring for her son and feeding her parents, all without any remorse and with the same fervour and zest I've always seen in her. She lives up to Maya Angelou's famous words: 'You may encounter many defeats, but you must not be defeated.'*

---

*Angelou, M. (n.d.). Quote widely attributed to Maya Angelou. Original source unknown.

Undying Spirit

Rahul had a fall while horse riding on his honeymoon. He was paralysed below the waist after the injury. He felt no sensation in his legs, and had lost bowel and bladder control. He had sustained a fracture of his seventh thoracic vertebra with an almost complete transection of his spinal cord. He was airlifted and transferred to our hospital within a few hours of the accident. His wife narrated what had transpired between sobs, and a quick look at the patient history and detailed examination later, I knew what we were dealing with.

'We will have to fix the fracture with a few screws and rods and relieve the compression from the spinal cord, but I haven't seen anyone with an injury of this nature being able to walk again. The purpose behind stabilizing the spine is purely to enable you to undergo extensive rehabilitation later,' I concluded, asphyxiating hope at the very beginning.

I don't know if I was being a blunt jerk, but knowing what we know, I'm often conflicted about what the right thing to say or do is when I know the chances of recovery are negligible. This was akin to the well-documented case of Christopher Reeve, acclaimed for playing Superman, who developed quadriplegia after being thrown off of a horse during an equestrian competition. He needed a wheelchair and portable ventilator to breathe for the rest of his life.

I attempted to soften the blow. 'The good news is that the location of your injury is such that your arms and breathing are spared.'

'What about injecting stem cells into the spine during surgery?' he asked, his eyes shimmering with unshed tears. Only 34, he had just been handed over the reins of his father's business of manufacturing bottle caps.

Stem cell research was in its nascent stages with no real proven benefit yet in a randomized control trial, I told him.

We went ahead and relieved the pressure from his spinal cord, removing a sharp spike of bone wedged into it and realigning the deformity with lots of metal. The surgery went off perfectly but, as expected, barring a flicker of movement, there was no improvement in the power or sensation in his legs.

When it was time to get discharged, he once again pleaded, 'Will I ever be able to walk again?'

Most surgeons brush off a definitely negative response with 'let's hope for the best', 'fingers crossed' or 'God willing'; in our country, the last one gets us out of difficult questions with ease and even panache.

In contrast to all the responses I could have relied on, with a straight face betraying no emotion, I said 'I doubt it' with unvarnished honesty. *There is a fine line between false hope and audacious optimism*, I thought, remembering all the cases of severe traumatic spinal cord injury I had operated on over the years.

Moving closer home, my uncle was diagnosed years ago with chronic leukaemia. Although it was under control with the help of oral chemotherapy, it recently relapsed fairly aggressively, transforming into an extremely rare variant. Most top doctors in India and the United States concluded that they had exhausted all options. As he was 73, palliation was the answer; a bone marrow transplant was certain to fail. The Americans suggested he enrol in a clinical trial with a very uncertain prognosis. He researched his condition extensively, learnt of the latest developments in the field and sent off a couple of hundred emails to various centres across the world, most of which were unwilling to accept him given the futility of treating this condition, but he didn't give up. Finally, he ended up in Israel and received a specialized, tailored transplant that resulted in complete remission. 'Every outlier represents an opportunity to refine our understanding of illness,' I remember reading somewhere.

Human beings faced with adversity are tenacious. Being resolute in overcoming insurmountable obstacles is what fuels the human spirit. As doctors, we often don't have an answer to many of the uncertainties we see; we tend to throw up our hands when things seem beyond our control. While scientifically documented advances through clinical trials are the sanctum sanctorum of medical progress, there is a growing body of evidence that the human body can heal itself from disease by simply changing one's perceptions. What the ancient spiritual leaders of our country practised with promise, faith and conviction, science will probably be able to prove soon. I am convinced that thoughts, belief and emotion have a huge impact on our health and our ability to heal. Cancer survivors, stroke victims and those who have miraculously recovered from physical, mental or emotional trauma have travelled a deeply complex and personal journey of healing—small footsteps towards the infinite potential of the human mind.

A few months ago, a well-toned, perfectly healthy man who appeared to be in his late thirties walked into my office with his wife. The face looked familiar.

'You don't remember me, do you?' he smiled. 'I'm Rahul,' he continued, turning around to lift his T-shirt and show me his scar. 'I came back to prove you wrong!'

I was in complete disbelief seeing him walk unaided. He told me that three years of extensive rehabilitation, machine learning, aqua and music therapy, meditation, spiritual practices and the power of visualization had helped him make this miraculous recovery. His one-point focus across this time had been to walk again, he said.

'No one,' I said, paraphrasing the Bible, 'labours in vain.'

I realize that these people are exceptions to the rule. But they also remind us that there are no rules. They are the ones who make the word 'impossible' seem like it's just an opinion. They defy everything we've learnt while studying to be doctors, all we know as scientific fact. And that's why they end up being the patients we admire and remember the most – because they teach us that the will to make a difference often makes the biggest difference.

Ominous Mercy

Pratima's son brought Pratima to me for the first time around three months ago. He was a big burly fellow with the gentleness of candy floss.

'She had a very fleeting speech disturbance a few days ago,' he described his 77-year-old mother's symptoms with a certain softness that has escaped today's world. 'The slurring lasted about five minutes and then she was absolutely fine,' he went on to explain.

I confirmed that there was no frothing from her mouth, upward rolling of her eyes or jerky movements of or weakness in the arms or legs – the additional features of a possible seizure or even a stroke. She sat beside him, a quarter of his size but holding her own.

'There is nothing wrong with me,' she insisted. 'I can cook, eat, bathe and go out on my own,' she asserted her independence.

'Then why are you here?' I asked with a smile.

'The MRI shows something,' she justified, as her son pulled out the films for me to see. There was a tiny bright dot surrounded by a celestial blush, a distant galaxy in the lower part of her left frontal lobe, which was the speech area.

'You look great, but this doesn't.' I explained, gently nudging her to get it removed.

'Can we not wait it out a little, given her age and the fact that she's doing well?' the son asked respectfully.

'You can,' I wavered a little, not entirely sure if this was as sinister as my first impression was, 'but it's taking a chance,' I added. We concluded that we would repeat an MRI after three months or before that if her frontal lobe decided to throw a bigger party.

Eight weeks later, when her son called me on the phone. I instantly recognized his voice because no one in this chaotic world had spoken to me that respectfully since I'd last met him.

'Mom's speech has gotten worse over the past few days,' he described. 'She's mixing up words, she repeats the same thing over and over again like a broken record and some sentences are incomprehensible,' he said, his voice dropping into an inaudible murmur.

'Repeat the MRI and come and see me,' I urged. When they returned the day after, I was a little taken aback to see that the dot on the MRI had exploded. The frontal lobe looked like it had been hit by an asteroid. It was like a galactic collision. The tumour had grown tenfold.

'We have no choice but to remove this,' I declared, and they agreed without any hesitation this time, without even a polite request to procrastinate.

Anushree, the bright-eyed over-enthused intern shadowing our team, took it upon herself to become Pratima's local guardian. She carried out a detailed evaluation, running cognitive tests that Pratima navigated with the charming grace of a tipsy ballerina. Words escaped Pratima, simple math became rocket science, but Anushree with the wisdom of an old soul, kept encouraging her: 'Perfect! Great going!' Sometimes, kindness can be a more effective diagnostic than any score.

Pratima's brain, much like the world outside, had gone to war. Grade 4 brain cancer. Survival estimate: less than a year. Yet there she sat, a radiant beacon of hope, smiling and asking, 'I'll be alright, won't I?' Because no matter how hard life hits us, despite all its vicissitudes, no one wants to die. We all want to rewrite our script, even if it's written in invisible ink. She was a child in a 77-year-old's disguise, holding on to hope like it was a precious, fragile bird.

I operated on her on my birthday.

'Couldn't you have taken the day off?' Anushree, the medical student, wondered.

'This is the best birthday gift I can give myself – there is no greater joy than to be able to rid this lady of her affliction,' I explained to the medical student, who was eager to be a neurosurgeon but didn't yet have the experience for neurosurgery to flow through her veins. I fixed Pratima's head on a clamp, ready to open it up. While we performed the craniotomy, I explained to Anushree all the rainbow-coloured tracts circuiting the tumour and the importance each of them had in speaking. All the functional areas of her brain had been drawn with an AI algorithm and were visible on a giant screen in front of us while we were operating.

'If I damage even a sliver of normal brain, she could lose her speech completely,' I explained, as I monitored each part before making incisions.

'Mapping miracles!' she whispered in awe from behind me. The surgery was seamless, a beautiful dance between precision and preservation. We differentiated the debris of the dirty tumour from the pristine whiteness of the normal brain and removed it completely, protecting the multitude of fibres that were threatening to get in the way. Astral harmony was restored.

As I walked out of the OT, a tiny doubt gnawed at me. What if I had been firmer two months ago and insisted that I operate then itself? But deep down, I knew it wouldn't have changed a thing. I often marvel at my own inability to stand my ground, giving in to a patient's desire to buy time, even when my gut screams otherwise. It's bewildering how some tumours can look like innocent angels on a scan, only to morph into full-blown demons before their horns even sprout.

'Never a dull moment in neurosurgery,' I quipped to Anushree, who was probably already daydreaming about her own heroic surgical adventures in the future.

The next day, Pratima greeted us with a denture-less smile that beamed like a thousand suns. With her shaven head and missing teeth, she looked even smaller next to her towering son. But then she spoke, fluently, about her wonderful sleep and the breakfast she had devoured, and we knew – her speech was back! She could name every object and repeat complex phrases, and her cognition scores had skyrocketed. Best birthday present ever.

'I'm going to go back to teaching social studies and mathematics,' she decreed with the authority of a queen reclaiming her throne. That's when I thought of what Christopher Poindexter, the Bohemian poet, once wrote: 'How bravely beautiful it is, that sometimes, the sea wants the city, even when it has been told its entire life it was meant for the shore.'* That's what she was – the sea – and the vast expanse of her resilience was reaching for the city and everything she loved about it. Her spirit, like the ocean, was unstoppable, and utterly magnificent.

---

*Poindexter, C. quoted on goodreads, (n.d.), widely attributed to Naked Human (Underwater Mountains, 2015).

Shared Humanity

Christ, the wandering sage, came to see me from the United States with his physiotherapist. He was a lean, athletic man with locs in his beard and his long hair tied in a gravity-defying bun. A T-shirt without sleeves framed his heavily tattooed arms.

'I've travelled twice around the world to see if someone can fix my human avatar, and finally, my search has led me to you,' he said in a deeply spiritual voice.

'And what's the matter with it?' I asked.

'I have this pain going down from my neck into my left arm, and it's killing me,' he confessed, having admitted to trying every possible remedy, including trying to self-heal. He winced as he spoke of his condition, a flicker of earthly pain momentarily eclipsing his spiritual aura. He was a professional rock climber, amongst other things, and was unable to pursue his passion because his fingers couldn't grip well and the numbness in his hand didn't allow him to get a feel for the stone.

'The legion of surgeons I've consulted across continents,' Christ continued, a hint of frustration colouring his otherwise serene tone, 'each one a fleeting stop on my global pilgrimage, have seemed hesitant. They've nodded gravely at the images of the two rebellious discs in my cervical spine, those tiny tyrants pressing against my spinal cord, but none has dared to offer a definitive promise. It was always a "we'll see". For a man whose lifeblood is clinging to sheer rock faces, "maybe" simply doesn't cut it.'

A slow smile spread across my face. 'You know,' I said, a

touch of amusement in my voice, 'with a name like Christ, it almost feels irrelevant offering the usual pre-op reassurance about divine intervention to you. It's like telling the Pope to say a few Hail Marys.' I chuckled softly. 'Seriously, though, is it … complicated? Carrying that kind of moniker around?'

'Are you specifically asking about my name, or the very misunderstood label that the separation group known as "Christians" have given an ancient consciousness?' he replied with a deep sense of purpose in the world. 'I grew up in a region of the United States called the Bible Belt, so as a kid, I learnt pretty quickly just to go by the name Chris. Kids are mean and they learn their ignorance from their parents. Now that I'm older and have a little thicker skin, I go by my name despite the feathers it ruffles,' he explained.

'My name is Mazda,' I gave him the corollary. '(Ahura) Mazda is the name of the God in our religion – Zoroastrianism. More than poking fun at the divinity of my name, most kids used to ask me if my brother was called Toyota,' I laughed, describing a bit of my childhood.

'All religion is man-made,' he interjected. He explained how religion was born from the fear of the unknown and the incomprehensible forces of nature that man had no control over. Man needed to be placated through certain behaviours, and hence 'God' was born. 'All religions were made by the political ruling class of their time, using the messenger as the leading figure, but constantly changing the message to suit their agenda – spreading fear, insecurity and guilt amongst their own followers and hate towards all non-believers,' he concluded.

Nothing has changed over millennia, I thought to myself.

'Who sent you to me?' I asked, intrigued.

'My spiritual guides from another realm, whom I have

communication with and gain guidance from, directed me to you to take care of my fleshy man monkey,' he explained clearly, knowing I wasn't ready for that answer. It was quite a boost to my ego, that while so many people on earth were completely unaware of me, my presence had been felt in the ether. 'I'm told that you are a Jedi in your field and will end the war going on within my body,' he surrendered, as we fixed a date for the surgery.

'Can I come in and see the operation?' Dr Lewis, his physiotherapist and a yoga practitioner, asked me as I walked into the OT.

'Sure,' I obliged, 'as long as you don't mind seeing us slit his neck,' I joked. Within the hour, we did exactly that, moving the carotid artery to one side as we reached the culprit – the disc that was badly pressed up against the nerve. We removed the fragment impinging upon the bruised nerve and, with perfection, placed a titanium cage to replace the disc. The neck was sealed back up such that the scar wasn't visible. His human avatar had been healed: he woke up pain-free, able to feel his own hand. A few months later, he went back to rock climbing as well as heavy duty carpentry.

And so, I had the distinct honour of mending Christ. It struck me then, with a quiet resonance, that I had also in the past operated on Mohammad and Ram, a trilogy completed not in dogma but in shared humanity. There were others in my surgical log too: Abraham and Raheem, Shiva and Parvati, Lakshman and Laxminarayan, Krishna and Balaji, Ganesh, Gautam and Gobind. Each arrived with their unique stories etched onto their faces, their external forms a vibrant tapestry of different hues and beliefs. Yet, beneath the surface, the blood flowing through their veins was indistinguishable. Their ailments varied, their pains were unique, but their fundamental desire was the same: to be whole and free from suffering. None of them inquired about the tenets I upheld or the rituals I observed. Their focus transcended the boundaries of faith; they simply yearned for peace within their own bodies, and by extension, perhaps, in the world around them. If this unifying desire for well-being can eclipse our differences when we are vulnerable, when pain strips away our pretences, surely we, in our moments of health, can reach for a greater harmony.

Let us then, in our strength, choose hope over hostility, understanding over aggression. May the peace these people sought within themselves blossom outwards, bridging divides and silencing the drums of war. May we not simply strive for peace, but actively cultivate it, nurture it and fiercely love the very essence of it, until it permeates every corner of our shared existence.

Unvanquished Fate

She was a single mother. She carried him horizontally in her arms. The *pallu* [loose end of a saree] of her dishevelled cotton sari covered his head to prevent attention from inquisitive onlookers prying into her plight in the crammed outpatient clinic of the public hospital where I once worked. One of the men, showing some rectitude, scooted up the wooden bench to give her six inches on the edge of the plank. She sat heavily, the weight in her arms seeming infinitesimally lighter than the solemnity of her expression.

I could see her through the slit of the half double door of my cabin, which swung open and shut constantly, typifying the busyness of a government hospital imbued with patients wanting to be seen first. I gently gestured for the crowd to ease off a little and allow for her to come in as a priority. They acquiesced gracefully. The civility that indigent people display to accommodate their own often transcends that of the affluent.

She thanked me with an unbridled smile as she gently lifted the veil on her child's head – a move that summed up for me the months of her anguish. His head was twice the size of his body. The skin over it was tightly stretched out and the scalp veins dilated enough to insert an intravenous cannula into any of them. His eyes were sunken, like the setting sun, a dull grey because of the raised pressure inside his head. He was 18 months old and emaciated because of delayed milestones. I could count his ribs without feeling them. I pored over the sheaves of tattered papers she was carrying with her after having visited multiple doctors in the village.

She removed a folded and crumpled CT scan film that showed an abnormal accumulation of cerebrospinal fluid due to a humongous tumour in the cerebellum, which obstructed the normal outflow of brain fluid. The brain was pushed to its edges, leaving only a thin mantle, and was unlikely to assist in the development of a fully functional child. The pressure of the fluid within prevented the skull bones from fusing, allowing me to palpate the contour of his pulsating brain over the vertex of his head. We call this area the fontanel, which in normal children is soft and sunken, but in this case was tense and bulging.

I pulled out a measuring tape. Active babies get extremely irritated when you measure their head circumference, but he lay there lethargic, numbed by the pressure within his internal world. His head circumference was 56 cm, comparable to an average healthy adult. When a baby is born, the diameter of its head measures about 33–35 cm, reaching about 46–47 cm by their first birthday. This child's head was growing exponentially and the rest of his body seemed like its appendage.

Surgery was the only option, I explained in fractured and mangled Marathi, describing in detail the risks of an operation in a child of this nature. A few sentences in, I was perplexed by the smile on the mother's face and so I paused.

'*Aap Hindi mein baat karenge toh bhi chalega* [You can talk in Hindi, it's okay],' she said wryly. I was pleased to bring momentary relief to her tormented world with my poor language skills and proceeded in Hindi. Being a Parsi, I must confess that this was not the first time such a request had been made. What's even more embarrassing is that on a few previous occasions, Hindi was what I had started with.

When we counsel the poor and helpless about the dangers of complex brain surgery, the possibility of death is the first thing we mention loud and clear, which annuls all responsibility of minor aberrations. When we do the same with the educated and prosperous peerage of society, we list out a menagerie of minor complications, very deftly mentioning the macabre possibilities somewhere in between. We must admit that we cannot escape our biases.

A few days later, after optimizing the child's nutritional status and temporarily draining some fluid from his head to release tension, we wheeled him into the operating room, his mother stoically standing as the door shut on her, relinquishing, probably for the first time in their togetherness, all her control over his fate. The anaesthesiologist clenched his wrist to bring alive his buried veins and secure intravenous access. They put a tiny breathing tube down his throat, flipped him over and strapped him down.

We made an incision over the back of the head down to where it meets the neck and held apart the layers of tissue with a retractor. The bone was so thinned out that we could cut it with scissors. We encountered the two bulging lobes of the cerebellum shaped like a healthy baby's bottom, a stark contrast to his own bottom which was malnourished. In a set of quick microscopic manoeuvres, we encountered the tumour that appeared like the rotten core of an Alphonso mango – after all, we were operating in May.

We debulked it amidst brisk bleeding. It appeared to be a high-grade cancer. In children this small and tender, even minute amounts of blood loss can be catastrophic. Adults have something called an 'allowable blood loss' that can be compensated for physiologically, but this child's allowable blood loss was zero millilitres. Through all the opaque barriers that separate a surgeon from the anaesthesiologists, I could visualize them squeezing the blood bag to hasten the transfusion. Pressures dropped, alarms beeped, but we managed to remove the tumour completely and were back in control. We closed safely.

After a few days of turmoil in the ICU, his condition stabilized and he opened his eyes wide enough to see. The bulging fontanel had saucered in. For the first time, one could see a semblance of a smile on his face and his limbs moved actively. We discharged him a month later after ensuring that he had gained some weight and was feeding well. We gave instructions for chemotherapy, but I didn't see the mother at follow-up. I assumed one of the others in the team must have.

A year and a half later, I recognized the same lady in the outpatient clinic with her baby wrapped in muslin and the head covered. Her face was imprinted on my cortex after all that we'd been through. Even if her identity was mistakable, her grief wasn't. I wondered why she still carried her child around when he should have started walking or at least sitting up. I lifted the shroud off his head myself this time, with self-congratulatory enthusiasm to keenly track if my surgery had done wonders. The head was still huge. But the baby was much smaller. I peered closely. This child was her second; the first had died six months after surgery from dissemination of the cancer.

The obscenity of heredity was on full display.

Section 2

CUTS AND BRUISES

These are stories from the frontlines of bruised bodies and battered egos – of falls, fractures, fluids, fainting spells and the fragile machinery we live inside. Here, pain is sometimes dramatic, sometimes absurd and occasionally self-inflicted, but always deeply human. These essays remind us that every cut carries a question, every bruise hides a confession and sometimes the deepest wounds are the ones we laugh about – because humour is our most reliable bandage.

A Hand, a Head and a Heart

'Which instruments will you use to cut open my spine?' Rasiklal asked me after I examined him for a herniated lumbar disc. I had just explained to him why he was a candidate for spine surgery. He was a tailor in his mid-fifties, slightly potbellied, and wearing a white shirt that, in his own words, 'used to fit him well before he put on some weight'. He had tried everything to avoid an operation – medication, physiotherapy, ayurveda, homeopathy, acupressure and acupuncture. He had visited a chiropractor, osteopath and even a '*baba*' who claimed to cure slip discs by kicking people on the bottom. Needless to say, his pain was much worse after that experiment, and now he was unable to cut fabric sitting on the floor. He needed to stand to do it, and even that he could do just barely before his back pain shot down his legs – the classical sciatica that people with disc disease describe.

When I asked him to sit, before doing so, he removed a large 10-inch pair of metal scissors from his pocket and placed it on the table. You could feel the intense sharpness of their blades just by looking at them. The bronze metal handles mixed with shades of silver had been softened by years of usage.

'This is my tool; I never leave my house without it. It's been part of my entire life. If I must have surgery, I need to know what you will be using.' He had made his point; I understood what he was trying to say.

'We do this operation with what we call minimally invasive technology,' I told him, explaining that we didn't have to cut any muscle like they did in the good old days. 'We'll first use a knife to make a 2 cm incision into the skin and then dilate the back muscles with a series of tubes, each a size larger than the other. We'll dock the tube on the bone of the spine, and using a fine drill that rotates at 60,000 revolutions per minute, we'll shave a portion of the lamina of the spine that covers and protects the dura' I described. He was listening intently. 'You need to have a rock-steady hand to be able to work the drill, because one slip and we could rip apart all the nerve roots of the spine,' I said, showing off slightly to make what we do sound more complex than it is.

'Then, we identify the nerve root that is being compressed by the disc, and once we expose the bulging disc, we cut into it with a sharp knife,' I showed him an animated video. Sometimes, the disc is just lying there, waiting to be popped out, and in those cases, we use forceps to grasp it and pull it out, thus relieving the pressure on the nerve root, which in turn relieves the pain. On occasion, we need to use a curette to scrape the disc, making sure there is nothing floating free to pop back out again.

'You don't ever need to use scissors?' he asked, slightly disappointed that we were neglecting his favourite tool.

'We do – to cut the stitches we make when we sew you back up,' I said to a look of delight on his face. 'If you don't trust the ones we have, we could use yours,' I joked, 'but actually, they're a little too big,' I dismissed the idea before he could agree.

'You don't use a laser?' he then asked. I wasn't surprised; this is another question every patient has, with the lure of having laser spine surgery.

'People use the term "laser" only to make it sound fancy and attractive,' I explained. 'The use of an actual laser is very limited in this field, but we do the entire operation with a high magnification and brilliant illumination microscope, and the focus point is a sharp red dot of light that looks like a laser, if it makes you feel any better!' I concluded.

'At the end of the day, while the tool is extremely important, it is what you do with your hands, your head and your heart that makes all the difference,' I said. 'For instance, I could never cut fabric the way you do if you gave me your scissors,' I tried to explain. I told him how clinical decision-making was the key to any successful surgery, and emphasized how one needs to have the heart and the courage to deal with a complication if it were to occur. But I understand why it is very important for some patients to know what a surgeon will use, especially if they use a tool themselves: artists and architects, plumbers and painters, cricketers and carpenters, musicians and maestros never cease to ask me what I will use to open up their spine or brain.

When we operate on the brain, we mainly use a suction device in one hand and an instrument in the other – varying from bipolar forceps for cauterizing the bleeding vessels and tissue, to micro scissors for cutting what we have coagulated, and an entire spectrum of micro dissectors of varying shapes, curves and sizes to get into nooks and corners of the brain that were once deemed unapproachable. We even have instruments that have lights at their tips to further illuminate what we're looking at so that we cut only what is intended to be cut. And we also use dyes that light up tumours and help us differentiate it from normal brain tissue.

There are several surgeons who, when they operate in different hospitals, travel with their own tool kit comprising instruments they are familiar with. The touch and feel of using your own tool (no pun intended) provides a certain sense of comfort and control. The joy of owning your own instruments and looking after them like you would after your own children is unparalleled. I know an orthopaedic surgeon who carries his own portable operating table with him for joint replacement surgeries. There is a neurosurgeon from Japan who uses only his own gold-plated microscope to perform his surgeries. In the interiors of India, just like farmers ask for a tractor in their dowry, surgeons ask for instruments, ultrasonic aspirators and microscopes. These are extensions of a surgeon's hands, head and heart; also called our second wives by a few of us, and first wives by most others. Don't ask me which group I fall into.

Rasiklal came for a follow-up two weeks after his spine surgery, completely pain-free and delighted that he could get back to doing what he loved the most.

'Here, try this for me,' he said, pulling out an elegant formal shirt and pant he had stitched for me. 'This is my gift to you for making me walk again.' His eyes brimmed with tears as he insisted that I try it on in front of him.

Without any reservation, I removed my clothes and put on his. They fit immaculately. 'But you didn't even take my measurements!' I exclaimed.

'Sometimes, you need more than just a tool – you need a hand, a head and a heart,' he reminded me of what I had told him. I spent the rest of my day in the clothes he had stitched for me so affectionately.

Mothers-in-Law

I plugged in the cerebral angiogram films against the white light of the view box and explained the imaging findings to Ryan. Ryan was a handsome 38-year-old software engineer. He wore rimless glasses, dark-wash jeans and clean dress shoes – a minimalist look that typified his profession. He had recurring headaches that did not seem to get better with 'regular' medication. His family physician had ordered a scan. The brain MRI showed a 5.5 cm tumour arising from the meninges, the protective tissue covering the brain, pressing down on it.

'This, in all probability, is a vascular meningioma,' I said with the modest authority that comes from pattern recognition, after having seen scans every day for a decade. 'Oma,' I went on to explain, 'means "tumour" or "growth". The word preceding it indicates the source or the cell of origin.' In his case, the source was the meninges.

A tumour is a collection of abnormal cells in the brain. There are a multitude of genetic, molecular and environmental factors that trigger this growth, but we haven't yet been able to fully understand what causes this to occur.

The angiogram was additionally performed on Ryan to determine its vascular supply and plan a surgical strategy around it; trace the main arterial feeders, tackle those first and the rest of the operation would be relatively bloodless. I ran my pointer along the edges of the tumour blush to delineate it on the angiogram.

'You can see that in this area, the extensive blood supply

comes early, stays late and is very dense. In medical parlance, we call this the mother-in-law sign,' I quipped to ease the tension I saw building as he tried to make sense of what was going on inside his head. He broke into a slight smile, flicking the sweat off his forehead with his index finger and thumb.

'So, what do we do about it?'

'Surgery is the only option. We will get the whole thing out, plus we will know the exact grade and aggressiveness of the tumour when we send it for histopathological testing.'

'Risks of surgery … ?' he interjected.

'Less than one per cent chance of death, paralysis, bleeding, infection…' I continued, with an entire laundry list that didn't seem to disturb him at all. 'Sometimes, these tumours can return after a few years even if we remove them completely,' I added as a word of caution.

'All the more reason to call them mother-in-law tumours!' he quipped, having by now eased into the consultation.

'Would you call this a cancer?' he asked after having processed the information.

I wasn't sure if he was taking the mother-in-law theme to the next level, but I went on to explain that 50 per cent of brain tumours are benign, meaning not cancerous. And 50 per cent are malignant. 'I'm pretty certain this belongs to the former category, but whether we need to give you radiation after surgery will depend on how aggressive this tumour is, which we will ascertain once we test it in the lab. Sometimes, radiation is needed even in the case of benign tumours just to ensure they don't become locally invasive. If I had to choose one brain tumour to have, I would choose this one,' I said.

A few days later, Ryan was in the operating room, his face the picture of calm and confidence. This positivity from a patient helps the surgeon perform better, I feel. After the induction of general anaesthesia, we fixed the head on a clamp, shaving his head only around the incision site. We went through the routine of cleaning and draping the sterile field, and then opened the skull to reach the main blood supply to the tumour, as planned.

Ryan's tumour was removed perfectly. As we controlled the last bit of 'nagging ooze' that we often see after excising tumours like these, I asked my assistant if he knew why these tumours were called mother-in-law tumours. I could see him smile through his mask as I buzzed the final bleeding point dry through the lens of the microscope.

'I *toh* love my mother-in-law,' he said out of the blue. 'She makes me my dabba every day.'

Ryan made excellent recovery with a complete resolution of his headache and was discharged within a few days. The post-operative CT scan looked clean. The final report turned out to indicate benign, low-grade meningioma, not requiring any further adjuvant therapy.

'Is there anything I can do to prevent it from returning?' he asked one final time as he got off the bed, thanking me.

'Be nice to your mother-in-law.'

Can You Hear Me?

'I can't seem to hear well from my right ear,' said a concerned 28-year-old air hostess poised gracefully in front of me. 'Initially, I thought it was because of the ambient hum of the airplane, but now I'm convinced it's a problem because I find it hard to decipher what people are saying on the phone as well. I've also noticed a bothersome buzzing in my head, as if a bee is bouncing off the walls within my skull with nowhere to go. There is also a subtle sway in my gait toward the right, but I'm not sure if I'm imagining it. The airline company doctor got me to do an audiogram and MRI, and has asked me to come see you with these results.'

I asked her to follow my index finger with her eyes by keeping her head straight, and noticed an abnormal jerk in her gaze when she looked to the right. Quick coordinated movements of her right hand lagged a little in dexterity when compared to her left side. When I made her walk in one line, heel to toe, the test made famous by the police to see if you're under the influence of alcohol, she stumbled, shuffling toward the right.

The MRI showed a 4.2 cm ice cream cone-shaped tumour arising from the vestibular nerve, one of the 12 cranial nerves that lead directly from the brain to various parts of the head and neck, and the one concerned with equilibrium. This is in proximity to the auditory nerve, hence the intricate association of balance with hearing. The other nerve that is at close quarters in this byzantine anatomy is the facial nerve that controls all the muscles of facial expression. I quickly made her clench her eyes tightly and puff her cheeks to check for facial weakness.

I explained that given the size of the tumour, she needed surgery. If it had been around 2.5 cm, we could have tried zapping it with radiation. The only concern with the surgery was that because the tumour was adjacent to an already stretched-out facial nerve, she would experience facial weakness after surgery, but it would, hopefully, recover over time.

'Hopefully?' she stopped me. 'I won't have a job if half my face is paralysed.' She stared back almost angrily, unable to comprehend the association between a vestibular nerve tumour, hearing and facial dysfunction. After about an hour of explaining the complexities of a surgery of this nature, we agreed to remove as much of the tumour as was safely possible without any risk to the facial nerve. If parts of the tumour remained, we would consider radiating at a later stage.

After the induction of general anaesthesia, we connected electrodes to the facial muscles to get real-time feedback while we peeled off the tumour. A tumour of this size is often imperceptibly merged with the nerves; even with the multifold magnification and intense illumination of the microscope, it is difficult to discern the difference between a thinned-out nerve and tumour capsule. We often joke that attempting to simply spot the nerve is enough to cause a facial weakness, let alone the outcome after handling an already compromised nerve for a few hours.

We debulked a large amount of the tumour using an ultrasonic aspirator, which briskly gobbled up chunks of it, giving us some space to be able to identify normal anatomy. We then used a high-speed drill to core out the internal auditory canal, the point of origin of the tumour, and gently rolled it over the vestibular-auditory complex of nerves, while the electrophysiologists in the room constantly gave us alerts regarding the integrity of the nerve.

We identified the facial nerve slapped thin over the anterior surface of the tumour, a far cry from its normal round self that we see when we expose this region for other conditions. Removing the last part of this tumour is the most daunting because of the maximum adhesion of the tumour to the nerves here. Four hours of diligence can be nullified in four seconds.

The young girl's face flashed in front of me. The questions she had fired at me played in my head. I held the last part of the tumour with a cup forceps while dissecting it off the nerve with another pointed forceps, hoping it wouldn't snap. The beating of my heart was a drum and in competition with the cantankerous sound of the facial nerve monitor, which went off like the gun of a soldier on the border before martyrdom.

Some time ago, a study was conducted at the New Delhi centre of the All India Institute of Medical Sciences (AIIMS) where they hooked up neurosurgeons to monitors while performing this operation. They recorded an astronomical rise in both the pulse and blood pressure of neurosurgeons during the crucial parts of the procedure. They concluded, 'Neurosurgery can induce a significant hemodynamic stress malresponse in the operating surgeon that appears to be greater than that induced by vigorous exercise. The correlation of this occupational hazard to long-term health and longevity remains to be studied.'*

The monitor silenced only after we removed the tumour

---

*Manish Singh Sharma et al., 'Intraoperative pulse and blood pressure recordings of neurosurgeons: a pilot study of cardiovascular performance', *Neurosurgery*, Vol. 66, 2010, pp. 893-899, https://pubmed.ncbi.nlm.nih.gov/20404692/, accessed 4 March 2026.

completely, the nerve hanging in there like an overburdened clothesline, weary but intact. Despite the anatomical and physiological preservation of the nerve, her face was weak for a few weeks, but I was confident it would improve.

When she returned in six months, I asked my neurologist to guess which side we had operated on. He couldn't tell. She had recovered completely and was back to work as usual. She smiled delightfully through her perfect teeth with tears in her eyes, reminding me of a beaming Julia Roberts. The pretty woman was back at her high-flying job.

Writing His Own Fairy Tale

Once upon a time, there was a boy named Arkojjwal. He was unlike any 13-year-old with a brain tumour that I have ever seen. In 2008, when I was an exhausted resident doctor training to be a neurosurgeon in Vellore, he was admitted to the paediatric ward that I was assigned to look after. He had a curly mop of hair that sat off-centre on his head, and wore a pair of thick glasses gingerly balanced on the tip of his nose, giving him the quintessential professor look.

'One day, whilst I was sitting in class, I suddenly noticed I had double-vision,' he said in his chaste Bengali–English as I noted down his history meticulously, 'and when I reached home, my mother saw a squint in my eye.' His MRI showed a craniopharyngioma – a tumour that is hard to pronounce and even harder to remove. It arises from the pituitary stalk and, in his case, had encased the right optic nerve, with chunks of calcium encircling important arteries of the brain. Not only that, it pressed firmly against the hypothalamus – the seat of consciousness.

It was unfathomable to imagine a monstrosity like this sitting inside one of the brightest minds I had ever seen. At the end of each day, way past midnight, when I used to sit down at the computer in the ward to type out discharge summaries for patients, send off investigations for the next day and pore through progress notes, Arkojjwal would pull up a chair and come sit next to me for an hour or two.

'Did you know Zoroastrianism is the oldest monotheistic

religion in the world?' he questioned, after finding out that I was a Parsi. I nodded, slightly befuddled. Each day, he would educate me with some trivia that broadened my worldly knowledge, and in return, I taught him to read MRI scans. He helped me file paperwork and write up lab tests for other patients. I indulged him with the anatomy of the brain and told him how we used to dissect cadavers in medical school. I regaled him with tales of how my 'dead body' was a British man because he had a stiff upper lip. We were a team. He was 13, and I, 26. He wrote me a poem every day to read out to me during our midnight rendezvous.

A few days later, I assisted my mentor with Arkojjwal's operation. His brain was softly dancing to the beat of his heart as we opened it. This gentle rhythmic bouncing that the brain does connects you directly to the cosmos. I watched in awe under the microscope as my mentor peeled off the tumour digging its heels into the optic nerve. I nimbly assisted as he removed small glistening pieces of calcium, almost like a miner unearths diamonds floating in fluid that looked like molten gold. The more we dug, the more jewels we found, until all that was left was the cyst wall stuck to the hypothalamus. As he peeled that off with the sleight of a magician, I found myself praying that Arkojjwal would awaken after surgery. Every bit of tumour visible to the naked eye under the magnification of the microscope was eventually removed. I was lucky to have witnessed such symphonic mastery.

Arkojjwal woke up just fine, reciting Shakespeare on the evening after the operation, as he was tethered to tubes preventing him from writing poetry. These patients, in whom such tumours are resected aggressively from the pituitary stalk (which is responsible for the transportation of hormones), develop sodium and water imbalances that can be laborious to treat, requiring the monitoring of their vital parameters every hour. After fairly tight control of his electrolytes, on the eighth postoperative day, his sodium levels saw a swift swing from rock bottom to sky high, and he slipped into a coma with alacrity, remaining in this state for over a month. The entire team was despondent, but we kept fighting on, reminded of something I had read a long time ago: 'In taking up another's cross, one must sometimes get crushed by the weight.'

When he seemed to awaken 56 days later, he couldn't move at all, except for an involuntary tremor in all his limbs. Owing to the rapid fluctuation in his sodium levels, he had sustained damage to his brainstem and the basal ganglia responsible for movement. After about three months of intense rehabilitation, which included his mother physically flexing him eight hours a day and talking to him about his past for another eight hours, there came about some semblance of an ability to walk and regaining of his lost memory. He was finally discharged on a great many hormonal replacement and growth hormone injections, as his body was no longer secreting hormones on its own.

He followed up with us in Vellore each year, walking a little better, shaking a little less, seeming a little sharper. Over the course of a few years, he underwent a hip replacement, as the steroids he was taking had affected his hip joint. His school allowed him to have writers so that he could complete his ICSE, and he took his exams lying down because he could not yet sit up. He had to replace 10 teeth in each jaw as the enamel had decayed from the side effects of the medication he was on. And then he developed a second brain tumour in his cerebellum, at the back of his head, which we also removed successfully. He was family to every staff member and every doctor in the hospital. He overcame every ineluctable failure inexorably with a fortitude worth emulating.

I left Vellore in 2014 and hadn't heard from him for a few years – until 2021, when he messaged me with a poem:

Dear Dr Turel,

You are always present in my mind to the extent that
none can reach,
The memories with which you teach,
How to overcome any problem,
And claim happiness by God's grace,
Sweeping away each and every sorrow,
Thus you've become to me an influencing hero.

Your beloved,
Arkoj

I was just a resident doctor at the time and not befitting of such praise, nor could I take credit for any medical outcomes or successes, but I was so excited to hear from him! I began reminiscing about all the wonderful times we'd had in the four months we had spent together in the hospital, two of which he spent oblivious. I picked up the phone and called him.

'Hiiii!' I bloviated, allowing for the time we had spent apart to collapse into a capsule, much like the ones he swallowed on a daily basis.

'I've completed my MA in English at Jadavpur University,' he said, in slightly more refined Bengali–English this time.

'Wow,' I exclaimed. 'What next?'

'I'm doing my PhD now,' he said with joy.

'In what?' I enquired, as that is the first question you ask anyone who tells you that they are doing their doctorate.

With a tender note in his voice backed by the certainty of a brighter future, he proclaimed, 'Fairy tales.'

P.S.: A few months ago, I got a call from his brother. He had fallen off the third floor of his building and died.

Bridal Hiccups

'I just got back from my pre-wedding shoot in Dubai last evening and I was perfectly fine. It was such a fabulous experience. The entire family went for dinner after that and we had a great time there too,' she recalled as she spoke to me lying on a hospital bed 12 hours after having the best time of her life.

'And then what happened?' I prompted her to continue.

'I woke up this morning with severe back pain, and realized I just couldn't move my legs,' she said, her face turning from a rosy pink to an ashen grey. 'Then, I vomited twice, and with each vomit, I felt like I had lost sensation: first in the ankle and then at the knee and hips. It's been several hours now, and I can't feel anything waist downwards. My hands are absolutely fine,' she finished, flicking back her professionally done-up hair over a face that still had remnants of her photoshoot make-up. I asked her to move her legs, and nothing. Zero. I gently walked a needle on her leg, poking it from her thighs to her toes to ascertain if she could sense the prick of a pin, and again, nothing.

Her physician had ordered an MRI of the spine and expeditiously sent her to me. I plugged the films against the scintillant light of the scan viewer as the anguished family waited for me to pronounce my verdict.

'There is a thick blood clot compressing the spinal cord at T-11, which has caused her to become paraplegic,' I said, pointing to the eleventh thoracic vertebra. 'There could be an underlying tumour or a vascular malformation, but that is secondary. It has to come out at the earliest,' I pleaded. 'It's choking the cord in full throttle. Time is of the essence in this. We should do it now.'

'Will she be able to move her legs?' the forlorn father asked, the anatomy of illness intersecting with the geometry of grief in his heart.

'That's the reason for rushing this,' I responded. 'The faster we decompress the cord, the better her chances of recovery – but how soon she gets better is anyone's guess. It could be a few days, it could be several months. There are a few patients who won't improve despite our trying everything.'

'She is supposed to get married in three weeks!' the mother burst into a torrent of tears, sobbing uncontrollably.

'Her fiancé is in another city and would like to speak with you,' said the brother, handing me his phone.

'Doctor *Saab*, tell me honestly: what are we dealing with here?' the fiancé asked.

I wondered if he had enquired with the subconscious trepidation of having committed his entire life to someone who might not be what he had imagined, if he sounded like he was ready to back out of the contract, but I quickly realized I was being judgemental without reason. I explained the reality of the situation to him while the operation theatre was being spruced up for her.

'Do your best, Doctor. I love her very much,' he entreated, trying to navigate the trifecta of sadness, uncertainty and hope from a distance as he hung up.

It was 6.00 p.m. I had already operated on two cases that day and realized I hadn't eaten a morsel yet. As the team prepped her for surgery, I decided to step out to the Udupi restaurant across the street to grab a quick bite. As I ate my idli sambhar, it dawned on me that this was the first time I was eating in a restaurant since the start of the pandemic. The food was gastronomically gorgeous. I was so focused on thinking about the case that, out of habit from having only eaten food at home for over a year, I picked up my plate and walked towards the kitchen till the waiter politely stopped me midway and took over. '*The lockdown has really rewired our brains*,' I thought to myself.

In the operation room, after the induction of general anaesthesia, we flipped her on her stomach and cleaned and draped her in the usual fashion, but with an added and intense swiftness. I cut down the middle of her back to get to the bone, which I drilled off with intention and urgency as my assistant irrigated the field to dissolve the bone dust. Once we removed the bone, we saw the thick blood clot sitting there stubbornly, stuck to the covering of the spinal cord. We gently scooped it out, giving the spinal cord its desired space and respect. We did not find an underlying lesion from which it had bled. After having satisfactorily decompressed the cord, we closed.

A few hours after surgery, we checked to see if she had regained any function. Nothing. Perhaps just a flicker of the toe, and that too if you imagined it hard enough. 'Let's wait and see what happens tomorrow,' I spoke with the despondent family and called it a day.

On my drive back home, close to midnight, I reflected on the famous adage about how someone's life can change in a day or even in a single moment. What must go through one's mind when one realizes out of the blue that they can't move their legs? Often, the cause is a viral affliction of the spinal cord called transverse myelitis, or an autoimmune condition affecting the nerves that supply the legs. In some rare cases, when the potassium level drops, it can lead to a condition called hypokalemic periodic paralysis, and gulping coconut juice can reverse the problem.

The next morning, when I went to see her, she waved at me with her ankles. There seemed to be a glimmer of hope. Two days later, she could bend her knees and hips. On Day Five, she could stand with a walker. When she started walking a week later, she said she felt the ground differently than before, but her sensations seemed to return gradually. She was discharged 10 days after surgery, walking independently, which is how she decided to leave the hospital. A spinal angiogram did not determine the source of her bleed. She had regained bowel and bladder function and exercised vehemently to strengthen her core, hamstrings and quads. She was determined not to postpone her big day. I went for the wedding. I'm glad she got her shot at her happily ever after.

Cushioned by Cushing

'I have put on an incredible amount of weight in the past two years,' said 38-year-old Tanya Patel, plonking herself on my office chair after barely managing a few steps on her own. She was bruised all over. 'Even a minor bump causes my skin to discolour and swell,' she said, showing me her arms with the words 'today I escape' inscribed on one in Sanskrit. 'I've had three fractures and two miscarriages and now I can't even conceive,' she lamented, her eyes grew moist. 'I have hair growing all over my body and I am ashamed to even look at myself in the mirror,' she burst out crying, covering her acne with the palms of her hands.

'I've had PCOD (Polycystic Ovarian Disease) for years, and doctors are attributing all my symptoms to that. My periods are irregular and I've been on hormonal medication forever but I'm tired and exhausted and annoyed and irritated and depressed!' she exclaimed as she emptied onto my table a bag full of pain killers, oestrogen and progesterone tablets, drugs for diabetes and hypertension, and mood elevators for her bipolar disorder. 'My sugars are all over the place, my wounds don't heal and I bleed profusely if and when my period decides to come!' she said, exasperated.

I examined her thoroughly after some more questioning. She had a very typical physiognomy. Her obesity was mainly truncal, while her arms and legs were lean. Her face was round like the moon. She had a bulge on her upper back where fat had deposited – in medical jargon, we call this a 'buffalo hump', classical of a certain ailment. I held her hands in mine and noticed that certain parts of them were very darkly pigmented. My suspicion grew stronger.

'I think you may have Cushing's Disease,' I posited. 'It's a condition where you get a bunch of these symptoms because of a tumour of the pituitary gland, producing excess cortisol. You can also see several of these features in people who are put on long-term steroids for either asthma or rheumatoid arthritis. But as you're not taking any, it's probably your body over-producing cortisol from either your brain or your adrenal glands. We must do some testing and get an MRI of your brain. If it is what I think it is, we'll have an answer to all your problems,' I left her with hope. After all that she had been through, that was the least I could provide for the time being.

She came back with her extended family a few days later, after completing the myriad tests that had been ordered.

'Bingo!' I snapped my fingers. The MRI showed an 8 mm tumour within the pituitary gland, off to the left. I pointed to it with a pen. 'That's the enemy,' I smiled.

'That tiny thing is doing this to me?' she asked, aghast.

I nodded, confirming after checking all the biochemical tests to corroborate my findings. 'We'll remove this via the nose using an endoscope and you'll be cured. In the place I trained, we probably did more of these than anywhere else in the world,' I said to boost her confidence. She looked at me with incredulity, still unable to believe that such a tiny thing could cause so much havoc.

A few days later, along with my ENT colleague, we made our journey through her nose. Navigating our way through the turbinates, we broke the posterior part of the nasal septum and entered a cavernous structure.

'That's the sphenoid sinus,' I demonstrated in 4K on a giant screen to some medical students interested in neurosurgery who were visiting us, standing on their toes in excitement. I had gotten them to see Tanya before the surgery and explained her MRI to them. They were shocked to know that a brain tumour can be removed through the nose.

I drilled the floor of the sella, the bony saucer that cradles the pituitary gland. 'You have to be very careful while you drill,' I cautioned them, 'as on either side of the sella are the carotid arteries, the main blood vessels of the brain, and if I damage them, the patient could die in an instant,' I narrated to add some shock and awe value and keep them engaged.

'*Shubh shubh bolo, sir* [Please don't say anything inauspicious],' my assistant prodded.

I cut the dura covering the gland widely and there it was – 8 mm of a cheese ball that we curetted fastidiously and removed completely. 'That's the normal pituitary gland to the right, pinkish and fleshy, a stark contrast to the tumour, which is soft and squishy,' I explained.

'Do you know who Harvey Cushing was?' I questioned the medical students while we closed in a meticulous fashion.

'He was the father of modern neurosurgery,' one of them replied.

I was impressed. 'Cushing called this condition the "diabetes of bearded women",' I enlightened them further. 'And do you know what his contributions were besides naming this disease over a 100 years ago?'

They remained silent.

'He was the youngest of 10 children, and he brought neurology and neurosurgery to the respect it has now. He used X-rays to diagnose brain tumours at the time and introduced to the United States, blood pressure measurement that he saw being practised in Italy. He described a definitive condition of raised intracranial pressure where there is a triad of bradycardia, hypertension and irregular breathing and named it Cushing's Reflex. He worked at both Johns Hopkins and Harvard, writing numerous papers on several important discoveries he made, designing several surgical instruments, describing new procedures, teaching surgical trainees and maintaining detailed records of his 2,000 brain tumour surgeries,' I lectured.

Harvey Cushing was nominated for the Nobel Prize in Physiology and Medicine 38 times, but never won. However, he won a Pulitzer Prize in 1926 for his biography of Sir William Osler. He died of a heart attack. Interestingly, his autopsy revealed a tumour-like cyst in his brain.

After Tanya was discharged, an endocrinologist took over her care to fine-tune her medication. But we stayed in touch over the phone and became friends. She came to me for a follow up a year later looking unrecognizable. She had lost 30 kg and looked well-toned, with glowing skin and dazzling hair.

'I'm two months pregnant and I only have you to thank!' she said, holding hands with her husband.

'Please don't thank me, the nose was the only orifice I entered,' I joked. 'Either thank him,' I said, directing my gaze to her husband, 'or thank Cushing, without whom we'd still be treating you for PCOD.'

'Cushing *zindabad*!' she cheered, and gave me a tight hug.

The Centre of the Brain

Everything revolves around a centre. The earth pirouettes around a molten core. The solar system hums to the rhythm of the sun. Cities pulse with life around their downtowns. A newborn baby at a family gathering is the centre of all attention And, in today's context, it's the one working charging outlet at an airport where a desperate cluster of travellers vie for their device to be the next to enter its precious electrical orbit.

Even our brain, the crowning glory of evolution, bows to this unassuming truth – life is regulated around its centre. Tucked deep within its protective vault rests a delicate core. Between the awakened pituitary and the sleep-regulating pineal gland lies the third ventricle ensconced by the thalamus on either side, the hypothalamus below and the union of the optic nerves guarding it – all quietly regulating sight, thirst, temperature, wakefulness and the hormonal symphonies that makes us 'us'. You mess with the centre, you rattle the entire axis.

Akshay, a 30-year-old tall and lanky chap, much to his brain's chagrin, housed a threat in exactly this location. I had seen him a year ago when he came to me with dull aching headaches. The ophthalmological exam, for the so-called 'window to the soul', had come clean. But we neurosurgeons know better – we are aware that behind every window is a wall. In his case, the MRI had revealed a small lesion trailing the optic chiasm, nestled near the third ventricle. Small. Subtle. Suspicious. And, more importantly, sentient, which I found out only after a year of watching it grow slowly but consciously. Due to the criticality of the location, him being relatively asymptomatic and the possibly benign nature of the lesion, I had refrained from recommending an operation. But now it was pushing against the optic chiasm, threatening to steal his sight. His sleep was a bit disturbed. He wasn't eating well. The centre was misbehaving. That's the thing about central problems: they start quietly but rarely stay polite. We had no choice but to turn to the heart of our craft.

'What is the risk of this surgery?' he asked.

'The tumour is smack in the centre of your brain,' I explained, detailing the anatomy lodged between hope and horror. 'Anything can go wrong,' I admitted, but then promptly jumped the fence from cynicism to comfort, reassuring him that nothing would. And here comes the dilemma: should we as surgeons project our fears onto a patient and their family or continue to showcase the false bravado that most of us often portray on the exterior? Is it okay to admit we're scared or is it our sole responsibility to make them feel safe?

'I have full faith in you, I know you'll do what's best for me,' he declared.

The real question was whether I had full faith in myself. I looked into my own centre for answers. It swung like a pendulum for a while and then replied, 'You've got this, Mazda!'

The day finally arrived. We mapped a corridor to the brain's secret chamber, parting the Sylvian fissure – a shimmering valley of veins – to reach the carotid artery. I gently dissected the silvery strands around it and reached the bifurcation, that glorious crossroad of risk and reward. The optic nerve, like a faithful sleeping partner, lies steadfastly next to the carotid artery. I dissected more strands, making more space. We surgeons are often in a hurry to get to the tumour, but like any climb to a majestic summit, the journey itself is what truly makes it spectacular. And, with this particular approach, the view is unparalleled. Speckled stardust on glistening white optic nerves is a visual treat, even if you witness it daily. As I made space between the carotid artery and optic nerve, the redness of the tumour became visible, encircled by a leach of serpentine blood vessels pulsating with a bit of wrath.

We had visitors that day in the operating room, medical students and surgeons from other countries who wanted to observe. It was the perfect case to showcase anatomy. But it was also the most frightening. As I was operating with a full heart and steady hands, I recalled the wisdom of Dr Harvey Cushing: 'A surgeon is surrounded by people who are watching him, but inside he is alone.' It was my centre connected to Akshay's; everything else was at the periphery.

The brain was still a little tight, like a stubbornly full suitcase. As the corridor narrowed, I opened up the anterior wall of the third ventricle and allowed for a gush of cerebrospinal fluid to reduce the pressure, akin to loosening a tightly tied-up corset in a cramped room. The brain relaxed, the tension dropped and the tumour's disguise began to fall apart.

This offered more space between the sleeping partners. I teased the capsule of the tumour and entered it, quickly destroying its core. Pieces of it came running into my suction device, eager to be swallowed from under the surface of the optic nerves. As we debulked the tumour down to its final sliver, the normal anatomy began to fall back to place. The hypothalamus gleamed from below; the pituitary stalk glistened anteriorly; and the brainstem waved out from behind, with the basilar artery pulsating as if to say thank you. The surgery took five hours, and it was five hours of symphonic concentration, transforming complexity into choreography, where we danced around vision, pituitary function, thirst regulation and life itself. We removed the tumour cleanly. Completely.

'We have to see how he wakes up,' I told my assistant as we prepared to close.

And that's the cruel paradox of neurosurgery. The brain can look perfect under the microscope and still hold surprises when consciousness returns. When Akshay woke up, his vision was perfect. But a few hours later, he began emitting a litre of urine every hour and had an unquenchable thirst – a sign of hormonal dysregulation. The brain was revolting because we had messed with its centre. The next few days were cautious but kind, as we externally regulated the centre till its internal compass recalibrated. A few days later, he walked out of hospital with a balanced core.

The surgical centre isn't a place. It's a metaphor. For precision. For courage. For reverence. For knowing that everything from gigantic galaxies to nano neurons spin around something vital. And if you guard the centre, you protect the whole.

Confused Awakenings

She came in wearing a Sabyasachi silk sari the colour of pomegranate peel, her salt-and-pepper hair twisted into an efficient bun, carrying a Bottega handbag that probably cost more than my last holiday. 'I'm not mad,' she announced before I could say a word. 'I just forget things I don't like,' said 70-year-old Mrs Gandhi.

Her daughter accompanied her. Far less flamboyant and living up to her last name in a khadi kurta that was more Fabindia than haute couture, she did most of the talking. 'She's been acting odd for a few months. Forgetting appointments, asking the cook if he's single, putting her keys in the fridge ... I know they're small things, but it isn't like her,' she declared, glancing at her mother, who looked like she'd just walked out of an art auction.

'And I've been baking too much cake,' her mother added with visible irritation. 'Apparently that's a symptom now.'

She was a feisty lady, single-handedly managing the family business up until a year ago when the kids decided to step in and take over. They had already been to a psychologist and a psychiatrist. Both had offered the same diagnosis of early-onset dementia, which, for someone in their seventies, is neither early nor a diagnosis anyone wants to hear. They had even started joint therapy – the new South Bombay substitute for family dinners.

'She needs help,' the daughter said gently. 'She's changed.'

'And you,' the mother interjected, 'need a less boring therapist.'

There was something off. But not in the way I'm used to seeing with dementia. She didn't have that blankness behind her eyes. There was sparkle. There was mischief. She remembered the name of her school principal but couldn't recall why she had tried to bathe the cat in coconut oil last week; I guess she wasn't named Velvet for nothing. I checked her smell and vision and both seemed fine. So, I did what I often do when things don't add up: I scanned her.

The MRI showed a 5 cm tumour sitting snugly on the base of the brain, nudging her frontal lobes upward like a snob in a sea-facing duplex. Frontal lobe tumours are curious things. They don't always announce themselves with seizures, strokes or headaches. They slip in quietly, altering personality, judgement and behaviour with the subtlety of bad politics. People become more impulsive, disinhibited, indifferent – just like regular politicians. They make promises they can't keep and tell neighbours what they really think of their children. They sleep in meetings. They laugh at funerals. They start baking (the country) obsessively.

When I showed her the scan, she examined it like a Sotheby's catalogue. 'So that's the little fellow causing all the trouble?'

'It's not little,' I said. 'And it's not trouble. It's pressing on the parts of your brain that control personality, planning and memory.'

She looked at her daughter. 'That explains your father,' she rued. I guess every South Bombay family is dealing with the same problems – chic on the outside and chaotic within. The saris may be Sabyasachi but the souls are slightly scrambled. The bags are Bottega but the baggage, *bhaari* [heavy].

'These tumours are typically benign – polite in nature, even if disruptive in behaviour. But they're often vascular and can be tightly adherent to the surrounding structures. The key is to debulk them from within, cauterize the blood supply and peel the capsule away without harming the brain or the nerves. It's like scooping *malai* off the surface of chai without disturbing the chai itself,' I explained.

They decided to go ahead with the surgery.

We made an incision hidden within the hairline and reflected the scalp forward. I drilled two burr holes and fashioned a frontal craniotomy, lifting the bone flap with care. Once we opened the dura, the frontal lobe came into view – pale, glistening, gently pulsating. We placed cotton patties and started the slow process of brain retraction; more than a forceful act, it was a conversation with the anatomy, with gravity doing most of the work. The tumour eventually revealed itself – yellowish-white, slightly lobulated, mildly vascular. I buzzed the base and began removing it. It felt soft, almost apologetic, like it knew it had overstayed its welcome. The ultrasonic aspirator hummed away as we cored out the central mass, shrinking the tumour from within. As it collapsed, the capsule started peeling off like the rind of an overripe fruit.

We removed it cleanly. No brain contusions. No bleeding. The dissection felt like a polite negotiation, not a battle. The frontal lobe relaxed back into place, grateful, as if someone had lifted an invisible burden. The microscope's lights glistened off a clean, dry surgical cavity.

She left the table warm, stable and intact, and it was as though we had pressed a reset button on her personality. She woke up from anaesthesia already halfway into a joke about the ICU nurse's eyebrows. Over the next few days, the transformation was nothing short of cinematic. Her memory sharpened, her language regained nuance and her sarcasm returned to its pre-morbid potency. By Day Four, she was giving unsolicited life advice to the junior doctors and correcting their Hindi grammar. By Day Six, she asked if she could run my clinic's reception. 'Clearly, your current staff can't spell "meningioma" correctly!'

I saw her two weeks later, in yet another silk sari but with none of the earlier confusion. She handed me a chocolate cake. 'Only three layers this time. I've calmed down.'

The final biopsy had confirmed what we had expected – a benign meningioma. No radiation needed, just annual scans to ensure it wouldn't return.

'Doctor,' she asked, pausing as she got up to leave, 'do you think I should go back to therapy?'

'Only if your therapist asks to see you instead.'

She laughed. 'I'll take that as a no.'

Bodily Fluids

'I have these drops of liquid trickling from my right nostril for the past week,' expressed Sheila, a very concerned, visibly overweight 45-year-old business executive. She was dressed in a suit and wore her hair in a tight bun, like a school mistress, as she leaned forward slightly and bent her head to elucidate what she was saying. Crystal clear driblets trickled down, one every few seconds like they do from a tightly shut but slightly leaky tap whose washer needs to be replaced. I collected a few bubbles in a sterile glass bottle to test. 'Initially, I thought that this was just a runny nose, but I have no other symptoms apart from a headache and this just felt odd, so here I am,' she gestured with animated hands, as most people do when something unexpected shows up.

'Do you feel a slight salty sensation at the back of your throat when you lie down?' I asked, to confirm my suspicion of this being no ordinary liquid but sacrosanct cerebrospinal fluid (CSF).

'Yes, yes, yes!' she interjected, relieved to know that I'd already diagnosed her problem. After a detailed assessment, I emphasized that she was lucky not to have had any fever; if the fluid got infected, it could lead to meningitis. I ordered a specialized MRI and CT scan to be able to pinpoint the specific defect in the base of the skull from where the brain fluid was likely to be leaking, and had her see me again at the earliest.

CSF is a colourless, odourless liquid that bathes the brain and spinal cord. About half a litre of this fluid is produced daily and gets recycled while nourishing the brain, washing away all the toxins that get absorbed via a drainage system curated flawlessly by nature. A slightly higher content of sodium and chloride gives it its saliferous taste. It also protects the brain by acting like a shock absorber for the central nervous system. A tear or hole in the covering of the brain (meninges) coupled with even a tiny bone defect in the base of the skull could cause CSF to seep out from the nose as it's all interconnected. In health, the nose is a 'stairway to heaven' as far as the journey of breath to the brain is concerned; in disease, however, when directions are swapped and there is an egress of CSF, it can potentially be a 'highway to hell'.

Sheila returned with her reports a few days later and, as expected, one could easily trace the exodus from a tiny defect in the base of the skull to the right nostril.

'We must seal the leak before you develop an infection that could be calamitous,' I forewarned. 'We'll do it through the nose itself, so we don't have to open up the head.'

'I'm ready when you are,' she replied resolutely.

The next day, alongside my ENT colleague, we navigated into her cavernous nostrils, an endoscope in one hand and an instrument in the other to flatten out the nasal turbinates against the lateral wall of the nose. Navigating through the nose with an endoscope is like driving a car. I remember my days as an assistant doctor: my chief would honk 'peep, peep!' which was an indicator for me to move the scope ahead or out of the way without bumping into any structure to avoid fogging the lens. We did a little drilling along Sheila's nose to smoothen out bumps and edges. After searching a fair bit, we could identify clear CSF weeping from a 3 mm defect in the base of the skull. A little bit of redundant brain was also trying to push itself out unsuccessfully.

Every surgeon has their cardinal body liquid, which often dictates the specialty they choose. Being fascinated and mesmerized by blood is not enough; that is simply a common denominator. For ENT surgeons, it's mucus and phlegm. The ophthalmologists are busy with tears. Dentists only have access to saliva. Hepatobiliary surgeons love bile. Cardiothoracic surgeons enjoy the pericardial fluid that cushions the heart. General surgeons are attracted to pus. Orthopaedic surgeons are drawn to the synovial fluid that lubricates joints. Cancer surgeons deal with lymph quite a bit. For nervous surgeons, their own sweat suffices. Gynaecologists are smitten by amniotic fluid. Urologists have urine, but they are also enamoured by prostatic fluid – the yellowish straw-coloured sticky juice that nourishes the sperm. Colorectal surgeons, unfortunately, need to be satisfied with diarrhoea. I, for one, am blessed to work with CSF.

CSF is the most angelic liquid present in the human body – spotless, sanctified and seraphic. It is, however, both the boon and bane of neurosurgeons. When handled tenderly and released gently, it relaxes the brain, allowing for surgery to proceed virtuously. When CSF flows over the tips of tiny metallic instruments, it looks like an immaculate waterfall inside the brain under the microscope. On the rare occasions when it isn't possible to create a watertight seal of the meninges, CSF seeps out from a cranial or spinal wound like a ghoulish adversary one has to fight till the very end for the patient's survival. Any infection of the CSF can turn into a lethal rampage. The sight of CSF within the brain or spinal cord is resplendent, but when you see the same fluid outside, it can be utterly demoralizing. After a valiant operation, to see a post-operative wound leak CSF is disheartening. Only another neurosurgeon can fathom the joy and exultation of a CSF leak ceasing.

In Sheila's case, we cleanly delineated the defect and sealed it using some fat, glue and a flap we had harvested from the nose itself. We injected fluorescein dye to see if there were any further leaks and inspected the entire panorama to ensure that it was dry.

'The first chance is always the best chance for any surgery,' I coached my assistant. 'Revisions and re-dos are never pleasant.' I concluded by reminiscing about two cases in which I had needed to go back a second time to seal the defect.

'Sir, every surgery of yours has a take-home message,' my assistant added wryly, cheekily imitating what I often say after each operation. We packed the nose with nasal packs, similar to tampons.

When we removed the nasal packs after 48 hours and saw no further leakage, we sighed in relief – both she and I, almost in harmony. Sheila walked around merrily, grateful that the sacred fluid was back where it belonged.

As neurosurgeons, we may not always have the luxury of applause or confetti at the end of a successful operation – but when a CSF leak finally stops, trust me, it feels like a standing ovation from the brain itself. And that, in my line of work, is as close as one gets to divine approval.

Size Doesn't Matter

'There is more than a 90 per cent chance that this will get better without surgery,' I told Nilesh, a 46-year-old gym instructor who had come to me with severe neck and left arm pain. He wore a tight black tee that delineated the curves of his torso. I've always wondered why people who pump iron go everywhere dressed as though they are still at the gym.

The pain had started a few days before he came to see me when he had lifted weights that were heavier than usual. It was now at a point where he could not lift his arm up, an act that unleashed an intense, undesirable pain. The MRI showed a large disc that had herniated out between the fourth and fifth cervical vertebra, compressing the nerve that supplied the muscles responsible for raising the right shoulder above the head as well as flexing the elbow, hence the pain.

'What you are experiencing is a combination of compression and inflammation. We will try a solution involving physiotherapy and medication, which works most often, but if it doesn't get better, we might have to consider surgery to relieve the compression from the nerve as a last resort. It's called an anterior cervical discectomy.' I explained.

'Surgery?' he sighed, folding in fear at my seemingly egregious suggestion. In my anecdotal experience, the people who are most apprehensive of surgery are well-built, middle-aged men. Taking an injection in their oversized gluteus maximus muscles is a nightmare for some. Those who are least perturbed about going under the knife are usually women, often lean and above

50. There must be an inverse relationship between external toughness and inner fortitude.

Nilesh tried all modalities of the treatment I had prescribed, but after a slight initial improvement, his condition remained unchanged. In fact, he started developing a numbness in his thumb and index finger, and felt little spiders constantly crawl over his arm. Even an injection that combined a steroid and local anaesthetic didn't work.

After about a month of trying a retinue of options, we agreed on surgery. As I explained what surgery would entail, his Adam's apple started to enlarge; most relentless gym goers have a prominent one. When I explained that we would have to cut through the front of his neck to reach the disc, his face blanched.

'Now would be the ideal time to take him to the operating room,' his resolute wife said, wondering why he was delaying the inevitable.

After a week of being cajoled by his family, he finally lay in front of us, ready for an incision – pinioned under anaesthesia with nowhere to escape. We transversely cut along one of the skin creases over the front of the neck so that when it healed, it would be camouflaged nicely. We buzzed some of the small bleeders on our way to dissect between layers of muscles. The anatomy of the human neck is wondrous: If one dissects the planes carefully curated by nature, each layer opens in front of you like a map mysteriously guiding you to a hidden treasure – illuminating and beautiful. However attractive a good-looking neck is from the outside, the inside is insurmountably more gorgeous.

We retracted the oesophagus and windpipe to one side and the carotid artery to the other, making space by snipping away at small strands of connective tissue that keep things together.

A surgeon needs an extremely diligent assistant to perform this retraction; the laryngeal nerve responsible for vocal cord functioning and voice production traverses in the region, and any undue stretch can result in a patient waking up hoarse, which is devastating. Any change in a patient's voice after this surgery silences a little something within the surgeon.

As I moved inward into the neck, I started feeling bone with my finger and cleared up the final bit of fascia (tissue) with a peanut – a local name given to a contrived instrument that has a small ball of tightly rolled gauze at its tip to help us rub along the bone and expose the concerned glistening disc space, which looks like a tiny speed breaker.

With an X-ray, we then confirmed that we were at the intended level of the spine. We cut into it by clearing off pulpous-looking gelatinous material until we reached the covering of the spinal cord. With a pair of forceps in my steady hands, I pulled out the fragment of disc that had migrated behind the bone and was tormenting the nerve.

'This last move has relieved one month of agony,' I pointed to my assistant. I took a ball-tip instrument to probe for any other fragments, but we were all clear. We placed a small implant to maintain the disc height and stitched him back up. 'Close the skin meticulously,' I instructed, 'or else he'll curse us for the rest of his lives!' Most often, after the pain disappears, the scar is the one thing that continues to bother some people because they can see it every day in the mirror. Here, again, it's the bulky men who have a problem; the women deal with it and move on (or have adequate armamentarium at home to conceal it).

Nilesh woke up with a significant reduction in the tingling and numbness in his hand. He could lift his arm high up above his head, completely pain free. I showed him the tiny fragment of the insolent disc that had been creating havoc in his life, the 2–3 mm of extruded gelatin that had devastated his day-to-day life.

'So, size doesn't matter after all,' he pondered profoundly in a clear voice – something we all end up realizing at some point in our lives.

Brave Heart

I did not know I was going to meet someone like her. She was all of 32 years old and sat in front of me with the poise of someone who had completed finishing school. Her white top enhanced her wheatish complexion. She crossed her legs one over the other with such elegance that even her linen pants did not wrinkle. Her ageing father watched her as she responsibly arranged all her files and papers on the table in front of us – the metaphysical barrier that allows a physician to maintain an emotional distance from their patient.

She had black wavy hair with streaks of silver. Her eyes seemed to have the accrued wisdom of several previous generations. Her face had the serenity of the Buddha and adorned a gentle compassionate smile. But the first words that came out of her mouth were earth-shattering to me.

'I have breast cancer,' she said with a composure I have never seen. From the corner of my eye, I could see tears rolling down her father's face. 'In both my breasts,' she added stoically.

'I'm so sorry to hear that,' I empathized, 'but what brings you to me?' the neurosurgeon in me inquired.

'My oncologist got a PET scan done to plan the course of treatment and they found a tumour in my brain as well. That's why he sent me to you,' she said. 'We also got an MRI dedicated to the brain to ascertain what tumour it is,' she continued as she pulled out the films to show me.

'Aren't you scared of all this?' I asked her, curious to know what was going on beneath that unflappable exterior.

'I have loved the stars too fondly to be fearful of the night,'* she smiled, impressing me with some Sarah Williams poetry. Literature is a great coping mechanism.

What fate delivered to her was so unfair, I thought to myself as I plugged in the films one by one to analyse the scans. She didn't have the slightest headache or, for that matter, any other symptom of the 6 cm gruesome brain tumour nestled within her, between the frontal and temporal lobes in a region of the brain called the insula. After careful thought, I announced that this wasn't a spread from the breast but a separate primary tumour of the brain.

'This is probably a low-grade glioma, a tumour that arises from the glial cells of the brain,' I announced.

'So, can we just leave it alone?' she asked with the curiosity of a child. 'Can I proceed with the chemo and then go ahead with my mastectomy as planned by my doctor?' She told me she was eager to get back to flying as a pilot, and that she'd been granted leave only for three months. I didn't have the heart to tell her that she might have to resort to a ground job in aviation.

Sometimes, there is no right answer. I thought for a while and explained that we would have to get rid of both tumours, and that we'd have to do it in quick succession. 'We could do either of them first,' her oncologist told me over a phone call, 'but if the brain tumour can wait, we'd rather do the breast,' he concluded.

I asked her what she would like to do. I remember my mentor, when faced with several options to choose from, always chose to tell his patients, 'Whatever decision you make will be the right one.' I have religiously followed that practice for over a decade –

---

*Williams, S. (1868). *The Old Astronomer*.

except I end up saying it more to my wife than to my patients.

'Let me get done with the breast and then we'll proceed with the brain,' she decided together with me.

I sat there in awe of her fortitude in taking life-altering decisions with such surety, although I was sure that a deluge of emotions might be erupting within. I find it tumultuous to deal with a flu, yet I see myself giving hope and strength to patients with brain and spine tumours on a daily basis.

We bid each other adieu with a plan to operate on her head once she had gone through a mastectomy and breast reconstruction. Chemotherapy was to start in a week. Yes, oftentimes in the treatment of cancer we need to administer chemotherapy to shrink the tumour before we operate on it.

Two months later, her father called frantically saying that she had had a seizure. She was unconscious at home. They took her to the ER of the closest hospital, which managed to salvage the situation. The day of the seizure was the day she had completed her chemo, and she was scheduled to undergo breast surgery a few days later. However, a repeat MRI of the brain showed that the brain tumour had grown marginally. We had a multi-disciplinary tumour board meeting and decided to go ahead with the brain surgery first.

A couple of days later, we opened up the head to enter an area that was once known as 'no man's land'; such was the danger that surgeons used to avoid going there. It was like the Kashmir of the brain: difficult to access, but once there, it enraptured you. We strode in bravely and could remove the entire tumour as it was, straddling the areas of cognition, motivation, fear, anxiety and happiness.

She woke up smiling broadly – a rarity after brain surgery. We discharged her in a few days and she was fit enough to have her second operation. Weeks later, she called to tell me that recovery from her brain surgery was a walk in the park compared to a double mastectomy with breast reconstruction.

'We only dug a hole; they erected a whole new structure,' I facetiously justified the hard work of my colleagues.

The *Financial Times* recently published an article on the unexplained rise of cancer among millennials. It mentioned that the past 30 years have seen an upsurge in cases of so-called 'early-onset' cancers in the under-fifties.* So marked is the increase that leading epidemiologists have suggested it should be called an epidemic. Scientists are not sure why, but changes in nutrition and ways of living hold at least part of the key to the puzzle. The consumption of food high in saturated fat and sugar is believed to alter the composition of the protective gut microbiome in ways that can harm an individual's health. Excess usage of antibiotics and other medication may also be responsible for altering the gut. Whether it will happen to one of us, only time will tell; now, it is also possible for us to do a whole genome sequence analysis to check if we could be at risk. 'Our graces don't stand to reason any more than our sins do,' I read on someone's X [formerly Twitter] handle.

She returned three months after having valiantly completed both her surgeries. Her long hair had now become a small frizzy bun, gracefully sprouting again after being jettisoned by the chemo. There was no tumour in her brain and her breasts were brand new. She beamed with confidence, hugging me tightly.

---

*Borrett, Amy, and Sarah Neville. *The Unexplained Rise of Cancer among Millennials*. Financial Times, 18 June 2023, www.ft.com/content/90d5f2e3-d539-4149-a503-2114ac3ef355. Accessed 3 March 2026.

'When can I start flying?' she asked like a little child eager to return to her playground.

Knowing that this was a permission I couldn't grant as yet, I replied, 'You're already soaring way above everyone else.'

Section 3

CLINICAL CROSSROADS

These are the stories that live at the junction where medicine meets morality, science bumps into superstition and the surgeon is forced to look inward before cutting outward. These are moments when patients, doctors, families – and sometimes entire belief systems – stand at a fork in the road and must choose which way to go. These essays explore the delicate art of standing still at the crossroads – when to act, when to wait, when to hope and when to simply sit beside a patient and share the uncertainty of being human.

Superstitions

'We cannot get admitted on a Thursday; Mataji *no divas chhe* [The day belongs to the goddess],' Mrs Desai said, vociferously objecting on behalf of her husband, who had agreed to a surgery to alleviate the accumulation of fluid in his brain, a condition we call normal pressure hydrocephalus. In his case, the fluid-containing cavities or ventricles were enlarging in size, causing progressive imbalance while walking, urinary incontinence and some degree of dementia.

The operation involved placing a thin silicone shunt tube into the ventricle of the brain, tunnelling it behind the ear and under the skin of the chest, and then inserting it into the abdomen to drain excess fluid.

'This is not an emergency. You can choose to get admitted any day you like and we will perform the surgery the day after – unless you have a preference for that as well!' I said in jest, not realizing what was in store for me.

'Of course, sir. Saturday is a good day, but we will have to make the cut before sunrise.'

I explained the logistics of the shift timings of operating room personnel and reasoned with the couple that even if I were married to an anaesthesiologist, she would not arrive for surgery before dawn for a routine case. Most surgeries start at 8.00 a.m.

'Sir, we are followers of Mataji. Kindly adjust.'

'I will do my best,' I promised, as I directed them to the reception for the paperwork.

'Sir, what brand of tube will you use?' he inquired. I was

expecting this question; patients like to hear the word 'foreign', although Indian products are just as good. 'Local, imported, no problem, sir. Just that the brand name should start with the letters A, M or K. These are Mataji's names.'

Their smiles touched their ears when I said 'Medtronic Company'.

I try hard to accommodate patients' requests, no matter how bizarre. I have replied to so many messages from patients' astrologers that the word 'neurologist' now autocorrects to 'numerologist' on my phone. It's unnerving to operate on someone on a Tuesday knowing that this is the worst day in the week for them. On the other hand, there are some who will only get operated on a Tuesday. Of course, at the end of the day, belief determines their disposition, but what is expected of the surgeon? Should the surgeon heed inconsequential requests or stick to protocol? I'm not brave enough to be dispassionate.

A few months ago, as one of my patients was being wheeled in for surgery, his mother grew hysterical and suddenly asked for the operation to not proceed. No amount of reasoning could change her mind. The relatives shared that a 'devi' had entered her '*atma*' [soul] and had instructed that the surgery be cancelled. We respectfully agreed, although the patient and the rest of the family had given their consent to proceed. He was operated elsewhere a few weeks later and suffered a devastating complication from the surgery. It could have very well been on my hands, I reminded myself. The customer is always right, be it at a hotel or a hospital.

Surgeons are superstitious too. Some don't operate on a full moon day. Others don't take emergency calls on *Amavas* [moonless night]. A colleague always carries an evil eye pendant in his scrubs while operating. Another puts on the left glove first while scrubbing in. Some surgeons don't indulge in sex the night prior to a major operation. I know of a few who turned vegetarian and gave up alcohol when a post-operative patient that wasn't faring well suddenly started improving.

Mr Desai finally did get operated on a Saturday before sunrise; I had to bribe my anaesthesiologist with an exotic breakfast after the case. He made an excellent recovery with significant improvement in his gait within a few days. Every morning, when I went to check on him, the gentle scent of incense filled the room. Soft *bhajans* [devotional song] played in the background. His wife fasted the entire week, having only a glass of water in the mornings after visiting a temple.

On a Thursday, five days after surgery, I told the family that he could be discharged the next day. They were not thrilled. The Desais conveyed that it was not a good day for them.

'But you got admitted on a Friday,' I said, groaning a little and exhausted by now.

'We can get admitted on a Friday, but not discharged. Please understand, sir.'

Clinical Equipoise

An elegant family of five walked into my office. The patient was the 80-year-old matriarch; let's call her Aunty ji. She was dressed in a bespoke white and gold salwar kameez with her hair tied back. She sat upright in the chair in front of me while her two daughters, probably in their fifties, planted themselves on either side of her. The two dutiful-looking sons-in-law accompanying them plonked themselves on the examining bed.

'We're two brothers married to two sisters,' one of them spoke up, introducing the fam jam.

'How's that going for the four of you?' I digressed before even trying to find out what was wrong with Aunty ji, in a bid to calm the nerves that were palpable in the room.

'Well, let's just say everything has its pros and cons!' one daughter replied.

'But there are more pros for sure,' the men jumped in to save the day.

'So, what brings you here?' I asked, finally turning to Aunty ji.

'I've been forgetting stuff,' she said, taking charge of the conversation. 'Sometimes I feel giddy and sometimes I have some imbalance while walking.'

'We've discussed it, and we don't feel there's anything wrong as far as her memory goes,' one of the daughters provided her perspective.

'But I feel something is not right with me,' Aunty ji asserted.

I examined her in detail and ascertained that her strength and coordination were good.

'We've gotten an MRI done,' a son-in-law pulled out the films and I raised them against the beaming light of the October sun peering through my window, which I often prefer to the boring white light of an X-ray box.

'You have a 2 cm tumour in your left temporal lobe,' I said, pointing at it, 'but it's mostly arising from the covering of the brain called the dura and not from the substance of the brain itself, so it isn't malignant,' I went on to explain. 'However, the swelling around it is a little more than normal,' I cautioned. I wanted to give all the details while I tried figuring out in my head what the best advice would be.

'We know all this,' the other son-in-law interjected. 'We've come here for a second opinion, rather a third,' he acknowledged.

'Because we are very confused,' his wife added.

'Let me explain the conundrum,' the son-in-law went on. 'We went to a senior doctor in one hospital, and he said we could leave it alone. "It grows 1–2 mm a year and she'll pass away from natural causes before the tumour can do anything to her" were the doctor's exact words,' he told me. They were then forced by their extended family to take a second opinion from another equally senior and renowned neurosurgeon in another hospital. 'He said, "This needs to be operated upon at the earliest, because she could have a seizure and the brain swelling could have deleterious side effects; it's better to remove it while she's well rather than when she starts having more problems,"' he reiterated verbatim what the second doctor had said.

'That's why we are so flummoxed,' the daughter added, while Aunty ji patiently waited for the verdict of someone with 25 less years of experience than the other two stalwarts in the field.

Strange as it may sound, this is an age-old occurrence in medicine – doctors, just like other people, will have differing opinions on how to proceed regarding something. I have seen time and time again, in my field and beyond, that medical professionals with identical qualifications and extremely similar levels of experience will often present diverse views on what to do next for a patient. We call this clinical equipoise – a state of genuine uncertainty. I have seen it with back pain: some doctors will prescribe bed rest, while others completely denounce it. Cardiac procedures present the same battle: some doctors prefer to stent while others simply give you blood thinners. In obstetrics, certain doctors are caesarean happy while others will have you labour it out. Like in many aspects of life and living, these seemingly contradictory suggestions are neither right nor wrong; they are simply honest but varying perspectives. I began to realize for the umpteenth time how hard it is for the common person to make decisions about their health when such conflicting opinions are presented. We must use our intuition, not our logical mind, when making important choices.

'There is a grey zone in medicine,' I clarified to Aunty ji and family. 'When there is no conclusive evidence toward one treatment paradigm over the other, surgeons tend to use their clinical judgement and experience to give you a recommendation. Unfortunately, sometimes, the true nature of the disease is only revealed in the due course of time,' I explained. Just like some people, I wanted to add, but refrained.

I could either agree with one of the two eminent doctors or present my own version and hope that I did not leave them even more confused than when they arrived. The Buddha in me decided to take the middle path, staying away from the indulgence of jumping into surgery and the self-denial of leaving this alone.

'Let's do some gait and balance physiotherapy for three

months and see if she's clinically better,' I suggested. 'I want her to be as physically and mentally active as possible, and also to take a walk every day and get some sun,' I added the standard cures of many of life's problems. 'We'll also repeat an MRI then to see if anything has changed in that time.'

The only commonality between the Buddha and me is that even though I am younger, I feel just as old. Unfortunately, in the field of medicine, simply feeling old does not count as experience. Nevertheless, adopting the Buddha's teachings that day brought with it a certain degree of peace. I stayed non-attached from either extreme – surgery and doing nothing – and assumed the eight-fold path with mindfulness.

The family looked reassured and immensely relieved with the middle path too, which, in my opinion, was the right thing to do. This is what most therapists also endorse: when in doubt, wait it out. It is still too early to say if this was the right or wrong choice, but the decision to wait comes from a good place, and the urge to do what is best for the patient persists. What happens to Aunty ji, whether she or her MRI worsen in three months' time or stay the same, and the decisions we take subsequently, will be revealed by time.

Aunty ji folded her arms with grace and dignity to thank me. As she left with all her children, one of them said, 'Thank you for allowing us to find a middle way.'

I couldn't help myself. 'Two brothers marrying two sisters is rather extreme, so it was time for something milder,' I joked, as we all had a bit of a laugh.

P.S.: Aunty ji has been managing well for the past five years – without surgery, and the tumour hasn't grown.

Healthy Matchmaking

She came to me with her father. They sat in front of me in my office for a consultation, looking at me a little tentatively. She looked like she was in her late twenties, hair parted somewhere between the centre and side, distinct enough for me to notice. Her dress had a valley of yellow flowers that resembled the golden fields of the south of France.

'This might seem like a strange consultation, but we wanted your opinion on the matter,' she said, looking sideways at her father, who gave her a supportive smile. 'I'm looking to get married and have received a proposal from a boy,' she said, clearing her throat. I wasn't sure what exactly was so embarrassing for them to treat the subject so gingerly. 'He's very nice. Has a good job. Earns well. Handsome also,' she pulled out a photo on her phone as if I were Sima Aunty from *Indian Matchmaking*.

'So wherein lies the conundrum?' I asked. They leaned forward – I'm guessing for me to repeat myself. 'What is the confusion?' I simplified.

'He told us that his father has Parkinson's. We want to know if Parkinson's is hereditary and if the boy can get affected in the future,' they asked, speaking frankly. And I assumed that if I told them it was, they would reject the proposal.

I started by explaining to them that Parkinson's was a degenerative condition of the brain, where dopamine, an important chemical, gets depleted, resulting in tremors and slowness of movement and some tightness in the limbs. 'It's very often controlled well with medication, and sometimes we can even offer an operation called deep brain stimulation if the tremors get out of control,' I laid out the basics. In the midst of my explanation, I remembered an elderly couple who had once confided in me not to over-treat the husband's Parkinson's because their sex life was marginally better because of it. But it was not my place to get into this in the current conversation, and dear reader, I request that you refrain from doing the same in your head.

'It's almost never hereditary,' I explained to them, alleviating their anxiety. 'And in the extremely rare cases that it is, it shows up early on in life. So, you have nothing to worry about if he's not shaking by this age,' I said with a gentle smile. 'Any other questions?'

'His uncle died of a brain tumour, he told us. Anything to be concerned about there?' the father added.

'Certain brain tumours have a strong genetic predisposition,' I cautioned, 'but it's mostly for direct lineage, as in parent to child, so you should be fine,' I said, seeing the relief on their faces.

'How many boxes will you check before you get married?' I asked, intrigued by the thought process of seeking a partner to spend the rest of one's life with. I believe we can only be one of two things in a marriage: lucky or unlucky. We can check as many boxes as we want, but we keep forgetting that they may all be Pandora's boxes. As Cheryl Strayed says, 'You don't have a right to the cards you believe you should have been dealt with. You have an obligation to play the hell out of the ones you're holding.'

'Any ailment in your side of the family?' I asked, mostly out of curiosity.

'No,' she said instantly, until her dad reminded her that her mother had breast cancer several years ago and underwent surgery, radiation and chemotherapy. 'But she's fully cured now, so nothing to worry about, right?' she assumed.

'Breast cancer has a pretty strong genetic disposition, especially if your mom had it when she was less than 40,' I said, and they concurred that she did. 'I don't mean to get you worked up; all you need to do is get screened regularly,' I advised.

'Is there any way to prevent it?' she asked.

'Regular screening and early detection are key,' I guided. 'Some people remove their breasts if they are positive for a certain mutation, but that might be too much. We now have whole-body genome sequencing for checking our predilection for thousands of diseases but, again, none of these is foolproof,' I said, lamenting that despite all the advances made by medicine, we continue to remain so far behind in providing certainty. Nothing is in our control, yet we're busy checking boxes.

'So, will you tell him that your mother had breast cancer?' I asked upfront, even though it was none of my business.

'I think I must,' she said, owning up to her end of the deal, and my heart was warmed.

'If you really want to discuss ailments, discuss mental health history in the family,' I stated, referring to its underdiagnosed nature. 'If you're getting married to a Parsi, there's nothing you can do about it,' I joked, 'but assuming you aren't, it might be worth discussing,' I mourned my wife's plight. 'Also discuss bills and money, credit and debt, parenting styles and what beliefs you'd like to instil in your children. Discuss how you'd deal with the extended family and what your financial and sexual expectations are. Talk about childhood traumas and check if they've been resolved. Speak about your careers and how you'd like them to take shape. Describe your bucket list, your dream home and your political views,' I listed out, my inner Sima Aunty suddenly surfacing. 'And if you really want to go the distance, then cognitive neuroscience allows you a detailed testing of your personality and can help identify the exact points of confrontation between the two of you. Knowing those in advance will help you understand each other better and divert the obstacle course ahead with ease,' I finished.

'We came here with such a simple question, but we're leaving so much more informed,' she confessed with a big smile.

'May you live happily ever after,' I wished them the myth.

Six months after that, they got married. Later, she brought her husband to me with back pain, which I treated with ease. Back pain in recently married couples has a specific diagnosis (excessive use of the front) but I gave him some exercises and told him he'd be okay.

'So, how's everything?' I asked at the end of the consultation.

'Parkinson's and breast cancer are the least of our worries, Doctor,' they both said smiling.

I understood. 'Marriage is just two people trying to stay together without saying the words "I hate you",'* I reminded them of what Jerry Seinfeld once said, and we all laughed together.

---

*Seinfeld, Jerry. Quote from stand-up comedy routine. Attribution widely circulated.

Organ Donor

'She was eating her lunch at home and collapsed on the dining table,' a panic-stricken daughter brought her 68-year-old mom to the emergency room. She was completely befuddled by what was happening. Everything had been fine just minutes before: her mother had been regaling her with stories of an errant uncle when, suddenly, she became unresponsive. Her blood pressure at admission was astronomical. She had to be intubated and immediately connected to a ventilator, as she wasn't breathing spontaneously. Her records showed she was on blood thinners for a cardiac bypass surgery she had had a few years ago. The CT scan showed a massive haemorrhage within the brainstem, the central core of the brain and areas surrounding it. Imagine drawing a giant brain the size of a *kabutar khana* [pigeon loft], where all the pigeon poop was blood.

I spoke with her daughter and son-in-law who were present. 'I would not suggest doing an operation, because surgery may at best save her life but will leave her vegetative,' I explained honestly.

'But we have to do something,' the daughter insisted emphatically. Most relatives want to go all out for their loved ones because the guilt of not doing everything possible leaves them devastated.

'We will give her medication to reduce the swelling in the brain and keep the blood pressure down, and see if she recovers any of her brain function,' I empathetically made them understand, because telling someone upfront that nothing can be done is equally shocking and can be perceived as giving up too soon.

The next day, she was declared brain dead. While all her other organs were working well with an external support system, the command centre of her body had completely shut down. This technically certifies that a patient is likely to never regain consciousness again.

'So how much time do we have until the heart stops?' the family asked, slowly coming to terms with the crushing news.

'A few hours to about a week,' I explained.

'What do we do until then?' was the next reasonable question.

'Allow for nature to take its course,' I consoled them.

As surgeons, we are not supposed to talk to relatives about organ donation. There could be a conflict of interest. A separate team takes over and explains to the family that if a brain-dead patient fulfils certain criteria, they could be eligible to donate their organs – eyes, heart, lungs, liver, kidney, pancreas – and help others who need these to survive. We've heard true stories of how deeply connected a spouse feels to a stranger in whom their loved one's heart has been transplanted, even though the law requires anonymity of the recipient. Esoteric. Enigmatic. But true. We've also heard stories of organ donors waking up on the operating table after having been declared brain dead just as doctors were preparing to harvest organs. Abstruse. Arcane. But true. Medicine is fraught with freakiness.

There are innumerable reasons for a family to decide in favour of or against donating organs. In India, very few people make their intentions known when they are alive, hence it is up to the next of kin to take a call. When I trained in Chicago a decade ago, as they made my identity card for the hospital, the first question I was asked wasn't my nationality, race, religion or orientation, but whether I would like to donate my organs if I were in a situation where they could be used.

'But I'm only here for a year,' I told the lady at the counter, a little petrified.

'Yes, sir,' she acknowledged, 'But you also know how life is,' she reminded me. I forgot I was in America – a country where more people have guns than gumption.

Our patient's family decided against donating her organs. 'We want the sanctity of her body to be preserved when we perform her last rites,' they justified. She passed away four days later. In some cultures, beliefs regarding life, death and rebirth influence the decision to donate organs. Others believe that the body should not be harmed after death. In many societies, death is surrounded by rituals and taboos. There are superstitions that suggest tampering with the body can invite bad luck or prevent the soul from resting in peace. I'm not sure if this is a myth or cultural stereotype, but I've heard that the Japanese rarely opt for cardiac bypass surgeries because they firmly believe that their soul would leave the body if their chest is opened.

A few years ago, I had operated on a young girl who came to us after two days of high fever. She was in a deeply comatose condition because of a possible fulminant brain swelling from an unknown cause. We were unable to salvage her brain, but her family made the decision to donate all her organs – including her hand, which was successfully transplanted in an amputee and continues to work well even today.

Recently, the mother of a physiotherapist in the hospital developed a spontaneous clot in the artery that supplies blood to the entire intestine. Within a few hours, she developed gangrene of the small bowel and had to undergo an emergency resection of 20 feet of the small intestine. The only way for her to be able to eat now would be to have an intestinal transplant, for which she would need a donor. Until then, she would have to get her nutrition intravenously, which has its own set of complications and can lead to premature death.

'She's recovering well, but we are eagerly waiting for a donor,' her son lamented. They were told that the hospital she was in often gets young adults with severe head injuries that cannot be salvaged. Many families of these brain-dead patients consent to organ donation out of goodwill and love. 'Someone who was considered recently was extremely obese with a lot of fat around the intestine and hence wasn't eligible. Another patient did not match her type,' he updated me daily. 'In such a case, we can't even use a living donor like we can with the kidney or liver, so that makes it even harder – or else I would have donated part of my intestine,' he stated, a tear rolling down his face.

'How does it feel to wait for someone to die so that your mother might be saved?' I asked him candidly.

He cringed, his face a grimace as his body went into a bit of a shiver. 'I would never wish for anyone to be hurt. I'm in the profession of healing, and here I am, praying for someone to show up for my mother,' he confessed. 'Probably someone even younger than her!'

Profane and sacred. Blasphemous and reverent. Material and transcendental.

Cybercrime

Shiv sat across from me in my office, a pleasant man in his mid-forties with a neatly mowed salt-and-pepper lawn atop his head. 'I got an appointment with you to ask about my mother's spine. I've been told she needs an operation, and I wanted a second opinion,' he said, pulling out his phone from a purple-and-silver-striped suit pocket to show me some reports. 'She's back home in Delhi and has severe lower back pain going down both calves. She's 70 and can't walk for more than 10 minutes. There are pins and needles in the feet, and her legs feel heavy,' he described all the typical symptoms of lumbar stenosis – nerve compression in the lower spine.

I began to type notes on my desktop.

'Wait! Before I trust you with her life, are you still running Windows XP?' he interjected.

I didn't know what the hell he was talking about. 'What's that got to do with your mother's spine?' I asked, a little perturbed.

'I can hack into your system and gain access to all your hospital data, meddle with patient records and tamper with billing,' he confessed.

'Why would you do that?' I asked, a little testily.

'Not me,' he smiled, easing me up a little. 'I'm a cyber security expert and my job is to catch the guys who do it. Cybercriminals aren't just locking up files for ransom anymore; they are shutting down life-saving medical devices, altering patient prescriptions and even targeting hospitals for sabotage.'

He asked me if I wanted to hear a shocking story. I nodded.

He told me it was about two rival hospitals in Mumbai. I asked him for names. He refused. A suspected cyberattack, possibly orchestrated by one hospital against the other, changed the medication dosage in the system from 50 milligrams to 500 milligrams. Nurses, following protocols, unknowingly gave patients incorrect dosages. Within hours, four patients had died, and the hospital was thrown into chaos. 'The news wasn't allowed to be reported by the media,' Shiv said grimly.

He continued. 'You won't believe me, but a cyber security colleague of mine is admitted in another city hospital as we speak, and she wanted to know why her surgery was getting delayed. She gained access to the entire operation theatre database on her phone, found out which patient was undergoing what procedure, what stage each operation was on and how much longer it would be for her turn.'

'What!' I exclaimed. 'In my hospital, even when I'm inside the operation theatre, I don't have all this information!' I joked. He pulled out screenshots on his phone sent by his friend to show me.

'I believe, purely on humanitarian grounds, just as the Geneva Conventions protect medical personnel and facilities in times of war, healthcare should be exempt from the cybercriminal world's attacks. There should be some value for the lives we're struggling to save. Regular medical complications hurt patients (and doctors) anyway, and now we're adding cyberattacks to the mix,' I lamented.

Shiv went on to narrate how in 2020, somewhere in Germany, a cyberattack crippled a hospital's systems, forcing emergency patients to be rerouted to another facility 32 km away, which resulted in one patient dying. In June 2024, a major laboratory services provider for NHS hospitals in London was hacked, leading to mass cancellations of surgeries and blood tests and jeopardizing thousands of lives.

'You have a robot in your hospital?' he asked. I acknowledged that we did. 'I could gain access to it from my phone and make it cut 2 cm deeper than you programmed it to,' he told me.

I suggested in jest that perhaps he should perform his mother's operation himself.

'Did you know that Putin won't take a dump in a foreign hotel?' he ignored me and continued, as I stared at him aghast. 'Instead, his bodily waste is collected and transported back to Russia to prevent medical details from being analysed by hostile intelligence agencies.'

This extreme level of precaution underscores how medical data is a goldmine for adversaries, containing insights into a person's health, genetic vulnerabilities, psychological state and even undisclosed conditions that could be used for manipulation. I wish my shit was that valuable.

'Listen, can I have your number? I feel I might need your help before you need mine!' I told Shiv.

'Of course, happy to help,' he responded, as we fixed a date for his mom's procedure.

I picked up my phone to save his number and entered my password to unlock my phone.

'Is 123456 really your password?' he asked with his mouth open. I looked at him in sheer embarrassment. He took my phone to start changing it. 'Don't worry,' he said. 'I won't use your date of birth either!'

Zeitgeist

Every few years, surgery gets a new obsession. A decade ago, it was keyholes. Then came lasers. Now, the flavour of the month, or perhaps of the decade, is robotics and AI. Everyone's either getting robotic surgery, selling robotic surgery or secretly Googling whether a robot will replace them.

Patients have begun to talk like tech critics. 'Doctor, do you use the robot?' they ask, the way people ask if you've upgraded your phone. If I say no, they look mildly betrayed, as if I've confessed to using dial-up internet. If I say yes, they beam as if my robot and I cohabit.

Last week, a gentleman with a slipped disc told me, 'Doctor, I want robotic surgery.'

'Sir,' I inquired, 'do you mean minimally invasive surgery?'

'No, no,' he replied, 'I'm talking about the one where you don't do anything – the robot does it all.'

I told him that in that case, he should just stay home and let his washing machine operate.

We are living through what philosophers call a zeitgeist, a German word meaning 'the spirit of the times'. The term first appeared in the eighteenth century and was used by thinkers like Hegel and Goethe to describe the invisible cultural current that shapes collective thought. Every age has its own: the 1920s had jazz, the 1960s had revolution, the 1970s had disco, the 1980s had bad hair and the 1990s had Nokia phones that could survive the apocalypse. The surgical zeitgeist today is one of automation and precision, where machines promise to remove the last traces of human error … and possibly the humans too.

The truth, as always, lies between the hysteria and the scepticism. Robotics, navigation and AI have genuinely improved spine surgery. They help us plan trajectories, reduce radiation exposure and improve the accuracy of screw placement. The robot doesn't tire, doesn't sneeze, doesn't flirt with the scrub nurse and never complains about the temperature in the operating theatre. But it also doesn't know when the tissue feels different, when the nerve looks unhappy or when a patient's anatomy politely decides to differ from the textbook.

In our quest for perfection, we sometimes forget that surgery is still a biological act. The human body isn't a 3D-printed file. It swells, bleeds and sulks. It can't always be persuaded to behave according to an algorithm. A robot can calculate; it cannot improvise.

Some years ago, a patient came in insisting on 'endoscopic spine surgery'. His neighbour had had one and was back to golfing within a week. I looked at his MRI and explained that his disc had ruptured into several pieces, compressing the nerve like a badly folded wallet. 'You may need a conventional microdiscectomy,' I explained.

He frowned. 'But isn't that old-fashioned?' he asked.

'So is gravity,' I said, 'but it still works.'

Give us a new gadget and we'll arrange a conference around it. Technology is seductive because it promises control, and medicine is full of uncertainty. The temptation to delegate our responsibility to a machine is strong. But if you depend entirely on it, you stop thinking. The danger is not that robots will replace surgeons, but that surgeons will start behaving like robots.

When used wisely, though, these tools are magnificent.

I've used navigation systems that guide screw trajectories with millimetric precision, and endoscopes that slip through incisions smaller than a buttonhole. I've also seen what happens when someone uses these tools without judgement; it is probably akin to watching a novice pilot attempt to take off in a jet because the manual looked easy.

A friend once said, 'Technology should extend intuition, not erase it.' That's the sweet spot. The best surgeries are still a symphony between hand, eye and mind, not a solo by silicon. The robot can aim, but it's the surgeon who must decide where to aim, and why.

Patients, too, are adjusting to this brave new world. One recently asked if ChatGPT could possibly plan her surgery. I said it could most probably write a very flattering post about it, but the sutures could turn out messy. Another wanted to know if I'd considered using a drone for spinal screws – it would be cheaper, he claimed. 'Only if it comes with Amazon Prime delivery,' I quipped. We used to measure surgical brilliance by scar length and then by incision size, but now we do so by the number of screens we can stare at simultaneously. Some of my younger colleagues reckon that if an operation isn't accompanied by a 3D animation, it may not be worth doing.

There's also the practical side. Robots don't complain, but they do malfunction. Once, midway through a surgery, the robotic arm froze. We restarted the console thrice, even called the engineer, but finally had to finish the surgery manually. The patient recovered beautifully. The robot, however, took longer to reboot – and probably still holds a grudge.

As a profession, we've constantly evolved. Trephination transformed into craniotomy, open surgery became minimally invasive surgery and microscopes gave way to endoscopes.

The best surgeons adapt, not because trends demand it but because improvement does. The trick is to stay current without becoming a slave to the current.

I tell my younger colleagues that being modern doesn't mean discarding the tried and tested. It means understanding the why behind the new. It means knowing that a robot can insert a screw straighter than you can, but it still needs you to know when *not* to insert one. It means remembering that empathy cannot be automated, and that no app can replace the quiet reassurance of a surgeon saying 'you'll be fine'.

Technology should help us see better, not think less. It should make our hands steadier, not lazier. And if it does replace us one day, I hope it at least inherits our sense of humour – because surgery without it would be unbearable. The zeitgeist will keep changing – from open to keyhole, from keyhole to robot, from robot to who-knows-what-next. The trick is to not resist it, but to not drown in it either. Surf the wave but keep one hand on the shore.

As I finished my OPD clinic one evening, a patient asked if I'd soon have a robot doing my job.

'Possibly,' I said. 'But until it learns to drink cold coffee, respond to WhatsApp messages from three family members of a patient all at once and smile when someone calls it Doctor Google, I think I'm safe.' The real trick, I told him, is simple: keep up with technology, but don't get carried away by it. Be its master, not its minion.

He nodded thoughtfully. 'So, Doctor, what do you call this approach?'

'The human interface,' I said. 'It's still in beta, but it's running quite well.'

For all its brilliance, AI still struggles with something

profoundly human – hope. It can predict outcomes, but it cannot promise comfort. It can read scans but not emotion. It cannot understand why a patient reaches for your hand before anaesthesia, or how a kind word steadies a trembling family in the waiting room. AI has surpassed our speed, our precision, even our memory, but can it look someone in the eye and give them courage? Can it look itself in the eye and accept failure? Surgery, at its heart, is still an act of faith between two people – one who trusts, and one who must be worthy of that trust.

Surgeons' Changing Room

'Hey, Mazda!' an orthopaedic onco-surgeon introduced himself to me while I was getting into my operation theatre scrubs in the surgical changing room. For the uninitiated, the surgical changing room is the sanctum sanctorum of any hospital, where all men (without exception) who are meek and silent at home disrobe from their submissive domestic attire and become loud and boisterous, adorning their superhero capes, getting ready to take on the egoistical world of saving lives.

'You probably don't remember me, but I operated on you around two decades ago,' he said to my surprise. The only operation I've ever had was to remove a benign (non-cancerous) tumour from a small bone of my left foot, I recollected. 'I was part of that team,' he smiled, reminding me of how nervous I was about an incision on my foot and how I have now gone on to cut people open daily. I was instantly reminded of the ordeal I had completely wiped from my memory. The surgical changing room is a great place to reminisce on old times.

'What surgery are you doing today?' I asked.

'I do only bone tumours now, that's my specialty,' he flexed a little, having progressed from the conventional world of knee- and hip-replacement surgery. 'We are removing a tumour from someone's femur and replacing the entire bone with a custom-made 3D implant,' he told me enthusiastically. 'What about you?'

'I'm doing an acoustic tumour,' I bragged a little. 'Going to remove a large tumour from someone's hearing nerve and try and preserve hearing,' I gestured with fine movements of my hands, not realizing I hadn't tied the knot on my pyjamas, which came slipping down. The surgical changing room is a great place to gloat. Surgeons often like to bluster about how complex their case is going to be and how many more cases they have than their peers. It's also a place where they whine about how long anaesthesiologists take to induce a case, while the anaesthesiologists do the same in the room next door, wondering when a surgeon is likely to finish a case.

Just then, our senior general surgeon walked into the room to change and jovially offered up his list of cases for the day. 'I'm busy putting my head in people's bums all day,' he rued, adjusting his mask so it sat well above his nose as he spoke to us about piles, fissures and fistulas. He narrated a story about how he had done an emergency surgery the previous evening to remove a dumbbell from someone's rectum. 'They told me it was a gym accident!' he said, raising one eyebrow. 'God knows what the kids of today are up to,' he sighed, as the rest of us conjectured about what might actually have happened. The surgical changing room is a great place for such gossip.

A cardiac surgeon sauntered in at the same time, and all of us changed simultaneously in what now seemed like a cramped space between the wall and the rusty lockers that lined the room. 'If one more person comes in, I'm sure our PPs will touch!' I said, using a cruder word, deciding to petition the hospital administration for more space. I was, of course, referring to polypropylene, a material used to make surgical gowns, but the surgical changing room is a great place for lewd jokes. We quickly bid each other the best for the day and charged out to appear important, as other doctors walked in screaming for tops and bottoms unavailable in their size or about finding holes in their apparel where there weren't meant to be any.

The surgical changing room is also a great place to alleviate frustration. You can redirect your anger at your wife towards an implant that hasn't arrived on time, and you can deflect your irritation at your kids' tantrums on the staff for not shifting the patient soon enough for you to start your case. You can crib about the stock market, the traffic or the weather, and you'll find someone to hear you vent, albeit while they scroll on their phone pretending to listen to you. Our theatre complex has a common changing room for all staff – ward boys, attenders, technicians and surgeons – so each day, there is a different array of torsos to view, sights to see, smells to savour and sounds to hear.

The changing room first thing in the morning is very different from the room one sees at the end of the day. In the morning, clothes are stacked neatly and there is a whiff of freshness in the air, while towards the evening, notices of 'Please keep your scrubs in the bin' are clearly ignored, with gowns scattered all over the place. As they walk in to change, you'll see tired surgeons rip their masks off as if they've just returned from war, and caps strewn around like confetti at a Coldplay concert.

The surgical changing room is also a place for hope and prayer. When surgeons return to it after surgery, wiping the metaphorical sweat off our brows, we analyse the operation in our heads and sometimes in our hearts. We hope we've done the right thing. We pray our patients recover the way we expect them to. As we get out of our scrubs into a more mortal outfit, it's time to surrender and oftentimes even invoke the divine for timely intervention.

When I was a resident in training, the surgical changing room would be the place where the most junior doctors would see their most senior professors in their *chaddi*s [underpants]. Stalwarts of surgery – professors you shuddered to ask questions to, and even if you did, they barely answered, or professors whose stern stare could make you pee in your pants – had no choice but to drop their guard and be one among everyone else. And once you saw them like that, in your head, you could poke fun at their flab or look at them fondly. You could place them on a pedestal or raze them to the ground. The surgical changing room is a great leveller. We all go out of it wanting to heal, but in the process, we also all hurt sometimes.

'We all share the same sun,' was doodled on Chris Martin's piano as he wooed Mumbai when he came here to perform. The surgical corollary to that is 'We all change in the same room!' The changing room for the female doctors is separate, though. And, thankfully, I have no idea what goes on in there.

God and the Surgeon

'Scrubbing in' is the act of cleaning one's hands and arms with antiseptic before a surgical procedure. A neurosurgeon – whose career typically spans about 30 years and roughly 300 cases a year – scrubs for 10 minutes before every operation. Do the math and you arrive at an unarguable truth: about 1,500 hours of life are spent standing at a scrub sink.

This gives the neurosurgeon, without contest, the cleanest hands in the family. It also gives him something else – time. Time to stare at his own reflection in the mirror, literally and metaphorically masked, and think.

When you are a resident doctor, scrubbing in is a period of quiet anxiety disguised as routine. Your mind runs through a rapid-fire interrogation, usually conducted by an imaginary version of the chief surgeon who is sharper, faster and far less forgiving than the real one.

What does the patient do for a living? Do they smoke? Drink? Is the name on the MRI the same as the name of the patient lying draped inside the operating room? Are they actually as old as the scan claims? When did the symptoms start? Which side was weaker?

The answers matter. Sometimes they change what you do on the operating table. Sometimes they save you from public embarrassment.

Those 10 minutes are also spent ensuring that nothing small has been overlooked – because small things have an irritating habit of becoming very big things during surgery. I would always check with the anaesthesiologist: is blood available? Have the antibiotics been given? Has the correct medication gone in? Scrubbing in was my time to go down my mental checklist, my way of making sure that the chief surgeon could focus on the difficult things without being derailed by the trivial ones.

As I grew into an independent surgeon, the thoughts at the scrub sink evolved. The questions turned inward. I began to rehearse the surgery itself, step by step, running the entire operation in my head. I would visualize the anatomy in three dimensions, imagine the length, breadth and height of the surgical corridor, anticipate which nerve or blood vessel would try to surprise me and remind myself of when caution needed to be upgraded to paranoia. I always had a Plan B. Over time, experience taught me that Plan B had a distressing tendency to fail as well. These days, I routinely arrive with Plans C and D quietly folded and ready in a corner of my mind.

In the final minute, as warm water trickles down my elbows and my palms are held up like I'm surrendering to the universe, I do one last thing. I pray. First, for the patient who is about to meet the knife. Then, for the man holding it.

I wouldn't describe myself as deeply religious, or even convincingly spiritual. But I do believe in a guiding force – call it intuition, grace, luck or something we have not yet found a way to measure. In the operating room, at least for me, there is an unseen connection between patient and surgeon, a quiet current that offers reassurance to one and humility to the other. On days when things don't go according to plan – when bleeding refuses to be polite and anatomy declines to follow the textbook – the three Ps that have stood the test of time come into play: pressure, patience and prayer. A little background music doesn't hurt either.

During my training at Christian Medical College, Vellore, I noticed a ritual that quietly moved me. Before each patient was wheeled into the operating theatre, the nurses would hold hands and whisper a prayer. One day, as I walked past, I heard them say: 'Take care of our patient, Mazda. Give him courage and strength. Help him recover fast. For this, we thank you, our Lord, our Mazda. Amen.'

For a brief moment, I stood there, unsure whether to feel flattered or deeply uncomfortable. I gently asked them to clarify – they were not addressing me. They meant *master* – the Lord above, which, in their accent, sounded suspiciously like my own name.

Some modernists argue that religion has no place in science. They may be right. But medicine is not pure science; it is beautifully, frustratingly ambiguous. And while I know outstanding surgeons who are deeply religious, I also know brilliant ones who are atheists. For them, their work *is* their religion.

Once, while scrubbing in alongside one such eminent surgeon, I asked him if he believed in God.

'What's the difference between God and a neurosurgeon?' he asked.

Knowing he was setting a trap, I smiled and waited.

'God doesn't think he's a neurosurgeon.'

At the scrub sink, I laughed. Then I scrubbed a little longer.

Loneliness

I'm a self-professed astute observer of human medical conditions, and this is one of them.

Hospitals are not lonely places, but they contain a lot of lonely people. Over the years, I've realized that recovery after surgery doesn't depend only on the precision of a scalpel or the dosage of a drug. It often depends on who waits for you outside the ICU.

A wound heals faster when there's someone to change the dressing with care, even if they use the wrong tape. The heart beats steadier when it recognizes another voice nearby. And patients who have someone to hold their hand recover sooner than those who have only hospital linen for company.

In most private hospitals, there's an unspoken hierarchy of caregiving. The wealthy outsource affection. Patients are looked after by nurses, ward boys, dietitians, physiotherapists and occasionally family members who make brief appearances between business calls. They arrive with hampers of dry fruits and the latest gadgets to 'cheer up Dad' before disappearing again into traffic.

The poor, on the other hand, bring devotion. I've seen old men sleeping under their wives' beds because there isn't another option. Sons spoon-feeding their mothers soup with the same reverence with which one might pay obeisance to a deity. Daughters massaging their fathers' feet as if trying to press life back into them. Their love is raw, inconvenient, unpaid and utterly medicinal.

A few years ago, an elderly couple came to see me. He was 92, she was 89 – both stooped slightly but were perfectly synchronized, the kind of couple that walks together without needing to speak. She had had a compression fracture in her spine after a minor fall.

'Doctor, fix her,' he said, as if I were a tailor and her vertebrae a loose button. We treated her conservatively, but age is a fragile thing. She developed a chest infection and passed away one morning. He was inconsolable. 'We were married for 67 years,' he said, his hands trembling. Three hours later, he collapsed and died too. His heart was fine. His will wasn't. The body, it seems, can only live so long when its reason for living leaves the room.

Loneliness doesn't just visit the elderly; it haunts youngsters too. During my fellowship in America, I was astonished at how often patients came in alone for major procedures. They'd drive themselves, park, sign the consent form, get operated on and then Uber home post-op, their discharge summary folded neatly next to a salad. No family, no fuss, no waiting arms. Independence taken to its tragic extreme.

In India, we do the opposite. We arrive with entire neighbourhoods. Aunties bring food, cousins bring opinions and all ask if there is free parking. It's chaos, but it's a living, breathing kind of chaos – proof that we still care enough to crowd.

Even so, I often see old patients come to my clinic alone. They walk in with scans tucked under their arms, sit quietly on a chair and wait their turn. When I ask who's come with them, they say, 'No one, Doctor. My children live abroad.' They smile as if it's a badge of pride.

When I tell them they'll need surgery or prolonged care, the smile falters. 'Who will stay with you?' I ask. They look down. That pause, heavier than any diagnosis, is what I've come to recognize as surgical loneliness.

A few months ago, a widower in his seventies came in for a spine procedure. He lived alone in a flat filled with books and dust. After surgery, he insisted on going home the same day.

'Who'll help you up the stairs?' I asked.

'My Alexa,' he said. We laughed. The next morning, he called to thank me – 'Not for the operation,' he said, 'but for asking that question.'

Loneliness, like cholesterol, creeps up quietly. It doesn't show up on blood tests but corrodes everything that keeps us alive. You can see it in the eyes of patients who have no one to call, no one to text, no one with whom to share the fear that their next operation might be their last. Science doesn't yet have a metric for how effective love is as a cure, but I sometimes think it's the most potent post-op antibiotic.

Yet, amid the sterility of wards, I've witnessed small acts of human connection: a nurse who sings to an old woman while changing her bandage; a ward boy who feeds a paralysed man lunch, joking about cricket scores; a junior resident who sits with a patient long after rounds are done. These moments don't show up on discharge summaries, but they are where healing truly begins.

We are creatures wired for connection. When that connection breaks, so do we. Machines may monitor pulse, pressure and oxygen, but they can't measure hope. Hope isn't quantifiable. It's given quietly, in the way a hand rests on another, or in a voice that whispers 'I'm here'.

My all-time favourite singer Jagjit Singh once sang,

Mujhe tasalli na do, sirf baithe raho,
Waqt mere marne ka tal jaayega.

[Don't console me, just sit with me; time itself will delay my death.]

I've seen it happen – in ICUs, in waiting rooms, in homes. Sometimes, love keeps people alive longer than medicine does.

In the same ghazal, Anwar Mirzapuri writes,

Yeh kam hai ke maseeha ke rehne se hi,
Maut ka bhi iraada badal jaaye?

[Isn't it something, that the mere presence of a healer can make even death change its mind?]

However, even among doctors, there's a peculiar kind of loneliness. We spend our days surrounded by strangers. We talk endlessly but rarely speak. Our WhatsApp groups are busy, but our hearts stay in airplane mode. Loneliness isn't the absence of people – it's the absence of being seen. The business of a 16-hour day masks it all.

I recently read somewhere that medicine is considered to be the loneliest profession, because doctors rarely speak well of other doctors and colleagues are rarely friends. We attend the same conferences, exchange polite smiles, even click photos together. We're co-surgeons, co-authors, and co-panellists – but seldom companions. A possible reason for this is that medicine, unlike most professions, is built on rank and hierarchy. Only the 'toppers' get surgery. Only the 'best' are selected for postgraduate programmes. Only a handful 'make it big'. So, we start running – not to be better doctors, but to be better than other doctors. It's not malice, it's conditioning. But the repercussions are lethal.

Studies from reputed journals show that doctors report the highest rates of professional isolation compared to engineers, lawyers or corporate professionals. One study found that over 60 per cent of physicians have no close professional friends outside their immediate workplace. Besides the obvious mental health repercussions, this is damaging even on the professional front: when doctors stop trusting each other, they stop learning from each other. When envy replaces empathy, the whole ecosystem suffers – and everyone loses, especially the patients.*

Technology may let us replace joints, valves and vertebrae, but it cannot replace the presence of another human being. Machines heal the body; only people heal the soul.

We are all caretakers, whether we admit it or not. The question is: when the time comes, will we be the ones holding a hand, or the ones waiting for someone to hold ours?

---

*Medscape UK. "61% of Doctors Say Work Gets in the Way of Maintaining Friendships." *Medscape*, 21 April 2023, www.medscape.com/viewarticle/61-doctors-say-work-gets-way-maintaining-friendships-2023a100089r?utm_source=chatgpt.com&form=fpf. Accessed 3 March 2026.

I Had a Dream

A few years ago, I got a call from the Vatican. 'Hello, this is Alessandra Romano and I'm calling from the office of His Holiness, Pope Francis.'

'Yes?' I answered, both suspicious and surprised, proceeding with a muttered, 'How may I help you?'

'Am I speaking to Dr Mazda Turel and is this the right time to talk, *signore*?' he questioned in a thick Italian accent, the kind that someone might overdo while pulling a prank. I tried to quickly identify if it was one of my friends pulling a fast one on me, but we hadn't done something like that in over two decades now.

'Yes, this is Mazda,' I confirmed my identity.

'I am calling regarding a strictly confidential matter,' Alessandra continued in a serious tone, 'and we hope you will respect the privacy of His Holiness regarding the same.'

'Please go ahead,' I replied, still suspicious but now also a little serious.

'As you must be aware, our Holy Father hasn't been keeping well for some time now, which is also why he has reduced his public engagements and appearances. He has been having persisting headaches. The personal physician of the Pope, Dr Roberto Bernabae, has diagnosed him with a brain tumour after several tests were conducted, and the neurosurgeons here have suggested an operation,' he briefly summarized.

'Okay,' I replied, not knowing what the call to me was for.

'His Holiness Pope Francis wants you to do the operation,'

said the reverend, sounding a little confounded himself at the absurdity of this phone call.

'Is this a joke?' I asked, a little impatiently, but then quickly realized my own worth and switched to, 'Why me, when he could get anyone in the world?'

'Your name appeared to him in his meditations the previous night, and this is his personal request,' he replied in a formal tone. 'If you are willing, we will arrange a formal video consult with his doctors and then make travel arrangements for you and your team to come over at the soonest,' he concluded. During the phone call itself, my email inbox received an official communication from his office along with all his medical reports.

'I would like His Holiness to be on the call before I can make the decision to travel,' I added some meat to the conversation. A few days later, through very official looking communication, I got onto a call with the Pope and his medical team. He was in his ceremonial robe and everyone else wore a crisp suit, while I was in my scrubs sitting in my office. *I should have taken this a little more seriously*, was my first thought.

The surgeons took me through the case history and examination findings in detail while I sat there a little awestruck. They asked if I had any questions but everything was clear. It was a big but thankfully benign tumour pressing on the Pope's right frontal lobe.

'It's straightforward and he should be fine,' I said with brevity, maintaining decorum.

'Thank you and may God bless you,' were the Pope's only words before he left the meeting, allowing us to discuss the logistics. I was made to sign a non-disclosure agreement until the Pope could make his first public appearance after the surgery (which is why I can talk about it now).

We organized a four-member team from the hospital to go to Rome, which included me, my assistant, a nurse and the anaesthesiologist. On landing, we were escorted to the Vatican in a mini entourage. Our accommodation was arranged in the Apostolic Palace itself, ordinarily the official residence of the Pope, although it is this Pope's* personal choice to live in a guest house nearby, I was told. After an official lunch with the Pope's chief physician and a private tour of the palace along with a briefing of how it functions, we were escorted to meet the Pope.

He sat there in a sombre room devoid of all the grandeur of the palace. It was surreal being in a room with a man whom millions can see only from afar. There was an indescribable aura around him, but once he started speaking, he seemed like a regular chap going around doing God's work. He spoke to me in his Italian English, and I briefly asked him a few technical questions, carrying out a quick examination after taking his permission to make physical contact with him. I held both his hands in mine. They were soft and wrinkled. I put them on my head and asked him to bless me. He did so and kissed me on the forehead.

'I do have a confession to make,' I said, becoming a little chatty. 'Many years ago, when I visited the Vatican as a tourist, I jumped the three-hour line outside and sneaked in. I seek your forgiveness for that,' I quipped, and we both laughed about it. 'Out of curiosity, Your Holiness, why do you want me to do your operation?' I asked just before I left.

'That shall be revealed to you when the time is right,' he said, always a man of few words. We then visited the private hospital of the Vatican that caters to all the cardinals and pontiffs. We

---

*referring to the former Pope Francis.

were shown the equipment; it was all state of the art and I tried hard to not look enamoured.

The next morning, the head of the Catholic Church was under anaesthesia on a table in front of me with no news of this in the world press whatsoever. I have never felt this nervous before an operation. If something were to go wrong, I knew my career was over. 'Let's do this like we would do it for anyone else,' I told the team. Once he was under the drapes and we had opened the head, it looked like that of a regular pious 85-year-old. In a synchronized fashion, we removed the tumour effortlessly without a glitch. He was fully awake as we wheeled him off to the ICU within a few hours, a gentle smile on his face. As the ICU was reserved entirely for him, I slept the night on the bed next to him to ensure nothing went wrong. I spent the next three days by his side, having long and interesting conversations that I plan to compile into a book titled, *Parsi Communions with a Man of Christ.*

His Holiness was discharged within a few days and resumed some of his work in a week. He even made a brief appearance at the large balcony at the centre of St Peter's Basilica to ensure that none of his devotees were concerned about his health. The night before we left, our team was felicitated in an extremely private yet opulent ceremony on the palace lawn. The air was crisp and the atmosphere filled with gratitude. It was such a proud moment for me, my community and my country.

I looked up into the sky and saw a shooting star whiz past. The harder I looked, the closer it seemed to come towards me. Within a few moments, it had doubled up in size and appeared to crash into the earth. I felt a huge thud on my body.

'Wake up daddy, wake up!' said my 20 kg daughter jumping on me. 'It's Sunday! Let's go out and play!'

Theatrical Conversations

'Here is my MRI and it shows a brain tumour, for Christ's sake. Why me?' implored Elton John, a visibly upset 60-year-old theatre artist. His real name was Eric Jamaspa, but he preferred to use his stage name. He was dressed in an effervescent floral shirt, ankle-grazer striped pants and below-ankle polka-dotted socks with white canvas shoes without laces. He donned black-rimmed, round Corbusier glasses and carried his reports in an oversized recycled Freitag bag – a company renowned for making items out of truck tarp, cycle tubes and car seatbelts.

How can someone who dresses like that ever be upset about anything? I thought.

I believe doctors are allowed to make a few harmless assumptions in a lighter vein about the people they meet. We encounter personalities from varied backgrounds on a daily basis – those who dress peculiarly, smell weirdly, behave oddly and have mixed (often indiscriminate) opinions about their doctors – so why can't we make quick, seemingly rational conclusions about our patients in jest?

As neurosurgeons, we sporadically see patients who are of the firm belief that there is something wrong inside their head despite completely normal scans and reports. Excess 'gas', panic attacks, ulcers, insomnia and even erectile dysfunction are often attributed to something structural changing or going on 'up there'. Quick analytical conclusions about various personalities are required to ascertain if the problem is organic or functional, followed by a referral to the concerned specialists, often psychiatrists.

'Why did you get an MRI to begin with?' I questioned, quickly attempting to resolve John's problem and alleviate his anxiety.

He widened his eyes, removed his spectacles in a lightning-quick move and placed them on my table. On closer inspection I noticed the glass had a pink tint on it. He pouted his lips and expressed that all he had was an infrequent headache.

'And?' I probed, wanting him to speak openly.

'And I used to forget some lines during rehearsals, but which guy my age doesn't?' he questioned with his hands flung open wide, almost toppling my computer.

I wanted to remind him that he was not on stage right now and should calm down, but I didn't have the heart. I was an amateur theatre performer once myself, and I could relate to wanting to have your moment. All the time.

I explained to him that all brain tumours do not necessarily present themselves with raised intracranial pressure. He instantly and animatedly narrowed his eyes and raised one eyebrow, which, I assumed, was a gesture asking me to explain further.

'You don't have to have headaches with vomiting, double vision or a seizure or weakness in the limbs to have a brain tumour. These symptoms depend on the location and size of the tumour. Often, if a headache wakes you up in the middle of the night, that's not a good sign. I usually recommend a scan for even a mild to moderate headache if it doesn't go away in a few weeks. However, MRIs tend to pick up several lesions on the brain, and not all of them require treatment. A lot of these are "incidental" findings and can be left alone or closely monitored. But what you have is probably a low-grade cancer in a relatively safe area.'

'Cancer?' he yelled. Two nurses left their workstations and ran into my room to check if everything was okay. I reassured them that all was in control. I had resigned myself to the fact that the conversation was going to proceed with a flair of the dramatic. I told him that he should be relieved that the doctor who had ordered the MRI had picked this up in its nascent stage, and that removing the tumour would result in a positive outcome. If we were to let it be, it would most likely advance to a higher grade, defeating the purpose of an early diagnosis.

'What have I done to deserve this?' he lamented, another question that we as surgeons are not unfamiliar with. Before I could say 'nothing,' he leaned closer and whispered, 'Has me being gay got anything to do with this? I've been completely faithful though,' he added just as vociferously, wondering if I was going to give him some karma BS.

'Absolutely not,' I asserted, reposing his faith that it was perfectly acceptable to make one's own lifestyle choices. Being gay was partly genes, partly environment, partly chance and, for some, partly luck, I reasoned. He pecked me on the cheek and repositioned himself in his chair, a little mollified. I, on the other hand, was still recovering.

All the world's a stage, said the Bard, and all the men and women merely players. He was playing his part and I was trying hard to play mine. Conversations with patients are never easy: some are filled with hope, others with despair. Most are emotional; anger is a rarity. Very few are as theatrical as John was. There is almost always an element of gratitude but, not infrequently, there is also criticism. Patients look to you for reassurance even in the terminal stages of an illness and yet expect integrity. I'm usually extremely optimistic, but I can recall quite a few instances where patients have cheered me up with the magnanimity of their hearts when there was nothing more I had to offer. Sometimes doctors need to be 'healed' too.

A lot of people ask 'why me?' when confronted with the diagnosis of a brain tumour. Besides the scientific answers (to simplify it, tumours are caused by mutations in genes), I've tried many others – from 'why not you?' to 'I don't know' and 'if I knew, I'd get the Nobel Prize'. None of these provide any solace or comfort, of course, but when I leave them with 'tomorrow, it could even be me,' there is the silent acceptance of the universality of nature's fallibility.

On Top of the World or the Bottom?

I had operated on a brain tumour exactly a week before I was scheduled to travel for work to Uzbekistan. This 66-year-old lady had a tumour growing from her pituitary gland that was compressing her optic nerves and rapidly diminishing her vision. We removed it with finesse using an endoscope through the nose. The family was delighted that her vision had dramatically improved after surgery. The day before I was to leave the country, I saw her in the morning and asked the floor doctor to process her discharge. She was chatty and chirpy, and happy she would be home soon.

'I'm going to be travelling for four days, so I'll see her after a week, as planned,' I told her daughter while conveying all the necessary post-operative care instructions.

A few hours before she left the hospital, she collapsed in the washroom. Luckily, a nurse accompanying her prevented her from falling to the ground. When we rushed to examine her, her speech was slurred and she was facing weakness in the right arm and leg. She was having a stroke. Innumerable thoughts about what might have caused it crossed my mind as she was wheeled in for a CT scan after the medics ensured her vital parameters were stable. In contrast, my heart rate and blood pressure were through the roof. *It always happens ... something always happens before I travel,* I told myself. It is the experience of countless surgeons: something goes wrong when you least expect it to. Or want it to. It's nature's way of keeping you grounded every time you plan on 'flying high'.

Luckily, the CT scan didn't show any major bleeding in the region of the tumour, nor was there any evidence of reduced blood supply to the left half of the brain, which would have explained the speech disturbance and paralysis of the right half of the body.

'There's nothing that needs to be corrected surgically,' I assured the family.

'But Doctor, you're not going to be here,' the daughter lamented.

'If you want me to cancel my travel, I can, but we need to investigate this further medically, and our neurologist will take care of it,' I tried to alleviate their anguish. 'We have an entire team here looking after patients and no doctor is indispensable. Also, I'm always available on the phone,' I reassured them.

She steadfastly improved under the care of our specialist, although we could never identify the cause of her stroke. Patients with hypertension and uncontrolled diabetes are prone to such occurrences when their system is stressed beyond measure, which any kind of surgery contributes to. Thankfully, with timely intervention and medication, she made a complete recovery.

Two weeks later, I was scheduled to climb Mount Kilimanjaro, a trip that a bunch of us had planned (but not prepared for) over the past few months. In the days leading up to my trip, I promised myself I'd operate only on spine cases, as they are relatively free of any worry or post-operative complications. But, as luck would have it, in addition to my scheduled list for surgery, three massive brain tumour cases showed up. 'I'm not in town from Friday onwards and I'd suggest you get operated elsewhere, because this can't wait beyond a week,' I told all three patients when they showed up in my OPD on Monday.

The first patient was known to the principal of the nursery my children used to go to. She was a 29-year-old girl with a big tumour in the back of the head causing pressure symptoms – headache and vomiting. They insisted I do it. We slotted her for Tuesday and removed it with ease. The second patient had a haemorrhage inside his tumour and simply couldn't wait; his operation therefore, took place on Wednesday. That chap too made an excellent recovery.

The third patient was scheduled for Thursday but was told that I'd be travelling the day after surgery. This was a large tumour arising from the hearing nerve but pressing against the cerebellum, causing balance issues. They understood the risks of absence from the second day of surgery but insisted I do it anyway, as I was recommended to them by multiple sources. Nothing fans a surgeon's ego more than that, and it's a snare most of us succumb to, almost unfailingly.

The morning of surgery, I was informed that her platelet count was below the acceptable range to perform surgery. *This is God sending me a signal*, I thought. 'It's best to wait until we get the platelets up, because there could be a risk of torrential bleeding with a low platelet count,' I explained to the relatives. 'Once the platelets are normalized, I will get one of my colleagues to perform the surgery.'

They were convinced by my explanation, but just before I could cancel the surgery, the pathology lab called up to say that some people have large platelets that don't get counted appropriately by the machine, and when manually counting them, this girl's platelets appeared adequate. I went back to the family to tell them, and they requested I go ahead with surgery.

I didn't know whose side the 'higher force' was on. We went ahead and opened her up. We fashioned the bone removal behind the ear to get access to the tumour. The brain was tense and swollen, and even on gently retracting the cerebellum, tributaries of blood started filling up my field of vision, which, under the magnification of the microscope, seemed torrential. *I shouldn't have agreed to do this operation … This patient is going to land up with a complication. You saw all the red flags, yet you didn't pay heed to them …* I lamented to myself silently, all the while trying to control the bleeding. Through a narrow corridor, I found access to the tumour, which I quickly shrunk to the size of a raisin from that of a lemon, preserving the facial nerve it was stuck to. Throughout the surgery, her blood pressure surged and dropped, probably from the pressure on her brainstem. We ventilated her overnight and removed the tube the next morning; thankfully, she was perfect.

'Anything can happen over the next few days,' I cautioned the family, 'but my team will take care of it, as I won't have any network.'

Are surgeons allowed to take a break? Is it ethical to operate on a patient and travel the very next day? Where do we draw the line? Although patients understand that you won't be around, if something goes wrong, they might not be so forgiving. Even when we are away, we are thinking more about our patients than the ones we are travelling with. That's exactly what I did while climbing that mountain. I played on loop every single step of the last operation in my head whilst in the biting cold, even when it seemed impossible to put one foot ahead of the next. Even when it was hard to breathe. Even when it transiently felt as though my soul had left my body.

When I returned to civilization a week later, after successfully summitting the highest free-standing mountain in the world and the tallest peak in Africa (yes, I am showing off a little!), my phone downloaded a barrage of messages. The first one I opened was from my colleague: 'All patients are doing great. Nothing to worry. I hope you reached the peak.'

It was a different kind of high.

Section 4

CLIFFHANGERS

These are the adrenaline-inducing stories – the ones where monitors beep, blood pressure dips, families pray and we stand suspended between disaster and deliverance. In these essays, lives balance on a millimetre, a heartbeat and a stitch. Some cases race from despair to redemption, others from comedy to catastrophe and back again. They are tales of sudden turns, miraculous revivals and outcomes that could swing either way with a twitch of fate. This is medicine with its pulse racing – thrilling, terrifying, ridiculous – and occasionally redeemed by grace. These are essays from the surgical precipice – where we bargain with biology, improvise with courage and hope our luck lasts longer than our common sense. And just when you think the patient (or the surgeon) is about to fall off the edge – something extraordinary happens.

Super Highs and Extreme Lows

He cautiously walked into my clinic with his brother. Rajesh was just 27 years old and wondered why his legs kept 'giving way' while walking. 'I've had four falls in the past one month,' he moaned, perplexed about why this was happening to him when he was in the so-called pink of health.

I reminded him that he was over 100 kg and should refrain from using such a 'rosy' description of his well-being.

'My legs feel heavy and tight and I've stopped driving because I sometimes have no control over the accelerator – my foot just does its own thing,' he lamented.

I made him lie down on the examining table to confirm my suspicion. I intertwined my hands behind his knees to check for spasticity. His legs were like logs – stiff and unwieldy. Then, when I bent the knee and pressed against the ball of his foot, the ankle went into a rhythmic jerky contraction that wouldn't stop until I released the stretch.

'This is what happens when you drive, right?' I demonstrated, and he acknowledged that it did. 'It's called clonus – Latin for turmoil,' I elaborated to clear up his confusion. I completed the examination and noted that he had lost a substantial sense of touch below the torso, and when I made him stand with his eyes closed, he instantly buckled and fell to the ground.

I pressed his MRI against the fluorescence of the viewing box to corroborate the diagnosis I had made in my head – and there it was. A six-inch sausage-shaped tumour inside his spinal cord, T2–T8. A sliver of normal spinal cord circumferentially wrapped the tumour, like the silver foil that encircles an Indian *mithai* [Indian sweet] roll. The surgical task was to eat the sweet completely while preserving the foil entirely. Any deviation from that goal could result in paraplegia, and loss of bladder or bowel control and sexual function. We endlessly discussed all the options open to him along with all their macabre outcomes. And then Rajesh and his brother left, probably more dazed than when they had arrived.

I was told that the family, after comprehending the risks of surgery, had opted for alternative medicine, but Rajesh returned three weeks later with worsening gait and recurrent falls. My stance did not change. Surgery was the only option. He was admitted a few days later but, as I came to understand afterwards, his family was still not ready for surgery. They opted for a discharge the same evening. I was a bit irritated, as extensive coordination and preparation is required for a surgery this intense – but, at the same time, I was somewhat relieved that he would not be on *my* list of 'complications'.

A week later, when he was finally admitted and in the operating room, we flipped him prone and made a 1 ft incision down the middle of his back. This operation is performed with intra-operative electrophysiological neuro-monitoring of the leg muscles. If there is an undue stretch or distortion of spinal cord tissue during surgery, the physiologist fastidiously watching the computer informs us instantly and we subvert any potential harm by temporarily stopping the dissection or by moving to another area until the signals recover. Here, however, the team of neurophysiologists were unable to record any normal signal right from the start. We gave time for the muscle relaxant to wear off as we continued our exposure, cutting through bulky tissue and then sawing the bone to lift off 10 spinal segments in one piece to fix back later. An hour later, the dura, which covered the spinal cord, was exposed. 'Now try,' I said, hoping for some response. Physiologists usually bellow since they always think they are providing extremely crucial feedback. Their silence made me turn around – one of them shook her head to signal a no. They rechecked all their connections following the universal rule of hardware malfunction – almost everything works if you unplug it for a few minutes and plug it back. This didn't.

I was left to make an epochal decision: either proceed without signal feedback or re-attach his spine hinged at one end and close. I always involve my team in decision-making even if I subconsciously already know what I'm going to do.

'He's 27, you can't do this to him; he'll be paraplegic for life,' said my compassionate anaesthesiologist, vetoing my plan to go ahead.

'What if this is not a technical problem and he's too spastic for the muscles to send normal signals? It's going to be the same the second time around,' I tried to rationalize.

'Or, let's wait for a few months till the tumour causes the paraplegia instead of you causing it today!' the assistant interjected cheekily, clearly trying to wriggle his way out of a 12-hour operation if we decided to go ahead, something we've all done as 'juniors'.

'Knife, please,' I announced with my hand outstretched, and opened the dura, exposing the ballooned spinal cord. All the fibres of the brain converge into this bundle, thick as the width of a thumb, to form the spinal cord, which was pushed to its edges by the tumour – much like a younger brother's face pressed tightly against a wall by a bullying elder sibling. We zoomed in with the microscope for maximum magnification and made an incision along the entire length of the spinal cord to identify the tumour. Painstakingly, we dissected tiny strands off it, buzzing the small arterial feeders supplying it. Over the next eight hours, we laboriously isolated the entire tumour from the spinal cord and removed the 'hot dog' in a single piece – the silver foil seemingly intact. We closed in the normal fashion, laboriously restoring the anatomy we had defiled on the way in.

We flipped him over and the anaesthesiologist was quick to extubate him knowing we were all anxious to see if he moved his legs. And ... he didn't. His legs didn't react to the deep pain, not even a flicker, even after he was fully awake a few hours later. This can happen occasionally, owing to the swelling of already compromised nervous tissue, but when there was no improvement even a week later when it was time for him to be discharged, I had the realization that I'd made the worst decision of my life by proceeding with the surgery. As I saw him leave on a wheelchair (he had come in walking), I dug my palms deep into my eyes, cursing myself for being so frivolous with someone's future. I gave detailed instructions to the family on physiotherapy and other assistive devices.

These are moments when you question your craft. Your skill. Your ability to deliver in times of a complex crisis. You ask yourself if you are worthy of being in a position where someone's life is in your hands. 'It takes hundreds of good golf shots to gain confidence, but only one bad one to lose it,' said the golfing legend Jack Nicklaus. I was devastated. People assume that doctors are inured to complications and often annealed by them. I was heartbroken. I lost my sleep, hair and appetite. '*Ars longa, vita brevis* [Art is long, life is short]' Hippocrates tells us, 'and life is short; opportunity fleeting; the experiment perilous; judgement flawed.'

I operated on easy cases for the next few days before

venturing into dangerous territory again. I thought of Rajesh every day and spoke to the family patiently every time they needed advice, tracking his seemingly imperceptible progress. A book by Cheryl Strayed was lying on my desk; I flipped to a random page and read a random line: 'Most things will be okay eventually, but not everything. Sometimes you'll put up a good fight and lose. Sometimes you'll hold on really hard and realise that there is no choice but to let go. Acceptance is a small quiet room.'*

Six months later, on a sunny Tuesday evening, I got a video on my phone from an unknown number. It was of a man running and then climbing 22 stories. After the initial 30 seconds, I scrolled to the end. It was Rajesh. He had taken his own time to recover. Alone in my consulting room, I stood up, clenched my teeth and pumped my fist in the air six times. I had hit a Roger Federer backhand winner, realizing its brilliance about half a year later. Every 'cord' clearly has a silver lining.

---

*Cheryl Strayed. *Tiny Beautiful Things: Advice on Love and Life from Dear Sugar.* New York: Vintage Books, 2012.

Hey Jude

'No one in the entire continent is willing to operate on him,' said Jonathan, on arriving from Africa with his younger brother Jude. I glanced at the MRI films and wasn't surprised. *Gosh*, I thought, projecting composed confidence, as the two waited to hear the next words from me.

Jude was a 16-year-old pleasant kid. He had started having headaches a few years ago but had gotten a brain MRI done only recently, when he began to lose vision. The MRI showed a colossal 10 cm tumour within the ventricles of his brain, occupying 80 per cent of it.

Ventricles are cave-like cavities filled with cerebrospinal fluid that give buoyancy to the brain. They are the reason why you can carry 1.5 kg of it without feeling the weight, even if you are pig-headed. An obstruction in this normal pathway of fluid by a tumour within the ventricle results in raised intracranial pressure, which manifests as headache, vomiting and problems with vision.

'This is a very complex and high-risk operation,' I explained after examining Jude and noticing that his right arm and leg were slowly losing mobility. There was a greater-than-usual chance of complications since the tumour was in a precarious location, straddling the centres of consciousness. It was enormous in size and had voluminous vascularity. We went on to discuss the chances of death, paralysis and even a vegetative state – all the possibilities that could arise despite the best of doctors taking on the case.

'Whatever happens, don't let him die,' Jonathan said quietly, pressing my forearm.

I wanted to say that we wouldn't, but stuck to, 'We'll do our best.' I left the hospital that day with the image of that beast of a tumour in my head.

For the next two days, I studied Jude's scans from all angles, reading up about his specific kind of tumour and watching surgical videos. It might be scary for a patient to learn that the surgeon YouTube-ed the technicalities of the operation the night before surgery, but if one sticks to credible sources, I find this mode of research extremely useful and one that offers clarity. I also shared the scans via WhatsApp to my senior colleagues to check what approach they'd take. I received replies accompanied by the eye roll emoji, most likely at the monstrosity of the tumour.

The next morning, I was inside Jude's brain. The snowy spotless walls of the ventricle soon disappeared from sight as we saw the tumour rearing its ugly head in the form of a red ball of fire. Some tumours allow you to go around them, but this one we had to get into. From the moment we touched it, it started bleeding. The magnification of the microscope makes trickles of blood seem like roaring rivers. What seemed like a calm start instantly turned into a battlefield; it was like watching an episode of *Man vs. Wild*. The tumour had pearly lobules, and each of them burst despite delicate handling, flooding the field of vision.

'Get another suction in here,' I ordered, wanting to improve visibility. The nurses scrambled, sensing the tension building up. The monitors started beeping, suggesting a drop in blood pressure. The anaesthesiologists muttered among themselves about how to tackle the situation. They ordered more blood and administered medication to keep the blood pressure stable.

Just when we thought we were in control, another tumour lobule exploded. The blood pressure shot up this time owing to an autonomic dysfunction. 'Control the damn BP!' I barked. Mature anaesthesiologists never shout back at the surgeon, knowing well the duress the surgeon is in. They also don't make it known if there is a problem at their end, even when things are out of control, unless they need us to stop. They efficiently go about pressing buttons, turning down the volume of alarms, connecting bottles of blood and injecting drugs, like clockwork. Communication with the surgeon is constant, brief and firm. Unfortunately, they don't get enough credit for their competence. Often, lives are saved by them, not us.

A famous surgeon once said that there are four degrees of intraoperative haemorrhage. One: 'Why did I get involved with this operation?' Two: 'Why did I become a surgeon?' Three: 'Why did I study to become a doctor?' Four: 'Why was I born?'* In this case, I surged directly from stage one to four.

The only way to control the bleeding from an aggressively vascular tumour is to remove it completely and briskly. This took around six hours and six units of blood. I think I also aged six years in that time. Once we had removed it, the ventricles finally reappeared in all their glory and the cerebrospinal fluid flowed uninterrupted like an immaculate waterfall. The brain was soft and pulsating tenderly as we closed.

Jude woke up the next morning as we got him off the ventilator. He was paralysed on the right side but movement improved dramatically over the next few days. By the end of the

---

*Henry Marsh. *Do No Harm: Stories of Life, Death and Brain Surgery*. London: Weidenfeld & Nicolson, 2014. (US edition: Thomas Dunne Books, 2015.)

week, he was prancing, not realizing we had almost lost him. His chirpy disposition helped him recover faster.

'Surgery is not an art, it's a personality disorder; that's why we do what we do repeatedly!' I told his brother, quoting a line I had once read.

'How did you pull off such a miracle, doc?' he asked, hugging me.

'We had the Beatles playing in the background,' I said.

And we made the lyrics come true: 'Hey Jude, don't make it bad / Take a sad song and make it better …'

Nitwits

Rahul was a biker dude who limped his way into my office one day. He wore a French beard and a tight-fitting Harley Davidson T-shirt. An interlocking brass chain around his neck and steely skull-shaped rings on his fingers completed the look. He had formidable forearms, but they were wrapped around his puny sister, who helped him into a chair. His robust face was wrinkled with pain.

'I have very severe back and right leg pain,' he mourned, running his palm along the back of his thigh and calf to show me how it travelled. 'I can barely stand, sit or walk,' he continued. 'It's been going on for over a month. I initially took bed rest for a week but there was no relief. Then, another doctor asked me to start physiotherapy, which didn't help either, and another gave me an epidural injection, but it's only getting worse. I saw two other surgeons and they've suggested surgery, but I don't want to have spine surgery because of all the horrible things people say about it. Someone told me I'd get paralysed; someone else said my pain would only get worse,' he prattled on.

I sat there listening patiently to 'his story'. That is why this is called taking 'history'.

'I've also been feeling numb in my balls for the past two days,' he suddenly said, unfiltered. That made me sit up a little. I asked him if he had faced any difficulty in passing urine, to which he shook his head. I had him hobble over to the examining bed to check his motor function, which was good, but he said he was numb all over the back of his leg and around his buttock and groin – a term we call 'saddle' anaesthesia. Imagine riding a horse (or in his case, a Royal Enfield). The part of his body that made contact with the saddle or the seat was numb. It was an ominous sign. His sister took out the MRI films which I plugged into the viewing box only to find a very large disc prolapse pressing on the nerves that go down into the leg and also subserve bowel, bladder and sexual function. I put my fingers briefly on my forehead, much like a doctor in a Hindi movie about to declare bad news.

'You need surgery without a doubt,' I asserted. He asked if he could wait some more before deciding and I shook my head firmly. 'I think you should get admitted today and that we should operate on you at the earliest,' I replied, which is something that I say only a couple of times a year.

He laughed a little; perhaps he thought I was joking. I wasn't. Most patients with sizeable disc herniations and even severe pain can be safely managed without surgery and recover completely, but when there is a motor weakness or sensory impairment of this nature, immediate action is warranted. If the pressure increases beyond a critical point where the nerve gets irreversibly damaged, recovery of function is not guaranteed. Unfortunately, though, many patients are of the opinion that when doctors suggest immediate or urgent admission, they are out to fleece them or deter them from taking a second opinion.

'I'm going to have to discuss this at home and then get back to you in a couple of days,' he concluded, clearly keen on finding other avenues to avoid surgery. I accepted his decision and reminded him of the warning signs to look out for. I don't like to frighten patients, but this is important when they haven't understood the gravity of your advice.

'Surgery is a big deal for anyone; you can't just expect

someone to instantly agree to going under the knife,' a friend retorted when I told him Rahul's story. 'It's much easier for them to accept the notion of surgery when it's an issue with the brain, such as a head injury or stroke, and it's a question of life and death,' he reasoned.

'But isn't leg function equally important? Or bladder function, or erectile function?' I questioned. 'Which 40-year-old would be willing to risk not having sex for the rest of his life?'

'Maybe you didn't scare him enough!' my friend said and we laughed about it. The next day I completely forgot about Rahul, although subconsciously he lingered.

Three days later, it was 11.00 p.m. on a Saturday evening. I was out dancing at a friend's wedding when my phone rang.

'I'm Rahul's sister,' the caller quickly introduced herself. I walked out of the room that was playing my favourite retro music just then at full volume to be able to have a conversation. 'He's been unable to pass urine for the past few hours,' she said in panic. 'His bladder is full but the urine is not coming out, and he can move his legs but can't feel the ground he's standing on!' she said, somewhat ambiguously. 'Something is happening to him, but we are unable to figure out what!'

I knew exactly what was wrong. The disc had further compromised his nerves – exactly what I had been worried about, as I reminded her. 'Get him to the ER now. We'll have to operate on him urgently or he'll be bedridden for life,' I said, oscillating between anger and concern.

'Can we try and see if he passes urine through the night and then come tomorrow morning if he doesn't?' she asked.

I felt like smacking her over the head with a gong but instead hung up in frustration, uttering a few profanities as I did. She must have heard them, because five minutes later, she sent me a message saying they were arranging for an ambulance to pick him up. I informed the hospital to keep everything ready, and they arrived at the ER at 3.00 a.m. On examining him, we realized that his bladder had reached his nipples. The ER doctor stuck in a catheter and drained two litres of urine, indicating that his bladder had distended way beyond its physiological capacity, which had certainly damaged its walls.

Once we had completed the required investigations, we took him to the OR and flipped him on his back after the anaesthesiologist put him to sleep – something that we should also have been doing at 5.00 a.m., but we were dealing with one man's nitwittery instead.

'Why are you getting so irritated with him?' my colleague asked as we painted and draped him in the usual fashion.

'Because a perfectly healthy 40-year-old may have to live his life on a catheter when it was completely avoidable,' I countered, making a tiny incision into his skin and docking a 20 mm tube onto the bone through which we would operate. We drilled a bit of the bone and found the extruded fragment of the disc waiting to be pulled out. It was like a chunk of macerated flesh, and once I removed the disc fragment, the swollen and inflamed nerve which was stretched to its limit once again came back into position.

'You know what Albert Einstein once said?' I asked my colleague as we closed.

'What?' he said, exhausted from a night of being awake.

'Two things are infinite: the universe and human stupidity.' There was a silence at the other end. 'And he wasn't sure of the former,' I finished, taking the last stitch and then removing my gloves with a flourish, much like Dr Derek 'McDreamy' Shepherd does in *Grey's Anatomy*.

Rahul was pain-free a few hours after surgery. He walked again with the panache of a biker dude. Days later, we removed his catheter after a trial of clamping it and he was able to pass urine normally. He must have accrued some karma from a previous life, I reckoned. Three months later, he came back smiling because his numbness had also been resolved.

When he walked into my office, my desk was strewn with the paraphernalia of a science experiment; I was in the midst of a discussion with a college student who had come to get insights from me on a brilliant idea he had. Intrigued by the mess, Rahul asked what I was working on. Not having forgotten his behaviour, I gave him a bright, cheeky smile and said, 'A possible vaccine for stupidity!'

Babaji Zindabad

I remember patients more by the geography of their brain tumour than by the topography of their face. Vivek's tumour had been in the left insula – an island of brain nestled between the frontal and temporal lobes, a place that processes emotion, sensation and awareness. I operated on him in January of 2020. The tumour was excised immaculately, but as it was Grade 3, radiation and chemotherapy were mandatory for a decent outcome.

'We'll skip the radiation and chemotherapy,' the elder brother told me a few weeks after surgery. 'He's absolutely fine and has already gone back to his job,' he reasoned. Vivek was 22 years old at the time, a bright computer engineer with a full crop of hair that we had delicately preserved during the operation.

'Why would you do such a thing?' I fumed. 'This is our best chance at controlling the tumour, otherwise it'll come back for sure,' I warned them, the way you warn someone in Mumbai that the streets are likely to flood on a monsoon day even if the sun is shining at the moment.

'The elders in the family have consulted with Babaji and they want him to try some alternative medicine,' he argued.

'I've spent six hours operating on this tumour, removing every visible cell under the microscope and preserving all his functions, and I know for a fact that this tumour will come back,' I tried to explain.

'We understand, Doctor, and we thank you for doing what

you did, but we have instructions from a higher order,' the two folded their hands and left.

I understand that science does not have all the answers, but I would respect the ones it does. Thousands of researchers are working on hundreds of drugs that have reshaped the topography of cancer over the past few decades. Their research has not only extended cancer patients' survival but improved their quality of life substantially. Yes, there is an alternate world of healing that we are now increasingly exposed to, and I deeply respect it, but it is surely less consistent in its results than science is. Medicine works because of its reproducibility.

A year later, Vivek returned with his family and a fresh MRI of the brain. You couldn't tell he had ever had surgery for a malignant brain tumour, either on the outside or on the inside. He looked good and so did his scan.

'Babaji's medicines are working,' his father told me. Vivek had been promoted to a senior manager role in his company. His cognition was sharper than ever before and his memory crisp.

'If it was a Grade 4 tumour, it would have returned by now, but as it's Grade 3, these take longer to recur,' I explained.

'Maybe it won't,' was the argument.

'It will,' I said authoritatively, trying to sound less like a prophet of doom and more like a weary meteorologist predicting rain.

The famous Canadian writer Margaret Atwood once said, 'Having experienced both, I'm not sure which is worse: intense feeling or the absence of it.' That's how I felt. Should I rejoice that Vivek was thriving, or mourn the biology I knew too well? Or should I simply shrug it off with a friend's favourite line: 'not my circus, not my monkeys'?

They kept coming back. Each time I wondered why, because they did exactly what they wanted to anyway.

'He's doing much better than ever before,' the brother said, and strangely, I remembered Margaret Atwood again: 'Better never means better for everyone; it always means worse, for some.'

I took a look at the scan and informed them that I could see footprints of a tumour crawling back.

'Babaji has told us to continue with his medication,' they retorted.

'Then I have nothing else to offer except my love,' I said, 'but along with that I would still take the radiation and chemotherapy.'

Three years later on a Saturday afternoon, I got a call from the ER. 'There is a 27-year-old boy who was found unconscious at home this morning. The family says you operated on him five years ago for an insular glioma.'

'Vivek?' I instinctively asked.

'That is correct,' said the voice on the other end. 'He's unresponsive and one pupil is blown.'

I went down and scrolled through the scan on the monitor. The tumour had grown tenfold with a massive haemorrhage within it. I should have felt sorrow but all I felt was rage.

The family stood there with their hands folded. 'Do whatever it takes to save him,' the father said.

'It's unlikely he's going to make it,' I said sternly. The mother collapsed to the ground hearing those words. I contemplated whether it was worth operating, because even if he survived the surgery, he would never be himself. The family insisted I operate. In the next hour, as I performed a big craniotomy, brain squished out of the opening. I got into the tumour that was mixed with large clots of blood. 'There go emotion, memory and cognition,' I muttered to my assistant as we cleaned up all the debris from the site of the bomb blast. The damage was done. We wheeled him out from the theatre without a skull bone, allowing space for the swollen brain.

He did not wake on Day One. Or on Day Two. On Day Three, he opened his eyes. He could breathe without the ventilator. He looked around purposefully. His family was thrilled that he was alive. But he couldn't speak. I don't think he knows where he is or what his thoughts are. I'm not sure he can feel either. I am supposed to be filled with joy that I had saved a life. But I am angry. Very angry.

Still, patients don't need to know you're raging inside. They just want to know you won't let your scalpel slip, no matter whom they thank afterward – you, science or Babaji.

Because better never means better for everyone; it always means worse, for some.

P.S.: Vivek returned to normalcy in three months. Unfortunately, he succumbed to the cancer a year later.

Limited Edition

Mahesh walked into my office with a bit of a limp. 'My right foot is dragging,' he said, as he made his way uncomfortably to the chair in front of me. 'I have a lot of back pain and it's going down my right leg,' he showed me, gesturing with the palm of his hand. I listened patiently.

'The orthopaedic doctor we saw told us it's sciatica and suggested some medication and physiotherapy,' his anxious wife explained. 'And now that he's not better, they want to give him an injection,' she added, pulling out the MRI of his lumbar spine for me to see. Like most patients, she believed that's where all the answers were. I allowed the films to sit on the table for a while.

I'm delighted to have trained at a centre where we focused on clinical medicine. 'Talk to the patient, hold their hand, touch them, examine them and only then look at the scan,' the words of my teachers echo in my mind every day when I sit for hours in the OPD. I asked him to lie down and relax his leg, while I toggled my hands behind his knee and lifted it up a little to see it go into an uncontrolled jerky spasm. I took a reflex hammer and tapped the knee, and the leg was ready to fly out the window.

'Your leg is spastic,' I professed. 'This cannot be a problem in your lumbar spine; it has to be higher up,' I said, as I went on to check the sensations on his torso. The right side was entirely numb below his ribcage. I ordered an MRI of his thoracic spine instead, demonstrating a masterclass in clinical diagnosis.

There are very few days surgeons feel euphoric about sitting in the OPD; most of their savage joy is accrued from the OR. Mahesh got the thoracic MRI that evening itself, and the radiologist called me up excitedly. 'There is a ventral spinal cord herniation at T8,' he announced, referring to the eighth thoracic vertebra. Not only had I hit the nail on the head, but this was also an extremely rare condition, with me having operated on only one such case so far in my career.

'There are fewer than 250 reports worldwide of your case,' I told Mahesh when he returned a few days later with the MRI films. I drew a diagram to show him how a blob of his spinal cord had herniated through a defect in his dura (its covering) and that the forward traction on the nerves was causing the leg to drag. Being a mechanical engineer himself, he could fathom the dynamics with ease and understood that only surgery would fix this.

'I can't be off work for more than two weeks; otherwise, what I've built over 20 years will collapse,' he gave me a warning.

'We are used to working on ultimatums,' I humoured him a little. Soon after, I removed the T8 bone from behind and cut the dura. As I angled my microscope, I could see the spinal cord plunging into a 1 cm defect, much like a fat man falling into a manhole and getting stuck at the waist. We carefully pulled out the man and sealed the manhole by layering it with a patch in a slightly more effective way than the Brihanmumbai Municipal Council (BMC) does.

'I feel great!' Mahesh told me the next day. The strength was back, the sensations were getting better and he felt like he had a whole new leg. The family was so grateful that, more than the operation being successful, we were able to get the diagnosis right. I must confess I did pat myself on my back for my clinical acumen. Three days later the family went home,

Mahesh walking out unaided. 'Case number 251 in the world!' I told my team to add it to the list.

But a few days after that, his son called. 'He hasn't been able to move his right leg in the past few hours.'

My relationship with pride and glee bent under its own weight and broke with an exhausted thud within the span of that single sentence. 'Bring him urgently to the hospital,' I instructed, after asking a few relevant questions. I couldn't help but think what my good friend often tells me – that no good deed goes unpunished.

The MRI done upon arrival showed a large blood clot (or so we thought) at the operation site compressing his spinal cord. 'We need to take him back to the OR and relieve the pressure,' I said with a sense of urgency.

'Now?' his wife asked, alarmed, considering it was midnight.

'Unfortunately, we don't have a choice,' I clarified, requesting them to allow me to proceed.

'I shouldn't have had the operation to begin with,' I overheard him say behind the curtain as the family discussed their options. I had transmuted from an ace diagnostician into a failed surgeon within the span of one operation.

When we took him back to the operating room, we found no blood clot. In fact, the bulk of his own muscle had swollen and prolapsed onto the spinal cord causing epidural compression, which we relieved while also placing a titanium mesh over the bone to prevent the muscle from making contact. By the time the night gave way to day, the paralysed leg was moving again, anxious faces were composed again and the vanquished surgeon had been resurrected again.

Living on the Edge

'There is a 16-year-old girl admitted with vomiting,' the ward doctor called to inform. 'She also had some stomach cramps, and the medicine guys worked her up for a gastro bug, food poisoning and typhoid but found nothing,' he added.

'Could she be pregnant?' the curious cat in me inquired.

'They ruled that out too with a test,' he confirmed. 'Since yesterday, she also started complaining of a severe headache and was unsteady on her feet, so the consultant in charge ordered a brain MRI and found a large tumour in her head. Hence, we are calling you,' he gave me the gist.

When I went to see her, she was sitting with her head in her hands. *This is not a good sign*, I thought to myself. I peered into her eyes with a fundoscope, a device that allows you to see the optic nerve head. It was fuzzy and red as opposed to sharp and white, suggesting raised pressure inside the brain. She spoke coherently with a gentle smile even though she was in pain, respectfully doing her best to answer all my questions. I was pleasantly surprised; I don't expect anything civil or gracious from today's teenagers, even if they are unwell. 'There's something wrong with the world today / I don't know what it is' – a song that Aerosmith sang 30 years ago often plays in my head on loop when I see the kids of today.

The MRI showed a large heart-shaped tumour at the back of her head in the cerebellum. I circled the tumour out for her father, a short bald guy, who stood there with hands folded but held slightly apart as if to catch every word that came out of my mouth.

'It's filling up the entire fourth ventricle and blocking the normal fluid outflow pathways,' I explained the reason for the headache, showing him how the normal slit-like ventricles had ballooned up. 'It is also pressing against the upper part of the spinal cord, which is why the imbalance. We'll have to remove this with an operation,' I said, detailing the need to do this at the earliest.

'Can't we try some medication to see if it melts?' he asked; understandably, like most people, he wanted to avoid surgery for his daughter.

'Not only do we need to do it, but we need to do it tomorrow,' I pushed. When doctors press for surgery, relatives often have their antennae going up. 'They are only here to make money … they are scaring us … someone else we know got better without the operation that two other doctors insisted on … we must take another opinion …' are all thoughts I've heard screaming from inside their heads without actually being articulated. 'Something's wrong with our eyes / We're seeing things in a different way / and God knows it ain't his …' the Aerosmith song continued to play in my head.

'At least shave her head to be on the safe side in case we need to do something urgently,' I instructed the ward doctor before I left for the evening to go to a friend's wedding anniversary dinner.

'We'll get back to you in a day or two about our decision,' the father told me. As I drove away, I didn't blame him because this is a pathology that can remain stable for a few days or even weeks, but can also get worse at any time. As surgeons, we tend to act before the situation deteriorates because then we have a better chance at recovery. It's going to be a while before patients can universally trust a doctor's intuition. 'There's something wrong with the world today / The light bulb's getting dim,' Steven Tyler crooned in my ears.

I had a fabulous dinner. I walloped succulent lamb chops. Picked on peppered prawns. Munched on mutton. Nibbled on noodles. Hugged friends I hadn't seen in ages. Danced a lot, sweated a little. I drove back home with my windows down, the cool late December breeze blowing in my face. As I parked my car, I got a call from the hospital.

'The barber came to shave her head, and she's not waking up,' the ward doctor paused, not saying anything after. Neither did I, waiting for him to continue. 'There is no response even to deep pain,' he added, waiting for me to say something. I remained silent. 'Her pulse and BP are okay,' he added, to tell me she wasn't dead, but still waited for me to respond.

'Living on the edge (You can't help yourself from falling) / Living on the edge (You can't help yourself at all) / Living on the edge ...' blasted at full volume inside my head – the electric guitar, keyboard, percussion, everything. If you grew up in the nineties or are an Aerosmith fan or even a fan of Tyler's daughter, you'd know what that would sound like on full volume at 1.00 a.m.

'Activate the entire team and shift her to the operation room now!' I commanded. 'Don't wait for consent or clearance from the billing department. If we don't do this now, she will die,' I warned, softly but very sternly.

'Hey, Siri, play "Living on the Edge" by Aerosmith,' I instructed, as I turned right back out of my lane and reached the hospital in the six-and-a-half minutes that the song lasted. To my surprise, the patient was already on the operating table. I changed and scrubbed, and cleaned, draped and bore a hole into the skull as bone dust swivelled in the air. I took a tube and inserted it into the ventricle to drain some cerebrospinal fluid, releasing the pressure in the brain. Fluid gushed out at such high pressure that it sprayed my mask wet. She instantly opened her eyes. I connected the tube to a system to let it drain at a constant slow rate.

I told the anaesthesiologist to keep her ventilated overnight and told the father we would operate early next morning to remove the tumour if he was willing. 'I don't have a choice, do I?' he asked.

'Not really,' I replied.

Eight hours later, we took her back to the OT, flipped her prone and opened the back of her head. Pearly white tumour slurped into my suction, begging to be removed. We cleanly separated it from the cerebellum and, as the last bit came out, it unplugged the fourth ventricle with a clear egress of cerebrospinal fluid, restoring balance in the brain. We closed in the usual fashion, and she woke up bright and crisp the next morning. All the tubes and pipes from her body were removed as she was discharged in perfect health a few days later, the MRI showing a complete removal.

'I don't even remember what happened to me,' she confessed.

'Just think of it as having taken a good night's sleep,' I told her.

'Thank you for saving my daughter's life,' the father acknowledged with reverence.

I couldn't help but think of the song of the moment again: 'There's something right with the world today / And everybody knows it's wrong!'

Will You Marry Me?

'There's a 62-year-old lady in the ER,' I got a call just as I was leaving late in the evening after an exceedingly active day. 'She was sitting behind on a two-wheeler at a signal when she lost her balance and fell backwards, the back of her head slamming into the road,' the physician in the emergency told me quite casually in contrast to his gruesome description of the fall.

In a matter of seconds, I had already imagined in my mind a fractured skull with brain tissue splattered all over the road, had cancelled the dinner I was supposed to go out for and was wondering – for the umpteenth time – why pillions don't wear helmets. 'How is she?' I asked to verify if my imagination matched the reality in front of him.

'She's absolutely okay!' he said, probably wondering why I sounded so edgy. 'She's fully alert, quickly obeying commands and moving all limbs well, and her pupils are briskly reacting to light,' he described, giving me the low-down on her neurological examination. I promptly uncancelled the dinner in my mind, replacing it with an image of the spare ribs I was so looking forward to.

I lugged my backpack over my shoulder and left my office to swing by the ER before I could call it a day. Apart from a tiny bruise on her occiput, she was immaculate. I was intrigued to see that her hands were covered in ornate mehndi from the tips of her fingers up to her elbows. It was so fresh that I could smell cloves from two feet away. I asked her what the occasion was.

'My son is getting married tomorrow afternoon,' she said, the longing to be present at the wedding clearly visible in her eyes, 'and I need to go home tonight,' she requested.

'I would have sent you home, but your CT scan shows a thin sliver of blood in the brain, so it's better that you stay the night and go home tomorrow,' I reasoned. Her overbearing family started loudly concluding that nothing was wrong and that she would be taken care of at home. Just then, she vomited once. 'We should not only keep her overnight but also watch her in the ICU,' I cautioned sternly. They found it hard to argue with that and reluctantly agreed. Most patients, I suspect, think that when we suggest a hospital stay for something mild, we're less concerned about recovery and more about funding the hospital's next coffee machine.

As I left to feast on burgers and spare ribs with truffle fries, I promised her family that I'd come see her the first thing in the morning and discharge her soon after. At dinner, I asked my friends if they had ever been advised admission by their doctor when they thought they didn't need it, and three of the five raised a hand. They couldn't elaborate because their mouths were stuffed with chunks of meat. We had the kind of meal that induced a food coma the moment I reached home way past midnight.

At 3.00 a.m., while I was in the deepest stage of sleep, my phone rang. I picked it up with my eyes still fully closed. 'Kamlaben has suddenly become unresponsive and she's not moving her right hand and leg. She's not able to verbalize,' the intensivist reported.

'What does the scan show?' I slurred.

'The blood has massively increased, causing severe pressure on the underlying brain. I've sent it to you,' he said, raising his voice slightly to awaken me.

I scrolled through the video he had sent me and sat up startled. 'Get her to the operating room now,' I instructed, putting on my scrubs to go to war. Over a few phone calls, the army was deployed. The OR was prepared, blood was arranged, her head was shaved. She was intubated and shifted for surgery.

Within the hour, I entered the hospital with a heavy heart and an even heavier stomach. I spoke to the son, confirming that we had to operate or else she would not survive. He wished me luck. I wished him back – in case he decided to get married.

'Thank God I insisted on admitting her,' I told my colleague as we made a big skin flap to expose the bone. We drilled a few holes in the bone, the burning dust smelling like the charcoal on the barbeque that was still being digested in my belly. The brain was tense as we lifted the bone off. As I cut open the dura, a large subdural haematoma – brain bleed – delivered itself like an overweight baby way past its due date. There was a large contusion within the lobe that we removed, after which the brain regained some semblance of normalcy.

'Would you get married if your mom was undergoing surgery on the morning of your wedding?' I asked my colleague as we started closing.

'I don't know about my mom, but if my mother-in-law was undergoing surgery, I would,' he joked.

As we placed the final stitch to close the skin, we placed bets on whether they would go ahead with the wedding; I said they would, my colleague said they wouldn't.

As we wheeled her into the ICU from the OR, we saw the son waiting outside, his mehndi-laden hands folded in prayer. I told him that the surgery had gone well and that she should recover, but it would all depend on how soon we'd be able to get her off the ventilator.

'How is it possible that she was okay for the first seven-to-eight hours after the fall but became unconscious later?' he asked me, clearly having pondered this while waiting outside.

'There is something known as a lucid interval in patients with a head injury,' I explained. 'After a transient unconsciousness from the impact of the injury, patients are fully okay. If a CT scan is done immediately, it may not show too much blood. But if active bleeding continues in the head, the pressure builds up and patients deteriorate after a few hours.' I wanted to tell him that these patients are often termed 'talk and die' in medical parlance, but I didn't want to burden him with negative thoughts. In cases of a mild head injury, it is sometimes a dilemma even for the doctor to determine which patients should be admitted and which can be sent home.

While it is mandatory in most countries for the driver of a motorcycle to wear a helmet, fewer countries have put laws into place for the well-being of the pillion rider, even though statistics show there is no significant difference between the head injuries sustained by motorized two-wheeler drivers and their pillion riders. In fact, before the Motor Vehicle Act of 1988 came into effect, a study found that only 0.6 per cent of all pillion passengers in India were helmeted. While Delhi made helmets compulsory for even the pillion rider about 30 years ago, Mumbai brought this rule into effect only in 2022. It is for each one of us to recognize how vulnerable the pillion rider is and insist on a helmet whenever we ride pillion. After all, Kamlaben hadn't even been in an accident; she simply fell off the bike.

We saw the son return in the evening, straight from his wedding; I had won the bet. He had on his vibrant wedding headgear. He also wore a nose ring and multiple earrings in both ears. Chains adorned his bare chest, and he wore a piece of golden cloth that looked like a combination of a dhoti and kilt. Without asking, he applied the ritualistic *haldi* [turmeric] and kumkum on his mother's forehead and left a box of sweets by her bedside, holding her hand for a while.

The next morning, Kamlaben woke up with a smile on her face, surrounded by her loved ones. She heard in great detail about the wedding she'd missed while her new daughter-in-law fussed over her and pressed her feet. A gentle-mannered woman, she thanked me profusely for saving her life and asked when she'd be able to have a bite of the celebratory *mithai* [Indian sweet] her visitors had brought her.

'One tiny bite, right away. The rest of it, once you're out of here!' I joked, patting her hand.

Paisa Vasool

A 72-year-old man was escorted into my clinic by his two able-bodied sons, each of them holding their father's hand and elbow to support him better. He walked with a robotic tightness but with very little control over where his next step would fall. After about eight minutes of trying to shuffle into a chair, he finally sat with a few moans. 'Everything hurts,' he lamented. 'My neck hurts, my back hurts and I just can't walk without support,' he groaned as he tried to adjust himself through his aches. 'I feel like I'm walking on cotton wool,' he explained, narrating what many patients with cervical spinal cord compression report.

'Any other problems?' I questioned. I usually allow my patients to finish saying everything they have to before I ask any leading questions.

'My hands are weak and numb, and stuff keeps falling from them; I can't button my shirt and my handwriting is like a drunk man's,' he replied.

'How's your control over passing urine?' I asked.

He shook his head and the corners of his mouth drooped with embarrassment at having to talk about it in front of his grown-up boys. 'I'm extremely unhappy with my life,' he concluded.

With patients who have multiple complaints, I usually ask them one direct question to help me with my surgical decision-making. 'Out of all your grievances, if there is one symptom I could help you recover from the most, what would it be?'

'I want to be able to count my money,' he said without the slightest hesitation, adding, 'especially the ₹500 notes. They just keep slipping out of my hand.' To lighten the conversation a bit, I told him that I faced the same problem, but without any hand weakness to blame.

His MRI showed an overgrowth of bone and thickening of ligament that was compressing his spinal cord from the third to the sixth cervical vertebrae. I pointed out to him the pencilling of his cord at those four levels. It was like a tourniquet that needed to be released for his spinal cord to be able to breathe again. Owing to the abnormal curvature of his spine that was visible to us, I explained that we would need to realign the spine by inserting a few screws and a rod to contour it back into an elegant lordotic curve.

Within a few days, he was lying prone on my operating table with his head firmly fixed on a clamp. We use intraoperative neuro-monitoring for these cases that allows us to know if we are causing any damage to the spinal cord, because even a little movement in a compressed cord can lead to catastrophe. After cleaning and draping him in the usual fashion, we cut deeply down the centre of the back of his neck and separated the muscle from the bone. We then placed the screws as needed and cut a fine trough on either side of the four vertebrae to lift off the compressing element as a single block. This was executed to perfection, but as soon as we decompressed the cord, there was a loud bellow from the back.

'We've lost all our signals!' the physiologist exclaimed. This, in regular parlance, meant that the patient was completely paralysed – in both hands and both legs. My heart sank into my stomach. This is the most unnerving piece of information you can ever give a surgeon in the middle of surgery.

The old man's words, 'I'm extremely unhappy with my life,' struck me even harder because I had potentially transformed that into abject misery. He would be awake but quadriplegic. I suddenly remembered a quote I'd read somewhere: 'That's the thing about unhappiness. All it takes is for something worse to come along and you realize it was actually happiness after all.'

Instead of being emotional and fraudulently philosophical, it was time to recalibrate and see if this could be reversed. I asked the anaesthesiologist to bring up the blood pressure and we started a steroid infusion. I always pray when I'm in deep shit. Within 20 minutes, the signals reappeared, and my heart began to gently rise back to its normal position. Sometimes, sudden decompression of a chronically compressed cord can result in precipitous changes of perfusion (the passage of blood) to and within the spinal cord. This can be disastrous if not recognized and dealt with immediately. To my absolute delight, the patient promptly woke up without any damage. He stated that he felt much better, and by the time he was discharged, he said he felt less 'tight' and more secure in his balance.

Imbalance while walking is not something that should be attributed to old age and left undiagnosed. Deficiency in Vitamin B12, especially in vegetarians or alcoholics, can afflict the spinal cord, resulting in the same imbalance that a physical compression would. Diabetes damaging the nerves can cause one's feet to burn and make them feel unsteady. A lumbar spine stenosis or even arthritic knees can make it difficult to walk. A disruption in the balance centres of the brain, certain brain tumours or simply an excess accumulation of fluid in the brain can also make one's gait unsteady. A detailed neurological examination is warranted before it can be attributed to old age;

it would be negligent to miss out on corrective treatment for something that's readily reversible.

Six months later, my patient walked into my clinic with his two sons, this time without holding their hands. He removed a bundle of crisp ₹500 notes from his pocket and began to count them in front of me – effortlessly and cheerfully. Just when I thought (obviously in jest) that I would be at the receiving end of a few of those notes, he stuffed the stack back into his pocket and gave me an empty but firm handshake. His grip was better than mine, and the power and function in his limbs were back to normal. To me, that was priceless.

Jehovah's Witness

'We were lying in bed, fast asleep at night with our backs facing each other,' started Peter, wanting to narrate exactly what happened to his wife. 'That is how we usually sleep, since we've been married for 12 years,' he continued, not wanting to spare any details. 'Suddenly, I heard her make a grunting sound that partly woke me up, and I, in my deep sleep, simply thought she was snoring, so I kicked her to keep her quiet. And usually this works!' he explained, giving me an insight into the dynamics of their relationship. 'But the sound continued, so I turned around to pinch her nose and found that my hand was wet. I immediately turned the light on and saw her frothing at the mouth. Her eyes had rolled up and she was breathing heavily,' he gestured with animated hands, 'and then the breathing stopped!'

I nodded, listening patiently.

'I tried to wake her up but there was no response. I didn't know what was happening. I called my kids from the bedroom next to ours and she didn't awaken to their calls either. She was dead, we thought. The three of us were simply holding hands and crying profusely, saying our final prayer ...' he trailed off.

I almost sported a ridiculously goofy smile on my face. I could afford to grin because his wife was sitting right next to him in perfect health while he was narrating something that happened two weeks ago.

'While we were wiping our tears, we heard a moan from her,' he continued. 'It was as if Christ had heard our prayers! She was back to life, but still not conscious, so we decided to rush her to the hospital.' Peter went on to narrate that somehow, they managed to seat her in their car and drove 20 minutes to get to the nearest hospital in the middle of the night. As soon as they reached, she opened the door to get out and asked 'Why are we here? What happened?' with no awareness of what had happened to her.

'When the doctor in the ER examined her, he found nothing wrong. He explained that what she'd had was a seizure,' he looked up at me and saw me nodding in agreement. 'For you it seems ordinary,' he countered, looking at my nonchalant expression, 'but for us ... we've never seen something like this and still don't know how to deal with it!' he exclaimed, shaking his head. I comforted him and told him the good news was that his wife was fine and that was all that mattered at the moment.

He handed over the pile of blood reports and MRI films of the tests they had been asked to perform in the city from where they had travelled to come see me.

'You do know you have a big brain tumour in your head,' I confirmed with one glance at the scan.

'But we were also told that it is not malignant,' they counterchecked with me. I agreed. I explained to them that it was a meningioma, a growth arising from the meninges covering the base of the brain near the temporal bone and extending towards the orbit. It measured 5 cm in width and height and was stuck to the internal carotid artery, the body's most important blood vessel, which nourishes half the brain. I also explained that these are extremely vascular tumours and bleed profusely, and simultaneously instructed my colleague to arrange for three bags of blood instead of the usual practice of reserving only one every time we open a head.

'Doc,' the husband held my hand. 'There's one problem.'

I waited for him to continue.

'We can't give her any blood,' he said, pulling the rug from under my feet.

I allowed for the depth of that statement to seep in before reacting. 'Are you a Jehovah's Witness?' I asked, having seen a few in the United States where I trained but none so far in India.

Jehovah's Witnesses are a Christian denomination with beliefs distinct from mainstream Christianity. A staunch conviction of theirs is the refusal of any blood transfusion, considering it to be a violation of God's law. 'We believe that life is blood, and if God wants me to live, he will do so with my own blood,' the wife spoke for the first time in this conversation, calmly and clearly standing her ground.

I respected her belief but couldn't help but wish she had an easier tumour to remove; this one was sure to need a blood transfusion. 'How about we draw your own blood, allow your haemoglobin to build up over a few weeks and then operate so that we can transfuse it when you need it?' I suggested, coming up with a brilliant plan that I had implemented previously for someone with a very rare blood group.

'Not allowed,' they vetoed it instantly.

'You go ahead with the surgery, doc. I'm willing to consent for death on table but I won't take the blood,' she said, emotionless, while my emotions were playing football in my chest. We are so entrenched in our beliefs that what seems completely logical and straightforward to one person seems outrageous to the other, yet surprisingly neither is wrong. Two surgeons had refused to operate on her, and we could do the same thing. The question was, what did I want to do?

I excused myself for a bit and went out to discuss with the

team. 'Even if the patient is willing, I don't want a death on *my* hands,' I justified.

'How will she know if we've given her blood? Just don't tell her,' innocently reasoned a colleague.

'If she gets the blood of a Parsi, she'll be cursing for the rest of her life and then she'll know!' I laughed, trying to make light of the situation.

Trying to make up my mind, I decided to speak a little longer to the courageous woman who was willing to die for what she believed in. A few conversations later, she convinced me to do the operation.

The evening before surgery, she held my hands and said, 'I have two little kids to go back to.'

I nodded and quipped, 'Thank you for adding more pressure to an already complex situation!'

As we wheeled her into the OT the next morning, she was happy to see the pleasant wallpaper view of a scenic beach and mountains that adorned the walls of the OT. 'If this is the last thing I get to see before I die, it's worth it,' were her last words before the anaesthesiologist put her to sleep.

'Does this lady want to live or die? I'm very confused,' I said aloud, while everyone got to doing their part.

From the moment we opened her head, it started bleeding. We used all the tricks in the book to stem the blood flow, ably assisted by our anaesthesiologists, who reduced the blood pressure for us so that we could minimize blood loss. We quickly drilled the bone and, in a set of coordinated moves, cut off the blood supply to the meningioma by buzzing all the vessels feeding it with a bipolar cautery, turning a red ball of fire into its ashen counterpart. Coring out the inside, I kept shrinking it until only a shell remained. I held the shell with an instrument and with the other hand peeled it off the internal carotid artery, removing the tumour completely without needing a single unit of blood.

She was fully awake by the time we wheeled her out of the operation room. 'I hope you didn't do a blood transfusion?' was the first question both she and her husband asked me in sync.

Back to my usual filmy self, I replied, 'The only blood I gave her was mine!'

The Illusion of Closure

'It's a really huge tumour encasing the major arteries of the brain and circling both optic nerves,' I said to the family sitting in front of me. This was after I'd intently and repeatedly scrolled back and forth through the MRI images loaded on the computer in front of me. The growth was arising from the pituitary gland but had invaded into the nose below and brain above, chewing up the bone at the base of the skull.

Betty, who had come in with her mother, was 48 and rapidly losing vision. She was finding it difficult to look after her five-year-old daughter not only because of her deteriorating vision but also her deteriorating decision-making and executive functioning. 'It's probably due to the tumour pressing on the frontal lobe, which is responsible for these functions,' I said. 'We'll have to operate on this through the nose and by opening up the head simultaneously. It's going to be a major deal.'

'Will she be okay?' her mother asked.

'Of course,' I said, following it up with a laundry list of possible complications. Our interpretation of how any operation will pan out is often filtered through the lens of our own experience.

A few days later, two teams operated on her synchronously. The ENT surgeon put in an endoscope from below and then prepared the passage through the nose. The tumour looked right back at us – quite pale and deceptively well-behaved. But the moment we bit at it, it bled like a pig. The only way to control the bleeding in such cases is to briskly remove the tumour, and we proceeded to do just that. We then opened up the head and removed the monstrosity from above, gently separating it from the arteries it was encasing and freeing up the optic nerves till we encountered the cavity in the nose.

Once we removed it completely, we could see right through from the brain into the nose and right up the nose into the brain. With the radiant light of the endoscope shining directly onto the brain through the nose in a darkly lit room, the skull looked like an art installation. The ENT surgeons then repaired the defect in the base of the skull to isolate the two compartments. This closure is the most crucial part of the operation.

The next day, Betty was alert and awake, could see better and looked really happy despite being connected to tubes and pipes in the ICU, which we got rid of over time. Her mother was thrilled that she was ready for discharge within a week. However, just one day before that could happen, I noticed two drops of water trickling down her nose. It was no ordinary water leaking out, but cerebrospinal fluid from the brain. My heart sank into that elusive pit in my stomach where it makes knots when disaster is around the corner.

'We have to repair this urgently by sealing the leak again,' I said with certainty.

'Another operation?' her mother questioned.

I nodded; the longer we took, the higher the chance of getting an infection, and I wasn't about to waste any time. We went back in and redid the closure, tracing a gentle stream of cerebrospinal fluid meandering from the brain into the nose. But she developed an infection with fever – no ordinary infection but full-blown meningitis. She became drowsy, irritable and almost comatose, but with the appropriate antibiotics over three weeks, we got her back in shape and she was discharged in pristine condition. Every day for those three weeks, we fought for her survival even when her family was convinced she wasn't going to make it. She went home with a new vision – literally and philosophically. She was back to taking care of her daughter with gusto.

A month later, she landed up in the emergency department with severe headache and vomiting. The CT scan showed that her ventricles had blown up – a condition we call hydrocephalus – and worse, they were full of air, air that was seeping in from the nose into the head. More sophisticated testing confirmed it.

'We have to go back in and fix the problem,' I proclaimed, albeit a little helplessly. Why this had happened after such a meticulous closure was hard to fathom. Was there another area of the bone destroyed by the tumour that was sucking in the air? Was it the pressure from the hydrocephalus that was not allowing the seal to heal? Whatever needed to be done had to be done now, before it was too late. We took her back to the OT and put in an emergency tube to drain the fluid, re-repairing the leak even though we didn't find the spot it was leaking from. But she wasn't improving.

I was razed to the bone of my resilience, yet I told them I wasn't going to give up. 'We'll fight this thing together,' I told her forlorn family. I saw her four times a day; checked on her an additional eight times. After doing a few small operations to change the external tube, we did another operation to internalize the shunt tube and then another to set its pressure right.

After another month, the CT scans looked perfect and so did she. She started talking, eating alone and walking with support. She asked about her child and gave instructions on how she should be managed at home. We cut a cake for her a day prior to discharge. The family was effusive in its affection, for our grit and her grace.

But the next day, she had a seizure; her head was full of air again. She was unconscious. We got another senior ENT surgeon to repair it but that closure didn't work either. We tried once more a few days later. Three months and 10 operations later, she was gone. And I still can't get over it. It's like the laceration of a heart that barely feels bearable.

In medicine, we are often told to detach. But no one teaches you how. She was an appendage of my mind and body and it is impossible to forget her. The popular mode of thinking is that if you work hard enough and follow certain steps, you're able to get over your losses. That might be true for most, but some losses don't follow such models. It was famous psychologist Pauline Boss who cautioned us about the nature of such loss: 'Its ending is never perfect, even in the best of times.'

Patients sometimes leave, but how they leave always stays. And often, the illusion of closure is exactly what it is – simply a myth.

Striving for Perfection

We were operating on a ruptured intracranial aneurysm in the middle of the night. In such an operation, the intention is to place a clip on a 9 mm aneurysm, which, in effect, prevents it from bleeding again. While doing so, one has to ensure that the parent vessel from which the aneurysm arises is not compromised. To witness the astounding anatomy of the brain under a microscope at any time of the day is special, but there is something rivetingly enchanting about it at 1.00 a.m. The obstreperous buzz of the operating room is doused at night. There are fewer people. Exits and entrances are less dramatic. You talk softer, you communicate less and you can even hear your assistant breathe.

We neatly dissected silvery strands off the blood vessel and identified our target. I took a slightly curved titanium clip and, in a gentle, nimble move, opened its fangs and placed it gingerly along the entire length of the neck. This is the operation. That's it. We were done. I then carefully inspected the anatomy with an endoscope to get a 360-degree view, to ensure there was no remnant hiding opaquely out of sight. Unfortunately, about 2 mm of the neck still lay unclipped.

'We have to advance the clip a little,' I spoke out.

'Leave it, sir, it'll thrombose eventually,' proposed my assistant, who usually believes in my sagacity more than I do. After all, everyone desires a good night's sleep. When I was a resident in training, I remember trying to convince my boss that the operation was 'superbly performed' so that he would leave and allow me to close quickly, such that I could catch a few winks of much-needed slumber before the brightness of the next day loomed over us.

'Neurosurgery is a precision sport. It demands exactness,' I lectured now, succinctly, at 2.00 a.m., as I advanced the clip to be perfect. When I withdrew my hand, the clip applicator failed to disengage from the clip and I ripped the parent artery in the bargain. In three seconds, the brain was full of blood. From cruising on an empty highway, we were suddenly in the middle of a massive pile-up. Alarms jarred, the ECG on the monitor convulsed and we got in an extra suction to clear the blood and another nurse to scrub. William Halsted once said, 'The only weapon an unconscious patient has against an incompetent surgeon is haemorrhage.'* But we had a capable team.

After a few minutes of the catastrophe, I was able to locate the bleeding point and stop it by suturing the wall, but I had narrowed its calibre in the bargain. We had to perform a rescue bypass to augment the flow to the normal brain to ensure that he didn't have a stroke later. I finally removed my gloves at 7.00 a.m., when just a few hours earlier, I had visualized myself lying peacefully in bed long before then.

After every surgery, no matter what time it is and how effortless or torturous it may have been, I sit in solitude for a few minutes to carry out an in-depth analysis in my mind of every step of the operation from opening to closure. I close my eyes and play out every move, lingering over the manoeuvres that are

---

*Hammond, Kerry, and David Margolin. "Surgical Hemorrhage, Damage Control, and the Abdominal Compartment Syndrome." *Clinics in Colon and Rectal Surgery*, vol. 19, no. 4, Nov. 2006, pp. 188–194, https://doi.org/10.1055/s-2006-956439.

more frangible. If there is a complication, I debate whether or not I pushed the envelope too much, and if I should have erred on the side of safety. As surgeons, we strive for this perplexing balance every day. In this case, did I do what was best for this patient in my hands? Was it really necessary to adjust the clip, or, in the wise words of Paul McCartney, should I simply have 'let it be'? If the applicator hadn't gotten stuck to the clip, we would have been done in a few more seconds, but it did and it ruined our night. Luckily, the patient recovered swiftly and was discharged after a slightly prolonged hospital stay.

A few months later, we were removing a tumour from the insula, a small region of the brain buried between the frontal and temporal lobes. The deepest portion of the tumour was abutting the area that controls the movement of the left arm and leg. After having removed most of it, we kept resecting the tumour at the depth guided by the neuro-monitoring signals that alert us if we are causing any potential harm. My intuition signalled me to stop but the normal signal feedback we got was cushioning my gut. The more of the tumour that you remove, the better the patient's chance of survival, and so we removed it to the extent dictated. But the patient woke up paralysed on the left side. In those moments of solitude after every surgery, cloistered in the confines of an operating room corner, you sometimes need to ask for forgiveness (from the patient and their family) and hope that what makes your heart ache now will ache a little less later. However, as one of my favourite writers, Cheryl Strayed says, 'Forgiveness doesn't sit there like a pretty boy in a bar. Forgiveness is the old fat guy you have to haul up a hill.'* And every surgeon has a mountain

*Strayed, C. (2012). *Wild: From Lost to Found on the Pacific Crest Trail.* Knopf.

to climb after every major error, no matter how inadvertent.

Not long ago, I was operating on a patient with a large lumbar disc herniation, a facile surgery done by me a few times a week. I decompressed the root diligently but, as the disc was calcified and causing compression on the other side, I tried to decompress it a little more so that he wouldn't face problems in the future with the opposite leg. In the process, a rent was created in the dural tube, from which spinal fluid leaked out and nerve roots started popping out like spaghetti in a clear soup. We spent the rest of the day repairing the rent. The patient healed well but I ended up ageing quite a bit.

Too often, we strive for perfection where excellence will do. Most neurosurgeons obsess over the nitty-gritties of everything. The way we do one thing is the way we do everything. While this may seem great on the surface, it has the potential to harm when looked at closely. With this attitude, it is possible that we might hurt our patients, do a disservice to our personal relationships and battle with our own peace. Over the years, therefore, I've come to soften my stance on perfection by transforming it as Maya Angelou suggests: 'Do the best you can until you know better. Then when you know better, do better.'

Section 5

CONUNDRUMS

These are stories from the grey zones of medicine, where every decision carries a twin shadow – of hope and consequence. They wander into the moral maze of modern medicine, where the right choice is rarely obvious, and every decision carries both healing and heartbreak. Here, law wrestles with compassion, autonomy debates with authority and doctors discover that the scalpel cannot always slice through ambiguity. These are stories where philosophy sits beside physiology, and both must learn to coexist. This section peers into the quiet rooms where choices are made, and reminds us that healing is not always about cure – sometimes, it is about conscience.

Law and Medicine

'If a surgeon, known or not known to you, messed up a patient's case, and you learnt of it, would you tell the patient or take a neutral stand and protect the surgeon?' a lawyer friend asked curiously.

'Are you asking me as friend or lawyer?' I inquired.

'Stop behaving like a lawyer. Answer the question!' she interjected.

Maybe that is her forte, I thought, but I also sensed the need for a heart-to-heart. Lawyers are tricky but important friends for doctors to have in this day and age, where every patient is a potential litigant. 'To me, the answer is simple. I would always protect the surgeon.'

'Even if the patient was a relative or close family friend?' she asked after an uneasy silence.

'Yes,' I said with conviction, subconsciously hoping that other surgeons would do the same if someone whose condition I had worsened came to them for a second opinion.

'But the patient will never know the truth. How does one find closure over a loved one who lost their life or was left debilitated after an operation?' she continued, suggesting I lacked empathy and morals.

'I wouldn't know the truth either,' I said. 'It's unfair and inappropriate to assume what might have transpired during someone else's surgery, or the exact nature of the problem and corrective measures taken ... I have no knowledge of the preoperative discussion with the family, the intraoperative sequence of events or the post-operative details. There are innumerable possibilities, and the story of the hurt family is likely to be tipped in the patient's favour. No surgeon in the world would operate on someone with the intention to harm. Complications are an unfortunate, sometimes unavoidable part of surgery.'

I offered a legal parallel to make my point stronger. 'Don't you send someone to jail for a crime they didn't commit, and sometimes acquit a person 20 years later because of lack of evidence? Is that any less of a screw-up?'

'I don't practise criminal law, so stop lecturing me!' she shot back. 'I'm asking because a client came to me for a second opinion after the first lawyer failed to spot glaring loopholes in his case, and asked for the wrong relief. As a result, the judgement went against him. Should I tell the client that the lawyer didn't do justice to his case or leave him believing that the Indian judiciary is ineffective? As lawyers, I believe we owe the client the truth and must be aware that we are part of a system that people must believe in.' It was too intense an explanation for me to handle. Lawyers love to lecture.

'You should read a book by neurosurgeon Henry Marsh,' I suggested. 'It's called *Do No Harm*. In it, he talks of how, despite our best efforts, things don't always go according to plan in neurosurgery. Whether one accepts it or not, some patients will always be part of a surgeon's learning curve. Neurosurgical disasters can be cruel: a patient can wake up and appear healthy, only to die a few days later of a stroke or a haemorrhage that's related, in "some unknowable way", to the operation. Nobody other than a neurosurgeon understands what it is like to have to drag yourself up to a ward and see, every day – sometimes for months – a patient whose life has changed for the worse and face his anxious family.'

Do you feel the same way about those wrongly convicted? I wanted to ask her but stayed silent. Instead, I went on to tell her the story of Mr Raman, an elderly god-fearing Tamil gentleman who had a tumour encircling and entrenched into his optic nerve. He came to me with declining vision. He could barely count fingers even from a close distance. Everything was a blur. During surgery, the tumour was like a rock, stuck to both optic nerves. After toiling for eight hours, I removed it, ensuring I preserved the integrity of both optic nerves. Unfortunately, after the operation, he went blind. The only statement from the pre-operative discussion that the patient and relatives remembered was my telling them that there was a 'small' chance of his vision worsening after surgery. Unfortunately, in his case, the small chance was 100 per cent. I had 'messed' up his case. I didn't need another surgeon to tell me that.

I guess, in law and medicine, where clients rely heavily on the expert's advice and expertise, we owe them an explanation when things don't go according to plan, but only one that we can fully vouch for. Every client chooses their lawyer and every patient chooses their doctor. Often, you win. Sometimes, you lose. Often, it's dharma. Sometimes, it's also karma.

Do Something or Let It Be

'If this was your father, what would you do?' I asked a few members of my team in an exercise I regularly indulge in to evaluate decision-making.

A 78-year-old previously healthy man had come in with a large hypertensive haemorrhage in his brain that had left him mute and paralysed on his right side. He was in a coma partly because of the location of the bleed, but also because of the pressure it was creating. We could remove the clot and that would probably save his life, but it was unlikely to alter his overall condition. He could be on a ventilator for weeks and discharged on a tracheostomy, but would still need months, if not years, of 24/7 nursing and continuous physiotherapy, and would have to be fed from tubes and made to pass urine via a catheter – condemned to an existence of meaningless metabolism he would probably never have wanted. If he made a meaningful recovery after all, he would probably still be dependent on others for his daily needs – doomed either way.

'I would do whatever it takes to save him. I can't live with the guilt of doing nothing, especially if there is a small chance of him making recovery,' appealed the senior resident unequivocally.

I turned my eyes to the next person, someone who loves to rattle off numbers, who argued, 'Literature suggests that long-term functional independence is achieved in about 10–30 per cent of such cases, with mortality rates of 60 per cent at one year. Unfortunately, these numbers do not help me decide.'

'It's easy to make a perfect decision with perfect information. Medicine asks you to make perfect decisions with imperfect information,' I recalled having read in an essay by Siddhartha Mukherjee.*

I stared into the eyes of the junior-most member of the team. 'If this was my father, I would not do anything, just keep him comfortable,' he adjudicated matter-of-factly.

'Why?' I queried, ragging him with 'is it because you don't know what to do?' Years of training in medicine makes you tough. And when you're on the other side and in charge, you need to ask tough questions even when you're all sailing in the same boat of uncertainty.

'If he passes away, he passes away. If he survives, my family does not have the means to support full-time nursing over a long period. And I'm pretty sure that seeing him like this for months is going to be demoralizing for everyone at home, leading to fights, discord and a perpetual state of unpleasantness. He's led a full life. I don't think we should mess with nature.'

Sometimes the most unassuming people take the most practical decisions, I thought to myself.

'Who are we to decide? Place the data on the table in front of the family, with the pros and cons of each approach, and let them take a call,' proposed another, concluding the discussion. It is easy for a surgeon to present published data in a manner that goads a patient and their family into make the decision that the surgeon wants them to. You can either speak with compassion or incite fear, especially if it's a question of surgery at a time of emergency, when relatives are emotional and unable to think

---

*Mukherjee, Siddhartha. *The Laws of Medicine*. Simon and Schuster, 13 October 2015.

rationally. But it is the surgeon's responsibility to help them make the decision that's right for them.

Who are doctors to decide who will survive and who won't? However, subconsciously, we make these decisions all the time for patients and their families. What is important when doing so is to keep one's own biases and opinions aside, and present things in a rational and unemotional way to relatives. 'When there's no place for a scalpel, words are the surgeon's only tool.' Paul Kalanithi wrote in his heart-wrenching memoir *When Breath Becomes Air*.

It's the same thing with Grade 4 brain cancer. If you don't carry out any surgical intervention, the survival expectancy is three to six months. If you operate and offer radiation and chemotherapy, survival can be one to two years. Of course, there are outliers who will survive a little longer, but would you offer the option of surgery to someone who has to sell their land or only cow, and have them exhaust all their savings just to have them spend the rest of their lives between home and the hospital? Even affluent people who can easily afford the works would think twice before opting for expensive and emotionally draining treatment options that may or may not yield results. It is not our circumstances that make us or decide our fate, but the way we respond to them. 'There is nothing either good or bad,' as Shakespeare wrote in *Hamlet*, 'but thinking makes it so.'

The relatives of the gentleman with the haemorrhage didn't opt for any aggressive treatment. He passed away three days later. While that week must have been full of turmoil for them, the son came back a month later to simply say, thank you.

Good Doctors, Unhappy Patients

'*Doctor Saheb, aa operation thi mane kai pan faaydo nathi thayo* [Doctor, this operation hasn't benefitted me at all],' said Mr Shah when he visited me for a follow-up three months after I had operated on his lumbar spine. Pre-surgery, his bones had degenerated, and the thickening of the spinal ligaments pressing down on his nerves left him with severe pain and a tingling in his legs when he walked. His vertebrae also had an abnormal movement. I discussed the options with him: a slightly larger surgery, which would require some screws and rods, or a smaller, minimally invasive one, where we'd simply release the pressure on his nerves by drilling the hypertrophied bone and biting off the compressing ligaments.

Given that he was 77, had osteoporosis, uncontrolled diabetes and varicose veins, he opted for the latter – and rightly so. The operation went off well, but after temporary relief, he was back to square one. He'd call me every few weeks. 'Sir, you said with a smaller operation I'd have a 70 to 80 per cent chance of recovery but I'm not even feeling eight per cent better.' He said he had approached me for a consultation because his neighbour, whose spine I had operated on, was doing very well. He wished he had gone to a more 'senior' doctor.

I saved his number on my phone thus: 'Mr Shah – unhappy lumbar spine'.

When patients don't do well despite the doctor's best intentions and efforts, it's gut-wrenching. I try and analyse, in my head and often in the heart, if I should have done something differently. I wonder about possible glitches in the process that could have led to a less-than-satisfactory outcome. *Would I offer the same options to another patient who came to me with the same problem?* I think. *Have I been truthful and transparent in decision-making? What do I do to rebuild the trust the patient had in me before he agreed to the surgery?*

I explored the regular route of pain-relief medication and continuous physiotherapy, and even recommended the larger operation. I suggested that he take a second and third opinion. But he received conflicting advice that confused him further. He decided never to have surgery again.

The spine is a complex part of the body. The pain generators can be in the muscle, bone, ligaments or the nerves. In fact, the cause of the pain is often a combination of these. In my opinion, the success of any surgery lies in choosing the right patient and operating when the radiology matches the clinical symptomology. Following this dictum, over 90 per cent patients do well; there will be a handful who will leave you miserable and drained, but they also keep you grounded. To see their name show up on your phone's display is demoralizing, but you have to give them your best each and every time. You have to work with unhappy patients and find alternatives to help them. You have to give them more time than you would to those who walked away happy.

Spine patients tend to be unhappy owing to multiple reasons: a complication in the primary surgery, the development of a post-operative infection resulting in prolonged hospital stay and agonizing antibiotics, or the next level adjacent to the one operated on undergoing new degeneration. National and international meetings are routinely held so that surgeons can discuss these issues.

Several months after a streak of success and perfectly performed surgeries on the brain and spine with excellent outcomes, I operated on Mr Daruwala, 83. He had a problem similar to Mr Shah, and his symptoms were not adequately alleviated either. 'I hate to tell you, but I don't feel any better. I would be lying if I said I'm okay,' he confessed. He felt he should have consulted me earlier, or it was his existing neuropathy that was interfering with the healing. 'I pray that Khodaiji [generic term for God among the Parsis] blesses you. May you continue to help the community and society.'

I turned red in the face. I was unable to tell if such a reaction from a patient was a harder blow than someone directly suggesting that I had used them as a guinea pig. Should I be relieved that this gentleman had taken the onus of the outcome on himself, or was he simply being kind to a fellow Parsi?

When I tried to find the answer, Philip Roth's words came to mind: 'All that we don't know is astonishing. Even more astonishing is what passes for knowing.'*

---

*Roth, P. (2000). *The Human Stain*. Houghton Mifflin.

TB or Not TB

'What is the differential diagnosis?' I questioned my team, raising my arm with an MRI film in hand, holding it up against the morning light that brightened up the patient's room. A differential diagnosis (or DD, as we like to abbreviate it) is where we list out multiple possibilities by weighing the probability of one disease against another, based on the clinical and radiological features of the patient's symptoms, to work towards an actual final diagnosis. It is a process of clinical reasoning that we exercise to determine the appropriate tests, helping us arrive at an answer.

Mrs Gandhi was a 55-year-old lady whose right eye appeared more prominent than the other. She felt pain while moving her right eyeball, and the tiny streaks of red we saw over the white of her eye looked angry and congested. The lower eyelid was swollen and appeared like a prosthetically positioned dark circle. An evening fever had been brewing in the background, but she had brushed it aside. She was capriciously told she had a tumour in the orbit and was sent to us.

The resident doctor peered at the scan, hoping I would shift my focus towards someone else or that my arm would tire waiting for an answer. When the diagnosis is uncertain, junior doctors don't like to speak up for fear of saying the outrageous.

'At least describe what you see,' I said, trying to instil some confidence.

'There is a fleshy-looking soft tissue lesion around the right orbit pushing onto the eyeball. It seems to have eroded the lateral wall of the orbit and a bit of the base of the skull, infiltrating the temporalis muscle as well,' he muttered, albeit correctly.

'So, what could it be?'

Once again, a couple of blank looks were exchanged, all in the presence of the patient who was nauseous with anticipation, eager to know what was going on inside her.

'Looks like a tumour to me,' he concluded sanguinely. Another doctor suggested that it could be a deposit from a lymphoma. The others posited that it could be something inflammatory. 'Anyone for infection – bacterial, fungal, tuberculosis?' I asked. They all nodded – some meekly, others mindfully.

Tuberculosis or TB should always be considered in atypical-looking lesions of the brain; the correct diagnosis comes from recognizing patterns and keeping an encyclopaedia of possibilities open. Most people think of TB as being a problem of the lungs, but TB can affect any organ that has a blood supply: the brain, spine, skin, muscle, bone, intestine, liver, kidney, spleen and even the heart; everything except the nails, hair and teeth. Given the endemic nature of this disease in our country, it always makes the list of differentials.

There was a time when TB or one of its manifestations or complications could be passed off as an answer to any question asked in an exam. Data suggests that 2,000–3,000 people die of TB daily in India, because the bacterium is becoming resistant to the first line of drugs available to treat it. There was also a time when many of the uncertain or unexplained lesions in the brain and spine were empirically treated with anti-TB drugs, and a vast majority would heal; that's how we differentiated many demonic cancers from a certainly curable diagnosis of TB. But in today's practice of medicine, almost every suspicion of the diagnosis of TB needs a biopsy to prove the same and document drug sensitivity.

I explained to Mrs Gandhi the possibilities of this being a tumour or infection, most likely TB. We would have to do an intraoperative histopathological analysis or a 'frozen section' of the tissue to decide on a further course of action. If the pathology of the mass during surgery suggested the presence of a tumour, we would attempt to remove it extensively. If it suggested TB, we would remove only enough to relieve the pressure on the eye without risking damage to neurological function, as post-operative anti-TB medication taken for a year would wipe out the residue effectually.

The next day, we did a craniotomy and removed most of the tissue as we waited for an answer from the pathologist, who was scrutinizing the cells under a microscope in a lab nearby. Sometimes, even pathologists may have a portentous time differentiating one condition from the other depending on the tissue they receive.

I once remember operating on a brain tumour in an HIV-positive patient. The scan looked like a lymphoma – a tumour that melts with a single dose of steroids and then some chemotherapy. We had decided, owing to the precarious location of the tumour deep inside the brain, that if the frozen section showed a lymphoma, we would not remove it completely, but if it were any other tumour, we would go after it. The pathologist decreed it to be a lymphoma and so we stopped. The next day, despite high doses of steroids, the patient had malignant brain swelling and died. A few days later, while carrying out assiduous testing, the pathologist entertained the possibility that the cells showed a high-grade brain cancer also known as glioblastoma. He was apoplectic that some of those cells had mimicked a lymphoma. I was devastated.

While we waited for the report to come in on Mrs Gandhi, we casually bet a coffee as we removed more abnormal tissue from her head. 'This looks like tumour to me,' I said, giving my final remarks.

My assistant disagreed. 'It's TB,' he announced, and he was right.

We finished the job and a few days later gave her the positive news that her TB was sensitive to the first line of drugs. She was back to work in a week, the scar perfectly covered behind her hairline; no one in the office could tell she had just had brain surgery. A year later, she was cured, a scan showing no trace of the lesions.

Medicine focuses on discerning the original and discarding the mimic. The word 'diagnosis' arises from the Greeks words *dia* 'apart, through' and *gignōskein* 'to learn, know'. It literally means 'to know apart'. A severe bout of gastritis can mimic a heart attack, and that of low blood sugar can imitate a stroke. A complex migraine can present itself in the same way a brain haemorrhage does. A simple lump can be camouflaged as cancer. If human beings at their very core are not true to themselves, how can we expect our illnesses to be? Or not to be.

First Responders, Second Opinions

An arterio-venous malformation is an uncommon lesion of inappropriately formed cerebral vasculature. A rupture of these vessels often results in a cerebral haemorrhage. Depending on the size and location, the nature of the bleeding can lead to varying results, from a severe headache to a catastrophic neurological deficit, the former being more common.

A sizeable portion of patients harbouring this malformation face seizures or epileptic fits that arise out of cortical irritation or haemodynamic alterations. Ravi, a 20-year-old engineering student, was brought to the emergency by his parents after one such convulsion that resulted in a sudden jerking of his left arm and leg, followed by a transient weakness in those limbs. By the time he arrived at the hospital, six hours later, he had already recovered most of his strength.

As we scrolled through the CT angiogram on the monitor, we identified a 3 cm vascular malformation with a tiny haemorrhage just in front of and not actually within the right 'motor strip', the area of the brain responsible for left hand and leg function. This was probably why the paralysis was transient.

'Based on all the characteristics of this lesion, there are a few options we have for treating this,' I explained to the parents with their son tethered to an IV pole beside us. Surgery, radiosurgery, embolization … I made clear what each entailed, concluding that this could wait a few weeks before deciding on an intervention.

The family was well-heeled. They expressed the desire to

take a second opinion. 'Of course,' I emphasized, giving them a detailed report of our meeting. A surgeon should always encourage a patient to take a second opinion rather than get offended by the suggestion. It offers security to the family and bolsters the first surgeon's decision-making when seconded by another colleague.

The family returned two weeks later after having seen a few 'top' neurosurgeons and interventional radiologists. They had also asked for and received suggestions from surgeons in the US and UK, I was told. I assumed that they had returned to be treated by me; after all, I was their first responder. I take pride in the discussions I have with my patients.

However, they surprised me with, 'Given your expertise in the field, we need you to help us choose between the two doctors we have zeroed in on.' *That's a first*, I thought to myself. Again, I realized, there was no reason to be insecure. Our job is to guide patients in the right direction with truth, transparency and trust. I analysed the notes and offered my advice.

In the past, I have seen a few patients who, after having consulted with me, have had surgery elsewhere. After the operation, they sometimes return to me for follow-ups. One can understand if they were not satisfied with the outcome of surgery and were seeking a fresh perspective, but in most cases, the surgery goes off perfectly and recovery is uncomplicated.

'Ideally, you should be seeing your surgeon so that you maintain continuity in treatment,' I often say, since most of us are keen on evaluating patient progress, recovery and health over the long term. In return, I sometimes get the response, 'We have seen him, but we also wanted to see you,' and I find nothing wrong with that approach either. All of us live our lives wanting to feel validated, so why not our patients?

Patients who visit a private healthcare facility and have the means to afford it often seek a second opinion, especially if it involves brain or spine surgery. Some like to make it clear at the very start that they have come only for a second opinion, while others like to reserve that information till the very end or not mention it at all, probably to be able to obtain an unbiased assessment. Unfortunately, patients sometimes pit one doctor against the other, like small children who dodge parents to get what they want. This can sour relationships. 'Never believe what a patient tells you his doctor said,' the famous Sir William Jenner said in the 1800s.

The online world is fraught with second-opinion clinics providing health solutions over remote consultations. Patients should be encouraged to seek opinions especially when the diagnosis is rare, as the world of academia may have physicians working on breakthrough treatments in the field. Insurance companies in the US also cover the cost of second opinions in order to reduce unnecessary surgery in patients with lower back pain. However, it is imperative that these opinions are sourced from credible institutions; there are enough 'quacks' selling treatments to those who are distressed or in pain, giving medicine the caustic reputation it is frequently taxed with.

Ravi and his parents returned three months after a successful surgery elsewhere to corroborate the advice given to them by their surgeon on tapering off and eventually stopping certain medication. I was with them throughout his illness, like the sidekick in a movie who is omniscient in every scene, uplifting the hero but never really getting credit for the film's success. I often wonder what must go on in the minds of patients who seek multiple opinions and in the heads of the countless doctors who give and receive them. But I also realize it is irrelevant:

all of us play a part in the life and treatment of each patient; sometimes, we play a key role, while sometimes it's a supporting role. No matter which it is, it's important to do the best we can.

Wants versus Needs

Sue demanded to be seen as soon as she arrived from Zimbabwe. She was escorted from the airport straight to the hospital and admitted in a deluxe room, typically reserved for overseas patients, complete with wooden floors, crisp linen, a recliner for relatives and a panoramic view of the verdant green racecourse and cerulean blue sea. Its neatness, however, was brusquely defiled by her messy way of unpacking and the acrid whiff of cigarette smoke that made the hair in my nostrils stand on end.

She shoved the cigarette packet under the pillow as soon as she saw me walk in – the kind of thing little kids do to ensure their toy is not taken away. Even though you've seen it ensconced, you're supposed to pretend you haven't. We exchanged pleasantries and I introduced myself and my team, politely suggesting we open up some windows.

She was in her mid-fifties. Her hair was short and wavy with dry streaks of white and gold. She had a raspy voice, which turned crustier when she began describing her story. 'I have this agonizing back pain that shoots down my buttock and the back of my left thigh and calf,' she said, tracing her finger along the site of pain distribution. 'It's killing me. I can't even walk for a few minutes.' She'd had a lumbar spine operation three years ago. When the surgery didn't make any difference, she was recommended another back operation, this time to insert some screws and rods to help rid her of her pain. She chose to come to India to get it done. 'Thank you for agreeing to do this surgery; I can't trust the doctors in Zim(babwe) anymore,' she said matter-of-factly.

One thing I learnt very early in my practice is never to believe what an unhappy patient says of their previous doctor; or, at the very least, take it with a pinch of salt. It's a trap. It's their often subconscious ploy to make you feel like you're the best – which is obviously incorrect. Another thing I learnt (this one fairly late in life) was to accept reality as it is, not as one would like it to be or even as one imagines it to be. This patient's pain was real. Her interpretation of its source was probably not, even though she had symptoms of sciatica with textbook fidelity.

After examining her carefully, I took a deep look at her MRI, scrolling back and forth on the computer, my discerning eyes scanning carefully. Apart from the tiny footprints of the previous surgeon, there was nothing on the MRI that could explain such agonizing pain. I had to squint hard to ensure I wasn't overlooking something miniscule pinching on the nerve. The X-rays did not show any instability even when taken in extremes of movement: flexion and extension of the spine.

As the photographer Richard Avedon says, 'All photographs are accurate, [but] none of them is the truth' – a lesson we learn over and over again from social media. The MRI was hers. The X-rays were hers. They were accurate. But did they tell the 'truth' about her condition? I needed to look for other causes, as I was convinced she wasn't faking her plight (which can also sometimes be the case).

I went back to her the next day to say I was certain she didn't need spine surgery. Her face changed colour, wondering if she had met another duplicitous doctor who was here to disappoint her.

'I flew 3,000 miles to have this operation. I can't stand for five minutes – my leg feels like someone's eating into it – and you're telling me you're not going to operate on me? I am not leaving here without surgery. Open me up again, take a look and see what you can fix. They tell me there could be some scarring. Even if I don't get better, at least I'll know I tried everything I could. I think that would be best for me.' She turned around and looked at her daughter, who nodded back in agreement at the finality of this decision.

I understood her despair and calmly asked her to lie down. I needed to examine for other possibilities. I held each of her feet in the palm of one hand. The left foot was distinctly cooler. On closer inspection, the colour too was imperceptibly different. The warmer foot was a rosy pink, while the cooler one was an ashen spectral white. I rolled my fingers to feel the contour of her pulse on the dorsum of the foot and behind the ankle: while it bounded on the right, it was entirely impalpable on the left.

'Smoking has damaged the arteries supplying blood to your legs,' I announced. 'They're crying in pain for oxygen and nourishment. We'll have to do a Doppler and CT angiography of the legs to find a block that we can open up. I will surely not operate on your back,' I reiterated, this time with the arrogance of finality. But medicine also requires a tender balance of firmness and kindness. 'Give me 24 hours,' I requested, 'and for anything we do to work, you have to stop smoking now,' I implored.

The angiogram showed a 5 cm occlusion of the left iliac artery, where it branched off from the aorta. There was severe atherosclerosis causing narrowing of the artery. We called a peripheral vascular surgeon who inserted a stent, opened up the vessel and started her on antiplatelets. Her pain was gone the next day – not a trace of it.

'It feels like I have a new leg!' she said with a smile on her face for the first time since she had arrived.

'You still want me to operate on your back?' I cheekily taunted.

'I'm sorry for being so silly,' she acknowledged, giving me a hug, ready to head back to Zimbabwe.

A while ago, I wanted to present this case at a clinical meeting and emailed her to check on the longevity of our procedure, so that I could be truthful about the outcome. She replied in a single sentence: 'Three years, no pain; thank you for not operating on my back.' I smiled, reflecting philosophically on the truth of the adage that what one thinks one wants isn't necessarily what's best for one.

Control or Surrender

'You'll have to sign here,' I instructed a chubby patient of mine, after I had explained to her the risks of undergoing surgery for a brain tumour. She had come in complaining of an unremitting headache, and the MRI revealed a tumour the size of a tennis ball in her right frontal lobe. She was 23 years old. After explaining the need for an operation, I began talking to her about the possibility of death, paralysis, seizures, infection or a postoperative haemorrhage requiring a redo surgery, wanting to give her a full disclosure of the possible complications any brain surgery can entail.

'Will you shave my whole head?' she asked, combing her hands through her pink highlights. I remembered George Eliot: 'Our vanities differ as our noses do.'

'We usually don't, but if you insist, we will!' I teased, and was rewarded with a priceless expression as her fair complexion turned pale. I hastened to comfort her. 'We'll make a tiny incision behind your hairline,' I pointed to where we would cut, 'and a few weeks later, no one will know you've even had an operation, which is the beauty of modern medicine,' I said, and watched as her face regained colour.

I later pondered upon what gets patients to agree to have surgery. Are they concerned about the part of their body being operated upon, the possibility of a mishap or the intentions of their doctor? Do they rely on their intuition or whom they've been advised by? Do they want to ensure that their expectations match what the surgeon is able to deliver?

When I trained at the Christian Medical College in Vellore, we treated a sizeable portion of Bengali patients having large brain tumours, and their primary complaint – obviously unrelated to the tumour – was constipation. It's the problem of all of East India. It didn't matter to them if we performed the finest operation to remove the most complex tumour from deep-seated cervices of their cranium; surgery was deemed a complete failure if we were not able to solve their 'gas problem'. '*Aye bodo operation toh theek aache, kintu aami paikhana korte paachi na, ki kori?*' [Doctor, the major operation – yes yes, that's all fine ... but I haven't been able to pass any stools! Now what am I supposed to do?]'

On one end of the spectrum are patients who don't want to know of all that can go wrong; they will stop you in the midst of an explanation of the risks involved. 'We have complete faith and trust in you. Please do whatever you deem fit.' These are the patients who, in my experience, sail through surgery like a breeze. On the other end of the spectrum are patients who want to know details down to the bone: they want to know numbers, statistics, how our complications match up with what's published in the literature and everything else one can possibly ask one's surgeon. When I trained in the United States, one such patient, who had an issue with her spine and needed a complex procedure, asked my boss how many of these operations he had performed. 'I invented this procedure!' he proclaimed. He really had.

The latter set of patients want a minute-to-minute low-down on what's going to happen, from the time of admission to the time of discharge and then every day thereafter as well. While I treat the entire spectrum without judgement, I (and most surgeons) can almost intuitively predict that something is likely to go wrong in this group, and it does, but thankfully, it's almost always something minor. But it is also often something you haven't spoken about while taking consent for surgery – like a fall in the washroom, diarrhoea from outside food sneaked in by a relative or a rash from a medication they didn't know they were allergic to.

Then there is the patient who complains about something post-surgery that you don't know how to respond to. A zesty young patient of mine had come to me for decompressing her trigeminal nerve (responsible for facial sensations) from an artery that was deeply indenting it, causing an electric shock to her jaw every few seconds. 'The pain has gone, but I can't feel sufficient sensation over the left half of my lips,' she complained. 'Every time I kiss a guy it feels so strange – and you never mentioned a word about it before surgery!'

The surgical consent form is now a medico-legal document. There are lectures conducted on how consent should be well-informed, the importance of the legibility of what is written down as risks and the alternate options to surgery. It is signed and sealed by the doctor, the patient and a witness. It is ceremonial. Even a marriage certificate is not this intense – and surgeons have to do this every day. It may also be heartening for a patient to learn that consenting to every single risk of surgery and signing the paper doesn't absolve a doctor in the court of law if something does go wrong.

In his book *Blink*, Malcolm Gladwell analyses why highly skilled doctors get sued much more than those doctors who make a lot of mistakes. Patients file suits not based on shoddy medical care alone but something else that happens alongside that. And that something is how they were treated by their doctor on a personal level when something goes wrong. After a successful operation, most patients thank the surgical team for taking such good care of them. In return, not only do we acknowledge the gratitude, we also thank them back for allowing us to operate on them.

The cumulative risk of any untoward occurrence in most standard brain and spine operations is less than five per cent. While we're explaining the risks of a surgery, patients' relatives often ask, 'what if he is paralysed or comatose after surgery?' or 'what if she doesn't wake up?' Even though with practice I've mastered the art of not letting a reaction show on my face, my response varies every single time. Sometimes I reiterate that it's an extremely unlikely possibility. Oftentimes I say, 'We'll do whatever it takes to resolve it.' If I've had a really long and exhausting day, I simply peer through the concrete ceiling of my office into the sky above and point my finger to the big guy in the sky. And then exhale deeply.

American author Henry David Thoreau said, 'In human intercourse, the tragedy begins not when there is misunderstanding about words, but when silence is not understood.'* Surgical consent is like that.

*Thoreau, Henry David. Quote widely attributed; original source unverified.

Sadness and Hope

'Will I be able to walk again?' Ronald asked me, peering deeply into my eyes as I stood next to his hospital bed. Three months ago, in another country, he was waiting at a red light on his bike when a truck lost control and thrust into him from behind, transecting his spinal cord and leaving him paralysed below the waist. He had surgery back home to realign the spine, in which they used some screws and rods to stabilize the broken fragments, but as expected, with an injury of this nature, there was no gain of function in his lower limbs. He was transferred to our hospital for extensive rehabilitation.

The short answer to his question was 'no'. The long answer was also 'no'. But how do you tell that to a 45-year-old father of two sprightly children, an image of whom I could see on the screen saver on his phone? He had left them behind with his parents and had travelled here with his wife, promising them that he would come home walking in two months.

'My hands are fine,' he said, raising them and opening and clenching his fists. He had rounded biceps and chiselled forearms, probably from using them to move his torso around. 'But I can't feel anything below my chest,' he mourned with a listless anguish. 'I don't even get an erection.' He pointed to the urine bag that his catheter drained into. It had flaky sediments that made the urine appear hazy; a consequence of prolonged catheterization.

I gently lifted the blanket off him to examine his legs. He had no power. He couldn't move at the hip, knee or ankle, even though the grimace on his face showed that he was trying. He couldn't even wiggle his toes. He had no sensation from below his chest to the soles of his feet. 'And yet, everything below feels so heavy,' he said, miserable.

I helped him onto his side as he wanted to show me his bed sore. Like an asteroid had landed on his planet, he had a crater on his buttock, with dying skin of varying hues sloughing away and tracking down to bone. 'This is what we need to fix first,' I told him. 'Without this, we can't do any physiotherapy. We'll get a plastic surgeon to clean it up and rotate a muscle flap over it.'

His melancholic expression told me that he wasn't interested in the technicality of any of it. 'I just want to be able to walk,' was his doleful one-liner.

'We'll get there,' interjected his wife, who was standing beside him. She was half his size but was astonishingly able to transfer him off the bed onto a wheelchair all by herself. 'What doesn't kill you makes you stronger,' she reminded him, summarizing the story of their togetherness.

I ordered some investigations and explained to them a plan for what we should do over the course of the next few months, which they agreed to. I walked out of the room and stared at my feet for a full minute. I stood on my toes, on my heels and did a squat. I thanked God. As neurosurgeons, even though we treat patients with spinal cord injuries all the time, this man's pain felt unbearable. The heartbreak in his eyes was as tangible as the dysphoria in his voice. However hard we try, we can never fathom what these patients must be going through. I sometimes wonder what's worse – to have an active mind in a paralysed body or a functional form with loss of insight, judgement and creativity?

Every year, about half a million people globally sustain a spinal cord injury. A majority of these are young adults. The social, cultural and economic burden of this is inconceivable. Its impact on the immediate caregiver is beyond belief. The assault on their emotional and sexual needs is just as devastating as the damage to their sensory and motor function. Physical barriers to basic mobility result in their exclusion from society, leading to a plethora of mental health issues. Billions of dollars are pumped into research to enhance recovery of spinal cord function with no promising results that can be universally applied.

'Why am I still not walking?' Ronald questioned me after a month. His bed sore had healed and his rehabilitation was in progress.

'We're building strength in your upper body so that it's strong enough to support your crutches when you stand,' I deflected. Every time we chatted, he spoke in the same monotone without blinking his eyes. Day after day, I went to his room and we talked for about 20 minutes or more. On some days, I took him down to the cafeteria and we spoke there. I got him a book to read. We cut a cake on his birthday and got all the hospital staff to sing for him, but it barely turned the corners of his mouth upward. 'How about we watch a raunchy film?' I tried, willing to sound inappropriate. He didn't concede.

I recalled lines from a poem by Australian author Erin Hanson. It starts with 'They say happiness will find you / But I think sadness will find you too', and goes on to say:

You can't remember how it started,
And you don't know when it will end,
But you know that you'd give anything,
To stand up on your feet again,

Sadness is that feeling,
When the falling doesn't stop,
And it saps your life of meaning,
And of the good things that you've got ...*

Every day, I would pause before entering his room. I would close my eyes and take a deep breath, then enter sounding loud and chirpy, but he looked at me with those brooding eyes and a tediousness in his voice, as though he could see through the facade. 'When will I walk?' his grief questioned me, almost making it seem like I was the one responsible for his infliction. The physiotherapist showed him videos of his improvement, but he refused to acknowledge those. From being unable to sit, he was now standing with callipers and holding onto a monkey bar, but he was nowhere close to walking, even with any kind of support.

On my rounds one morning, I saw all my patients on his floor but didn't enter his room. As I was heading to the next ward, the nurse reminded me that we hadn't seen Ronald yet. 'I can't,' I told her, defeated. 'It exhausts me completely and I have nothing to offer that makes any kind of difference to him,' I conceded.

We had failed him. His wistful eyes and his despondent voice told me so.

Ronald got discharged after three months. He still could not walk. Maybe he never will. But he hopes. As do I.

---

*Hanson, E. (n.d.). *When love arrives*.

Celebration or Suffering

It was a routine Wednesday and I was on my regular evening rounds to check on all my patients before I left for the day. I knocked and entered the room of a patient I had operated upon the same morning. I saw him sitting in a chair, his sizeable single room suddenly appearing cramped because of heavier-than-usual family traffic. His two-year-old baby (whom they must have sneaked in somehow, probably in a spacious IKEA bag) was plonked on his lap. His wife, a few sisters, parents, grandparents and a bunch of cousins encircled him. Only a few hours after spine surgery, he was in great spirits, rambunctiously guffawing away with his gang. My team and I were greeted by happy and smiling faces.

'Come, come, Doctor, you've come at the right time! Everyone, this is Rawnak's doctor,' his wife said, introducing me to the rest of the extended family, breezing through four generations in a jiffy. I was still a little bewildered as to what was going on until I saw a tall mango cake on the table with 'Happy Birthday' artistically piped on it.

Clapping hands, we sang the quintessential birthday song while the little girl on his lap wisely blew out the candle before the smoke detectors went off. They offered us a big piece that we readily gobbled. Rawnak fed his daughter, his wife fed him and then she went around the room, unloading a tiny bite into everyone's mouth in traditional celebratory fashion.

'Why would you choose your birthday to get an operation?' I asked aloud, intrigued.

Rawnak laughed out loud, his hilarity contained only by the stretch on his stitches. 'I was so bothered by this leg pain because of my slip disc and, like you know, I tried everything, but nothing worked. I just wanted a new lease of life, and what better day to do this than on my birthday!' he reasoned. 'I didn't want to spend my birthday in pain,' he said, devouring his cake. It was a strange perspective but an interesting one.

'What if something were to go wrong?' I mused, raising my brow, but before he could answer, I followed it up with something more positive. After some more conversation, the team and I exited. 'Good luck, buddy, have a great year,' I said, waving goodbye to everyone in the room. As I walked out, I realized I had completely forgotten to check on him and his pain and almost stepped back into the room to ask him, when my colleague stopped me. 'Let him enjoy his day, he's obviously okay if he's smiling so much!' was the justification.

As we walked down the corridor toward my next patient, I turned around and asked my team why anyone would get operated on their birthday, still trying to get under the skin of this viewpoint.

'It's the same reason why you make it a point to operate on yours,' my assistant retorted, reminding me of my quirk. Earlier in my career, when I didn't operate every day, I would make it a point to schedule surgery on my birthday, citing my unavailability a few days before or after stating any reason I could.

'That's completely different,' I argued. 'I want to start the year doing something I love. Nothing gives me more joy than operating!' I told them. But I understood what they were trying to say.

'By the way,' my assistant piped up, 'have you read the article published in the *BMJ* titled "Patient mortality after surgery on the surgeon's birthday?"'

'You've got to be joking,' was my reaction, and he pulled it up on the phone for me. I scanned the paper quickly. Apparently, patients 'who received surgery on the surgeon's birthday experienced higher mortality compared with patients who underwent surgery on other days. These findings suggest that surgeons might be distracted by life events that are not directly related to work'*. *Oops*, I thought, recollecting the outcomes of recent surgeries done on my birthday to confirm that I wasn't contributing to the statistic. 'From next year onwards, we'll keep these birthday cases short and simple,' I announced, unwilling to give up the tradition.

It has been my personal experience that patients put aside surgery for festivities. In the West, almost nobody has elective surgery in the last week of December. In India, hospitals see a drop in routine surgical admissions around Diwali (but injuries related to the festival make up for those). A few weeks ago, on the day of a planned admission, a patient called to cancel scheduled surgery for the next day. I was a little annoyed, as it scrambled a schedule I'd now need to rearrange, and in a slightly irritated fashion, I asked, 'Why?'

'Sir, there is an emergency wedding in the family tomorrow, so we'll get admitted the day after that!'

Amusement instantly replaced frustration. Their problems were clearly greater than mine.

---

*Anupam B. Jena, Andrew R. Olenski and Daniel M. Blumenthal, 'Association Between Surgeon Birthday and Postoperative Mortality Among Medicare Patients', JAMA Network Open, 3(8), 2020. https://doi.org/10.1001/jamanetworkopen.2020.12341

I'm not a big celebrator but I want to change that about me. I was inspired after I attended my daughters' school orientation. The principal emphatically spoke about celebrating the little things in your lives. She said, and I paraphrase, 'Even if your child comes fifth in a race, celebrate; if a parent gets a raise or switches a job, celebrate; if a family member excels in a hobby or even participates in something new, celebrate. Don't only honour and laud the big events, but rejoice in small victories, even if they cannot be measured.'

There is something miraculous about the mundane that we must celebrate. A simple surgery done well, a patient relieved of their affliction, a diagnosis cracked, a colleague's recruitment, a staff worker's promotion, the hospital's accreditation. If we are able to revel in small successes, we might be able to deal with failure more comprehensively. We might be able to treat the spectrum of emotions that accompany the highs and lows in a slightly more equanimous manner. We might be able to acknowledge the many ways in which we are human.

Rawnak got discharged the day after his surgery, completely pain-free and thrilled with his decision to get operated on his birthday. New beginnings are beautiful; sometimes terrifying, but beautiful nonetheless. I am now also planning to conduct a study on patient outcomes when they have surgery on their special occasions: birthdays, festivals, promotions, anniversaries, etc. Do I have any volunteers?

Black and White

Sam and Anita sat in front of me in my clinic. They were a couple in their early forties. He was a gym instructor and she was a teacher. Their physical appearance said they had little in common on the outside. They looked like the king and queen on opposite sides of a chess board but were on the same team in life. Seeing them I realized that true love sees no caste, creed, religion or race. After I heard their story, I figured that cancer doesn't either.

'Sam was diagnosed with a glioblastoma in his right frontal lobe a year ago,' his girlfriend started, holding his hand as she spoke, while I noticed his eyes were on the verge of spilling. A glioblastoma is a Grade 4 brain cancer. It is a ghastly diagnosis to live with. The median survival of this tumour is one-to-two years. 'He had surgery from another surgeon followed with 34 fractions of radiation and six cycles of chemotherapy,' she gave me the low-down. The previous surgeon had done a perfect job, with interim scans showing an immaculate resection and a wonderous initial response to therapy, but as expected in these ghoulish tumours, it had recurred.

'For two weeks, I noticed I was dragging my left foot and finding it hard to button my shirt,' he described, getting up from his chair to show me his gait.

'That's when we repeated an MRI and found that it had all come back,' Anita continued.

I examined him to find his left arm and leg slightly weak. As I peered at the MRI, it showed a large growth in the right frontal lobe that was pushing against the motor cortex, responsible for his weakness. It had also spread to the opposite side through fibres that connect the two halves of the brain. 'The tumour's not only come back, it's done so with a vengeance,' I announced.

'We know,' they said in unison, a gnawing sadness permeating the room. 'The previous surgeon simply said, "Nothing can be done about it."'

I recalled those being exactly the same words a dermatologist had used for me the previous day, when I'd asked her if something could be done about my premature balding, but I didn't think it right to mention this at this time, even though I have always believed that honesty and humour are the two greatest weapons in the face of helplessness. She had also advised me to 'accept it gracefully', and I wondered if that, perhaps, would be the appropriate thing to say here. They were an empowered couple who had done their research and were fully aware of the finality of this diagnosis. 'You could do more chemotherapy or attempt another surgery, but I'm unable to assure you or confirm if this will alter longevity and improve the quality of your life. It could also possibly make you worse,' I said, agreeing with the previous surgeon.

'We have a date to get married in three months,' Anita said, looking into Sam's eyes, surrendering to the anguish and anxiety of an uncertain outcome. These are such deeply personal choices that I refrained from making any comments, although I did briefly wonder why she wanted to marry a dying man.

'We've been dating for eight years, and a few weeks before my diagnosis, we'd set this date. We want to go ahead with it,' Sam said with a depth I was unable to fathom. Who among us would have the will to marry someone we know would die shortly thereafter? The answer to most things comes in not looking for one.

We discussed all the technicalities and, much to my reluctance, I agreed to another operation; I couldn't help but remember it was Voltaire who said, 'Every man is guilty of all the good he did not do.' I had to keep any personal judgement aside, because if we didn't operate, I was pretty sure he wouldn't make the date.

A few days later, we opened up the right side of his head. Everything about this tumour was macabre. It was dark and ugly. The veins in it had thrombosed and there were pockets of necrosis or dying tissue. There were engorged arteries feeding the tumour with the blood haemorrhaging in its core, which I buzzed and cut, buzzed and cut and buzzed and cut again. I kept removing it until I saw some semblance of normal-looking brain around, ensuring I had relieved the pressure on his motor cortex. The monstrosity was demolished, and the brain once again looked illuminatingly beautiful under the brilliance of the microscope. We had restored some normalcy, and hoped we had added a few checkered days to the duo's black-and-white lives. He woke up the next day with improved arm and leg function, but I was unsure of how long that would last. We scheduled him for some more chemotherapy as he got discharged.

'We're going to go for a holiday before we start chemo,' Anita smiled, giving me a hug to say thank you. They had transformed their suffering through their irrepressible vitality of spirit.

Cancer has been around for centuries. We have done so much to find a cure and yet, in the larger scheme of things, it has proven to be so little. It indeed is a great leveller. It respects nothing. Recently, I came across some research that elephants don't get cancer. The answer is, at least partly, that elephants' cells have an astounding 20 copies of p53, a cancer repair gene. Humans just have one. In a world where we see everything in black and white, it sometimes helps to be grey. 'The war against cancer,' noted physician and writer Siddhartha Mukherjee in his epic work *The Emperor of All Maladies*, 'continues to oscillate between being profoundly distressing and relentlessly exhilarating.'*

Three months after Sam was discharged, Anita sent me enraptured photos of them from their destination wedding in Bali. She was dressed in bridal silver. He wore a dark tuxedo. They were amidst flowers and friends of a myriad hues and glows. They were singing and dancing and living their dream. Several weeks later, I heard from her again. He hadn't made it. Everything was once again black and white.

---

*Siddhartha Mukherjee. *The Emperor of All Maladies : A Biography of Cancer*. New York, Scribner, 2011.

Creation and Destruction

I operate with AirPods nestled in my ears, a conduit to the hushed anxieties of the ward and the urgent whispers of the ICU. They also help me dispense advice to patients who might need it urgently without having to make them wait until the end of the day. It isn't as distracting as one might assume; it's the equivalent of talking to your assistant about his weekend while opening up someone's head, which is what we do when we have a brain tumour surgery on a Monday morning. Having said that, however, I often silence my phone during critical crescendos of an operation so that there are no inadvertent interruptions.

I realize that telling people you are available to talk on the phone while operating can be unnerving to some. Once, after boarding a plane, as the captain introduced himself, I recognized his name and voice and was quick to realize he was a friend. I sent him a message on his phone saying I was on the flight. He was so excited that he kept returning my messages as we were on the runway and about to take off. I finally stopped replying to calm my own nerves and be sure he'd focus.

On one such regular surgical morning, as I was performing a craniotomy – the removal of a part of the skull to access the brain for a complex aneurysm of the internal carotid artery – a call from the ICU pierced through the sterile air. Siri read out the name of the person who was calling in her sultry robotic voice in my ear. 'Answer?' she asked.

As I was burring a hole into the skull, I confirmed: 'Yes.'

'Good morning, sir. The lady you operated upon yesterday for a pituitary tumour compressing her optic nerve has a problem,' the doctor on the other end told me.

'What do you mean she has a problem?' I questioned almost angrily, because I had seen her an hour before starting surgery, and her face had been alight with the joy of her vision returning. Before surgery, she was barely able to perceive light, and when I checked up on her this morning, she could count my fingers at a distance of 10 feet.

'She says she can't see anything now,' he clarified, his voice laced with concern. 'She feels like a black curtain has fallen over her eyes. She's also breathing heavily and looks pale and scared.'

My heart sank as I continued to drill, bone dust swirling into thin air. The only plausible explanation would be that she might have had a bleed inside the brain. But a CT scan done earlier in the morning had been clean. I thought for a bit as I got the bone off, staring at the pulsating brain in front of me. 'Repeat a CT scan, and if that's normal, get an MRI and ask the radiologist to call me with the findings,' I ordered.

'Yes, sir,' came the military-like response from the other end.

'Also ask the ophthalmologist to rule out a retinal detachment,' I added, thinking of a rare possibility.

I sat on my chair, had the microscope brought in and began dissecting the gossamer strands separating the frontal and temporal lobes to expose the carotid artery, the main blood vessel that supplies blood to half the brain. While I did that, a parallel movie of the other patient being wheeled into the CT scan room played in another corner of my head. The weight of it pressed down on me. I pondered the possibility of returning to a patient barely a day removed from the operating table, all the while keeping watch on the aneurysm pulsing before me, knowing it could rupture at any moment and potentially cause an on-table death. It demanded an insane amount of equanimity to deal with the duality, this dance between creation and destruction.

Patients will always be unaware of the circumstances under which they are operated. No surgeon will confess to a late night of revelry, a tempestuous argument with their spouse before leaving the house, the gnawing anxiety of a looming debt, being jetlagged or even the simple human frailty of fatigue or distress. No patient will ever know that their surgeon's previous patient may be dying in the ICU on the same floor while they're being operated upon only a few metres away.

I had once scheduled a patient's major surgery for a Thursday morning. 'But isn't your brother coming down from the US in the wee hours of the same day?' the Parsi lady sitting in front of me asked, clearly having conducted a thorough background check on me.

'Yes, he is. So?' I asked, a little surprised.

'If you go to the airport to fetch him in the middle of the night, will you be fresh for my operation the next morning?' she continued.

'I've operated in more dire situations,' I told her, giving her a kiss on the head to assure her that she'd be fine.

The radiologist called to say that the CT scan was clear and there was no bleeding inside the brain. 'We are doing an MRI to check if there is any vascular insult to the optic nerves,' he updated. With steady hands, I navigated the treacherous landscape in front of me, carefully dissecting the neck of the aneurysm. Within its delicate walls, blood swirled like daredevil motorcyclists defying gravity in a metal sphere. The two parallel cases were looping vertically and horizontally inside my head. I asked for a 6 mm curved clip and placed it across the neck of the aneurysm, seeing the ball of the aneurysm shrivel in front of me as if the bikers had run out of fuel.

The radiologist called back. 'The MRI is also normal.'

'Then why the hell can't she see?' I muttered aloud. My colleague offered to close up the case so that I could go check on her.

Just as I walked into the ICU, I was informed by the team that her vision had returned to normal after knowing that the MRI was clear and showed complete removal of the tumour. 'She probably had a psychogenic panic attack after she overheard relatives of the patient in the next bed talking about someone losing their vision after surgery,' the doctor told me.

'What the … ?' I controlled myself. 'You have no idea what a surgeon endures on the other end of that phone when you deliver news like that,' I said, my voice tinged with the weariness of the morning. Yet I knew that, in their defence, they had followed protocol. The situation could have easily spiralled into catastrophe.

I stood at a distance of 10 feet from her and put up three fingers. She could see clearly. She was beaming.

'What happened?' I asked.

'I think I got very scared hearing that news and just blanked out,' she confessed. 'But now I'm happier than I have ever been,' she added, thanking me. Just then, I saw the other patient, the one with the aneurysm, being wheeled into the ICU, giving me a thumbs up. I realized I was helping patients live longer but ageing twice as fast myself.

That night, while I lay in bed with my kids, telling them about my rollercoaster of a day, I told them the story of how I was able to restore vision in someone who came in blind, and the mammoth smile she gave me at the end when she realized she could see. My 10-year-old elder daughter goofily asked, 'Was the smile bigger than her face?' While that isn't possible anatomically, I knew that physiologically and emotionally, it surely had transcended boundaries.

The Parsi lady, who had had the spine surgery and was discharged jubilantly a few days later, called one afternoon, in the middle of another operation of mine, to ask how soon she could start drinking.

'At least wait until the evening!' I told her.

Love and Death

He brought his wife to the hospital in a deep coma. They were both in their late sixties. I was called to see them in the ICU. 'She was absolutely fine when she went to work in the morning,' Sarosh Uncle told me with a dazed look on his face. 'But when she came home for lunch, which she does every day, her speech was a little slurred and she was talking gibberish, which is very unlike her. She complained of a terrible headache in her temple and couldn't complete the conversation we were having and collapsed,' he narrated. 'I immediately rushed to her side, only to find her completely unconscious. Our family physician and my two sisters got her here,' he said, limping from a bad arthritis of the hip that he'd been ignoring for years. He told me that she had been a breast cancer survivor for 18 years. We had noted her blood pressure to be 240/110.

'Did she smoke?' I asked.

'That was her only vice,' he revealed. 'About 15–20 cigarettes a day for the past 35–40 years. Otherwise, she was the life of every party: vibrant and full of vivacious energy. We've been married for over 30 years and there has never been a dull moment,' he volunteered information. 'But she never smoked in front of me,' he interjected. 'She knew I didn't like it, so she would only smoke in the kitchen, or if we went on a dinner date, she would excuse herself,' he told me with a look in his eyes as if they were still in college.

I examined her to note that she was completely paralysed on the right side. She didn't open her eyes even to deep pain.

No sound from her either. The CT scan showed an 8 cm haemorrhage in the left temporal lobe, the area responsible for speech, language and memory.

'We have two options,' I tried to explain. 'Either we don't do anything and let her pass peacefully, or we remove the haematoma and see to what extent she recovers, knowing that she'll never be normal again,' I said softly, bluntly but lovingly.

'Oh my God,' he replied, unable to fathom the gravity of the situation, several thoughts probably coursing through his mind. 'Being an editor myself, I'm an avid reader of all your columns, and you've saved so many people who were almost dead,' he said, searching my face.

'We always try our best,' I put my arm around his shoulder, 'and sometimes we win, but sometimes we don't,' I replied. I felt like a reluctant imposter, standing beneath the weight of expectations I couldn't fulfil. Over the next hour, we went through the entire spectrum of possibilities, from death to a persistent vegetative state to assisted living to the uncertainty of predicting to what extent she would recover. I was ambiguous about whether her speech would recover or if she would remember anything.

'We have so many things we still want to do together,' he told me. 'I would be completely devastated if anything were to happen to her. We are all we have,' he lamented. I asked him about his children, and he said that he hadn't wanted kids and she was ambivalent. 'I had often asked Ketayun who would look after us when we are old, and she used to say that we'd always have each other,' he said, a solitary tear running down his face.

'Can I accompany you inside the operation theatre?' he requested, explaining, 'I would not like to leave her side. I'll sit in a corner and won't be in your way. I just want to sit and pray while you're doing the operation,' he kept adding sentences, hoping I'd agree. I convinced him it would be best for him to wait right outside, and that we would be done in a couple of hours.

We finally operated on her and removed the large thick blood clot that was compressing the vital structures of her brain. The tense brain was soft again. As we wheeled her back to the ICU, I told him I was happy with the surgery and the nature of the brain at the end of it. 'We'll have to take it one day at a time,' I told him as I signed off.

He secured special permission from the hospital management to sit next to her 24/7. When I went for my rounds the next day, he was praying over her. I was so deeply moved by this man's love for his wife.

'Why don't you get some rest, Sarosh Uncle; this is going to be a long haul and it might wear you out. You have to be fresh and fit so you can look after her,' I tried to explain.

'In fact, I was going to request something from you,' he said to me. 'Can you please arrange for me to have a shower in the hospital? Because when I went home yesterday to change and shave, I was stricken with a profound grief for having left Ketayun's side for a few hours,' he shared, wearing his heart on his sleeve.

We arranged for him to be comfortable around her in whatever way he wanted. Over the next few days, we were able to get her off the ventilator and she began opening her eyes. She could not speak because she had a tracheostomy tube in her windpipe, but she was beginning to move her right leg. Every time I walked into the room to see her, she would break out into an enormous smile, which thrilled Sarosh Uncle to bits.

'She's making great progress,' I told him, as he adjusted the speaker that played healing sounds in her ears.

'Do you know, she's taken such good care of me,' he told me on one of my daily rounds. 'I often have these dizzy spells, so she used to constantly remind me to drink water. And if she knew who I was with, she would remind our friends to make sure I was drinking enough water,' he said with gleaming eyes. '"I live for you," she used to tell me. "And you are my life," I used to reply.'

I went home that day and told my wife I loved her. She probably wondered what was wrong with me. I narrated this story to her.

'They seem like a special couple. I would love to meet them,' she said. She met Sarosh Uncle and Ketayun a few days later, when we arranged a special musical evening for patients and their relatives in the hospital cafeteria so that they could forget about their worries for a moment.

'I must have done something phenomenal to deserve a wife like Ketayun,' he told her then.

'I also must have done something to deserve my wife,' I told him, leaving out the 'phenomenal' bit, as all of us laughed a little after three weeks of rigour.

As Sarosh Uncle and his beautiful wife Ketayun left our hospital to continue further rehabilitation and physiotherapy elsewhere, I couldn't help but remember the famous Russian poet Sergei Yesenin, who said, 'In this world you can search for everything, except love and death. They find you when the time comes.'*

---

*Yesenin, S. (n.d.). Quote widely attributed to Sergei Yesenin.

Section 6

CURIOUS CHARACTERS

These are portraits of unforgettable people – eccentric, dramatic, tender, infuriating and irresistibly alive. Patients who arrive with odd symptoms, unusual quirks and personalities that deserve their own medical textbooks. In these stories, biology misbehaves, comedy sneaks into tragedy and the human spirit – stubborn, fragile, magnificent – walks out of the clinic with its head held high.

The Man Who Couldn't Stop Laughing

'I got a little worried when he started laughing at his brother's funeral two weeks ago,' said a concerned wife, as Rusi, her 55-year-old husband, sat in front of me shaking his crossed legs with his hands clasped on his belly. He wore a chequered shirt with a grey pant that complemented his salt-and-pepper hair, and a confused look at why everyone was so perturbed about a few laughs.

'The other day, our cat had diarrhoea and defiled our expensive Persian carpet, and all he did was sit on the couch and laugh.'

'Not only has it been ruined, but it also doesn't smell as good anymore!' Rusi added with a huge grin followed by a raucous guffaw.

'See, isn't this ludicrous?' she pointed, almost instructing me to scold him for having switched from a caring and loving man to a callous embarrassment. 'He chuckles at old people being unable to cross the road. He has started behaving like that man from the movie *Joker*.'

'Not the Raj Kapoor one!' Rusi interjected as I burst out into a bit of a giggle myself. 'Yes, the actor whose name no one can pronounce properly,' he said, referring to Joaquin Phoenix. His wife sighed with exasperation as she pulled out an MRI scan of his brain that their family physician had ordered.

'So, he's laughing at all the wrong things,' I said, summarizing her woes as I plugged the MRI against the luminance of the

X-ray box, 'and this is why.' With the back of my pen, I went on to circle a 3.5 cm tumour arising from the trigeminal nerve and pressing onto the brainstem. 'A tumour in this location in known in extremely rare cases to produce pathological laughter,' I explained, as they looked at me befuddled. 'We'll remove it and he'll be fine.' My confidence came, from seeing during my training days, a similar outcome for this common tumour with an arcane presentation.

A couple of days later, we tucked under his right temporal lobe, drilling into a little quadrant of bone obscuring our vision. Neurosurgeons take a look into the glistening opalescence of the brain every day, but the view is a tad different each day. The brain is a variant shade of beige-pink, the nerves a diverse spectrum from white to yellow, and the corridors to access these tumours keep changing, making it a wondrous journey into enthralling nooks and crannies. There is a new treasure to be excavated every day. 'Can I cut this?' is the most common question I voice aloud to the amusement of the team watching the surgery on the big screen. Most often, you know what you're about to cut but, on occasion, you end up nipping something you can't identify in the hope that it's a part of nature's abundance.

We peeled the tumour off the nerve it originated from, and when we removed it completely, the dent it had made on the brain stem gently ballooned back to take its original form.

'You think he'll stop laughing after surgery?' I indulged my assistant as we closed, a time of the operation where we resort to prosaic yet philosophical questions of life.

'I think he has a great sense of humour; your surgery is only going to ruin it for him!' came the reply.

The morning after surgery, when neurosurgical patients are fully awake and alert, we check if they are oriented to time, place and person, and do a thorough neurological examination to check for motor or sensory impairment, seeing if things have become better or worse. In Rusi's case, we needed to say or do something strange to see if he laughed. 'We'll leave that for his wife to assess, after she spends the whole day with him,' I instructed as we wrote orders to transfer him out of the ICU and into the ward, which deemed that everything was perfect.

Two days later, we got a call from the emergency department about a 67-year-old lady who had begun crying violently and inconsolably for two hours after a glass of water slipped from her hand and smashed to the floor. On checking further, we realized that she wasn't hurt, and the glass didn't have any emotional value for her either. The psychiatrist who was called in to opine was also confused. Our astute neurologist ordered an urgent MRI that showed a stroke in the left thalamus. She was administered a clot-busting drug and we could see her tears dry up as the last few drops of medication entered her veins.

Pathological laughter and crying are uncommon manifestations of common neurological conditions. They don't have a motivating stimulus, nor are they triggered by an impulse that would not have otherwise led to this reaction. Scientists term this 'emotional incontinence' and it is often seen in patients with amyotrophic lateral sclerosis, a form of motor neuron disease. We have also seen this in patients with multiple sclerosis and Parkinson's, and in some brain tumours.

We went to check on Rusi on the day of his discharge. I could hear a roar as I knocked on the door.

'We haven't cured him, have we?' I turned to my colleague.

'Hi Doc,' Rusi smiled as the door opened.

'Is he still laughing at stuff he's not supposed to?' I turned to his wife.

'Nothing crazy so far,' she said, her hands folded in gratitude.

'Then what was he laughing at when we walked in?' I asked, my curiosity piqued.

'Someone sent him a neurosurgeon joke!'

'Let's hear it,' I said, preparing myself to be embarrassed.

'How many neurosurgeons does it take to change a light bulb?' he asked, and then followed up with the answer after a sly grin from me. 'Just one: he holds the bulb and the world revolves around him.'

I smiled, shaking my head at the comical impression people have of us, but appreciating the humour nonetheless.

The next time you see someone laughing nonsensically, don't hesitate to get a scan done for them. If the scan is normal, you can safely diagnose them to be Parsi.

The Son Who Couldn't Stop Crying

'My father has not been able to get out of bed for over two months,' lamented Jagdish Sanghvi, as his 90-year-old dad lay helplessly on a stretcher that jutted obliquely into my consulting room. In his tenth decade of life, the old man had a full mop of dishevelled silver hair and a perfectly chiselled face that wrinkled every time he winced in pain at attempts to adjust his recumbent posture. 'He had a fall eight weeks ago and has been unable to walk since then,' continued Jagdish amidst short ragged breaths and heaving sobs. I let him talk, handing him pieces of tissue and placing a glass of cool water on the table.

I have never been uncomfortable watching men cry in front of me. I, too, have cried when the occasion demanded it. It's a basic expression of grief across all ages and sexes. Why should stoic men be exempt from expressing it? Jagdish must have been in his mid-sixties and was unable to comprehend how his completely independent father, while remaining cognitively crisp, was reduced to frail dependency within a few weeks, physically worn out from the pain in his mid-back. I gently got him on his side and started pressing his back lightly, eventually reaching a point where it unleashed such an intense scream from the injured man that it got a few nurses running into my room. The area I had palpated corresponded to a compression fracture of the tenth thoracic vertebrae that was lit against the luminance of the X-ray box into which I had plugged in the film.

'There it is – that's the cause of his problems,' I told the son excitedly, pointing to a slightly collapsed triangular vertebra compared to the healthy and nicely squared others. I completed the examination noting the strength in the patient's legs, which was good. He wasn't moving only due to the pain.

'The family doctor said to just keep him comfortable, that no surgery should be attempted at this age, so we've kept him home. But it's only getting worse, hence we came to see you. The medication or physiotherapy is not helping at all,' he finished in a fresh burst of uncontrollable tears.

Both father and son had lost their wives and were each other's only pillars of support. The son bolstered the father physically and the father was his son's emotional strength; even through his own pain, he had a sympathetic smile on his face, silently conveying to me that it was his son who really needed to be taken care of and not he.

I explained to them vociferously that surgery was a very good option in his case. All we needed to do was inject some cement into the collapsed vertebra and fortify it; the heat generated from the cement would numb the nerve endings in the bone that generated the pain. 'We can do this under local anaesthesia,' I implored, setting to rest a gnawing concern of theirs. There were apprehensions about his age, whether he would be able to lie awake on his belly for the entire duration of the procedure and the management of his high blood pressure and diabetes ... I navigated all their copious questions and got them to finally agree on surgery.

'You must never sell an operation to a patient,' I remember a professor once telling me, 'you must get them to buy it.' More often than not, this is a philosophy I adopt, simply laying down the pros and cons and allowing the family to decide. But sometimes, when you have a cogent solution that will almost certainly relieve your patient of their malady, the only reasonable thing to do is to be unreasonable about it and goad them into making the right decision. The elderly are an extremely valuable asset to our community. They bring with them a grit and grace, a courage and compassion that comes with the wisdom of having lived a long life. There is a lot to learn from them. It is our moral obligation to care for them to the best of our ability.

The next morning, Mr Sanghvi lay prone on bolsters, shivering in a freezing operating room. We armed him with a warmer that soothed him a little. After cleaning and draping him in the usual fashion while our anaesthesiologist kept him preoccupied with the latest in the stock market, and after giving him some local anaesthesia to numb the area, I directed the needle to our target using intraoperative X-rays and injected 5 mm of toothpaste-like cement into the vertebral body. Live images showed the cement seeping into cracks and crevices, augmenting the injured area. Very rarely, the cement can extravasate into the bloodstream and enter the lungs, causing a sudden collapse, but – knock on wood – we were okay. I withdrew the needle and sealed the entry point with a stitch.

We flipped him over and asked him to wiggle his toes and bend his legs, the first thing we do after every spine operation to ensure we haven't caused any harm. He did so effortlessly, without even a wince. A few hours later, I went and saw him in the ward. He lay in bed smiling, chatting with his son.

'Would you like to try and walk?' I interjected.

They gawked in disbelief. I put the side rails down and extended my hand for him to get a grip as he seated himself at the edge of the bed gingerly for the first time in two months. Then, he reluctantly planted both feet on the ground and stood up, taking his first step. For his son, it was like watching Neil Armstrong take his first step on the moon; he once again wept vehemently. Tears are a most confusing body fluid: they express themselves the same way even in diametrically opposite states of emotion.

The next morning, Mr Sanghvi had taken a shower on his own, had oiled and neatly partitioned his dishevelled silver mop, completed a walk around the corridor and then sat upright in his bed reading the newspaper.

'How do you feel this morning?' I asked.

'Younger than my son,' he quipped, and his perfectly curetted face wrinkled again – not with pain but with a hearty laugh.

The Lady Who Sinned

'You need an operation in your neck, Mrs Smith,' I told the god-fearing 66-year-old lady after conducting a detailed evaluation in her hospital room. The medicine cabinet next to her bed had three different-sized photo frames of Christ, two rosaries and the Bible. The windowsill was lined with a picture of *The Last Supper*, and next to it were a couple of wooden crosses. There was gentle 'Praise the Lord' music playing on her husband's phone. I felt as though I had just walked into the kingdom of heaven.

Over the past year, Joanne Smith had started to complain of a difficulty in walking on uneven surfaces. She had tripped over and fallen a few times. She found it hard to cook, as vegetables and utensils kept slipping out of her hands. As a well-built lady, she was used to a large amount of physical labour, but most of her activities had been curbed owing to her ailment.

'I feel like I'm walking on fluffy clouds all the time,' she said in a despondent voice, describing the sensory impairment in her feet. I really was in the kingdom of heaven.

'Squeeze my fingers tight,' I instructed as I put them on her palm for her to grasp. Her hand slipped off easily, and her husband, who was standing stoically next to me, nodded his head, expecting this outcome.

I prophetically held the MRI films against the light streaming in from the window to show them where her cervical spine was being compressed by her thickened bone and ligaments. 'We will remove whatever is pinching on the cord and over the next few months, you'll regain most of your function,' I explained, apprising them of the usual complications that could arise with an operation like this.

'God has chosen you as an instrument for her healing,' her silver-haired, dark-skinned husband proclaimed.

'I will do my best,' I said with my hand on my heart, albeit a little nervous of their proximity to God.

The next morning, we flipped her on her belly, fixed her head on pins, and sliced down the back of her neck. I went ahead and meticulously drilled off the bone, punching out the thickened ligament to allow for her spinal cord to breathe again. 'I don't want anything to go wrong with this lady,' I said, which is what I assert loudly when my subconscious tingles that something might. The surgery went off well, and I sounded off the post-operative instructions as we closed. We shifted her to the ICU for overnight observation.

I saw her again in the evening before I left for the day. As I placed my hand over her forehead, she softly smiled at me and said 'thank you', still groggy from the anaesthesia. She was moving her arms and legs well, which was an excellent sign.

'Thank you, Jesus!' I said to myself for a change, a variation from the oft-used 'Thank you, Khodaiji,' hoping my Parsi God wouldn't mind. I drove back recalling the Smiths' belief in God and I wondered if atheists or agnostics recover just as well as devotees of the divine. It might be a study worth conducting one day, although I am convinced that providence plays a big role in successful outcomes, especially in the kinds of cases I do.

The next morning, I walked into the ICU with a bounce in my step and a freshness that comes from having slept deeply. After the previous day's successful operation, I was hoping to see Joanne sitting up in a chair and eating breakfast. But when

I walked over to her, I was aghast to see her lying flat with all four limbs restrained to the bed. She was thrashing around violently with a strength I never knew could exist in someone who was so weak before surgery. Her heart was thumping at 200 beats a minute and her blood pressure had the same numerical value. I looked urgently over at the ICU registrar and a couple of nurses who were around, my eyes wide open and arms up in the air, questioningly.

'She's become violent and aggressive over the past hour,' the nurse explained, showing me her own arm that had been clawed into by Joanne.

'She almost bit the ward boy who tried to help her,' another continued.

'Everyone here is trying to kill me!' Mrs Smith yelled at the top of her voice. I thought that looking at me – a familiar face – might ease things a little, but I was wrong; the screams continued. 'You are the devil and my murderer,' she growled at me with fiery eyes. The way she was moving her neck while chained to the bed made me worry that she might suffer a whiplash injury.

The junior doctor in the ICU came over to confer with me. 'We gave her something to calm her down, but it hasn't worked so far,' he said, pointing to her chart.

'We should shift her out of the ICU now, she'll be fine,' I announced it with the panache of James Bond, who knew exactly what might be going on.

'But her blood pressure and heart rate are uncontrollable; it might not be safe,' the doctor responded, trying to reason with me for the well-being of the patient.

I put my arm around him and said, 'Please shift her out. Being in the ICU is part of the problem.'

Post-operative psychosis is a rare but known phenomenon. A wide range of behavioural symptoms may occur after any kind of surgery, not necessarily only those performed on the brain or spine. Patients have been reported to develop depression, mania, hallucinations and impulsivity. In an ICU setting, listening to the constant beeping of various machines, the hushed voices of the nurses and the wails of some who are gravely ill, patients may experience disturbed sleep and start hearing voices, feel severe anxiety and see things that aren't there. This might result in them being severely disoriented, agitated and even violent. We call this ICU psychosis, and it shows up acutely. It is best treated by transferring the patient out of the ICU to somewhere they can feel the comfort of their loved ones. If life-saving treatment is still being administered and that isn't possible, appropriate medication is administered instead.

The next morning, Joanne greeted me with a cheery, 'How are you, Dr Turel?' exhibiting an effusive warmth that was oblivious of the apocalypse of the previous day.

I tested her hand grip and it was as strong as a beast's. My operation was a hit, but I wanted to get to the bottom of all the drama. 'Do you have any recollection of what happened in the ICU yesterday?'

She shook her head sideways, unaware. 'You were not a good girl in there!' I reprimanded her in jest, knowing fully well that what she had gone through was beyond her control.

'Jesus died for our sins,' she said apologetically.

'And it would be a complete waste of his time and effort if you didn't commit them!' I concluded in agreement.

The Gregarious Geriatrics

Gulnar and Armaity had a combined age of 175 years. Together, they were as old as the iconic Sir JJ Hospital that their ancestors had built. Both were in their late eighties and were like each other's appendages. The two Parsi ladies always accompanied each other for their respective medical consultations. Armaity looked like Jon Bon Jovi's mother, with fair skin and a bouncy salt-and-pepper bob cut. Gulnar, who was fondly called Gul by her friends (because she kept getting lost on the foreign trips she took with them), was like an adorable, huggable Shih Tzu transformed into a zesty Parsi aunty. They gingerly helped each other sit in the chairs in front of me in my consultation room.

'I have had this horrible back pain for the past 20 years,' Armaity told me. 'My buttocks are sore, my legs tingle and I just can't walk anymore!' she sounded exasperated.

I assessed her in detail and told her she had severe compression in her lumbar spine. The MRI she had reluctantly gotten done confirmed the same. 'Your X-rays show that your spine is unstable, and we'll have to fix it with screws if you consider surgery,' I explained.

'Surgery at 87 is okay?' she asked with trepidation.

'Only if you want to live to be a hundred!' I said.

'I don't mind!' she exclaimed, her Parsi genes kicking in, 'but not in this pain.'

'Then let's operate on you and fix it once and for all,' I proposed.

'But people say all these bad things about spine surgery …' she further cautioned.

'That's because all those who've had successful surgery are too busy enjoying their lives and don't have time to talk about how good they feel, but the handful of negative outcomes keep getting amplified,' I reasoned.

'I also have back pain,' Gul intervened.

'Do you also want surgery?' I joked.

'I'm a surgical veteran,' she told me. 'I had an emergency perforated appendix and had to fly back from my vacation in the Andaman,' she started.

'Luckily, you weren't lost at that time, and they found you,' I teased her a little.

'Then I had surgery for diverticulitis, where they removed two feet of my intestine,' she said, completely ignoring me and trying to complete her story. 'I had a pouch coming out of my stomach for nine months, which they finally internalized,' she made a face. 'Then, I had four dental surgeries interspersed with three falls, in one of which I fractured my nose and blood splattered all over my face,' she animated the scene. 'I also had four major hernias repaired, and recently, they found three polyps in my uterus, which they suspected were cancerous, so they removed the whole system including my tubes and ovaries – not that I need them anymore,' she flexed her biceps. 'Never a dull moment in my life!'

'So, for the time being, we'll avoid your spine surgery,' I confirmed with a reciprocal smile. 'You don't even need one,' I confirmed after examining her and seeing her images. 'We'll put you onto a good physiotherapist and that should do it.'

A couple of days later, we took Armaity to the operating room. I drilled out the bone and removed the thickened ligament pressing on her nerves, decompressing them meticulously. We put in some screws and connected them with titanium rods to realign the spine and give it back its native shape and form.

'Even though you've put so much metal in my body, I feel 10 kilos lighter,' she told me when she came two weeks later for a checkup. 'All the pain in my legs has vanished. My back is a bit sore, but I'm sure that'll go too,' she said with relief. 'I wish I had done this 10 years ago,' she concluded, echoing what most patients say when they get spine surgery done after avoiding it for as long as they can.

The elderly are some of my favourite people, because while they are the most vulnerable, they are also the toughest. They have accrued the wisdom and experience of several decades to know what's best for them. The youngsters who accompany them on consultations are often heard telling them to slow down or take it easy, which, I believe, is incorrect. The older you get, the more active you should be and the harder you need to exercise – physically and mentally.

Armaity had thought for less than five minutes before she decided she wanted to have surgery. I remember so vividly a 95-year-old man who insisted I operate on him for a haematoma inside his head while his children suggested it was best for him to go peacefully. He calls me every year on his birthday to thank me for adding another precious year to his life. He is 98 now. On one of his calls he lamented, 'I have a four-bedroom apartment on Altamount Road, but I live all alone. Both my children are abroad. I bought the house for ₹4 lakh in 1975, and now it is valued at over 15 crore,' he beamed with pride.

'Uncle, don't forget to write my name in your will!' I said in jest.

Three months later, Gulnar and Armaity walked into my clinic again. Armaity was limping and back to using the walking stick she had given up. She barely managed to seat herself onto the chair before lamenting, 'I was doing so well after surgery, but one day, while I was taking a walk in the garden, this silly giant of a dog chasing a ball dashed right into me and I toppled over.' She winced in pain while I examined her.

'Doesn't look like anything's broken,' I said, 'but we'll confirm it with an X-ray.' It came out to be clean. I gave her a few pills to take away the pain and asked her to come back in a few weeks.

'Give me also some medicines, na,' Gulnar, as usual, intervened. 'All my friends are taking medication and I'm not taking a single pill. I feel left out!' she made a Shih Tzu face. Both Armaity and I looked at her as if she were crazy. Then again, we are Parsi; if we don't have some kind of idiosyncrasy, we aren't doing justice to our genes. 'Give me some memory pills!' she requested. 'My friends call me Gul Golmaal because I keep mixing up stuff.' I gave her some multivitamins to go through in her last decade.

Another three months later, the duo was back. Armaity had no stick and Gulnar was beaming. They looked like they were reverse ageing. I was amazed at their spirit, which they passed on to me both literally and metaphorically; they handed me a bottle of Johnnie Walker whisky. I pulled it out from the bag to take a look and reminded them to do what the bottle says.

'What?' they asked. 'Keep drinking?'

'No,' I said, although I knew that was part of the reason they were so full of life. 'Keep walking!' I pointed to the label.

'You're our Santa,' they thanked me, 'and the best gift you gave us this Christmas was our health back.'

'Happy New Year!' we wished each other while doing a group hug, and I added, 'May you both live to be a hundred!'

'I'm going to write an essay about the both of you,' I warned as a parting remark.

The Real Hero

On a slightly weary Thursday evening, just as I was about to go into surgery at 6.00 p.m., I got a frantic phone call from a son about his 75-year-old father. 'For the past few days, my father's balance has been off. But since this morning, his speech has been slurring, and he's becoming incoherent and confused. It almost seems like he's slipping in and out of consciousness,' the son went on, slightly frenzied. 'We took the advice of our family physician and got a CT scan of the brain. We've been told he's slowly bleeding into the brain and needs an emergency operation,' came the vague description from the other end.

'Why don't you take him to the hospital closest to you,' I suggested, channelling my inner GPS.

'Doctor, we live in Juhu. Do you come to this side of town?' I politely declined. 'Even in his completely incoherent state, the only thing my dad keeps saying is, "Take me to Mazda. I've read every single column of his in the paper and I know he'll be able to fix me!" the son pressed on, almost panting on the other end. 'He's a big fan and a very stubborn one. Please do something,' he urged. 'He keeps chanting "Mazda, Mazda", as if it's a medical mantra.'

To be honest, I had a huge smile on my face, almost blushing a little. Until now, I thought my fan base consisted primarily of 70-year-old women, and it was good to have some male cheer – a dopamine boost mixed with some testosterone. It took away the tiredness of a long Thursday, after having done a six-hour brain tumour surgery followed by a three-hour spine operation.

'Bring him to my hospital and we'll see what we can do. I'm just going into surgery, but the team in the ER will evaluate you and then call me. I'll come and see him,' I said, hoping it would be a quick fix and not a full-blown renovation.

'Thank you, Doctor, we'll be there in an hour,' he sounded relieved.

As we were operating on our third case of the day, I told my colleague that I had started writing a few years ago to help people understand brain and spine problems so that they could make informed decisions about their health and become aware of what conditions to promptly treat and what could be ignored. 'Today, I feel we succeeded!' I told him, as we put a tube into the brain of a young girl that had an excess accumulation of fluid.

Two hours later, Aspi was in the ER with his two children who looked exactly like him. His wife was also present, a shawl wrapped around her neck. When I went to see him, he looked like he'd wrestled a bear and lost, a classic emergency room look: his hair was dishevelled and shirt incorrectly buttoned. Nonetheless, he recognized me despite his deeply confused state. Score one for the ego! I quickly examined him to make sure he was moving his hands and legs. 'But he can't walk,' the son interjected. The CT scan had showed a collection of blood on both sides of his brain that was building up after a fall he had had a few weeks ago that had now reached tipping point.

'He'll need an operation to drain the blood,' I said.

'When, Doctor?' they asked.

'Now-ish!' was my response.

'We'll do whatever you say,' they agreed, after I gave them a detailed explanation of the procedure and possible outcomes.

'He'll be home in three days,' I assured them. They looked relieved.

'*Achha*, Doctor, we forgot to mention that he had epilepsy for many years but has stopped his meds for over a decade, as he's been seizure free,' they added.

'Not to worry,' I said after inquiring about it in detail.

Within hours, the whir of the drill echoed in the sterile theatre as we punched two coin-sized holes through Aspi Uncle's skull, cut the dura, and let out a pool of blood that had collected below it. It was like an overflowing river whose floodgates had just been opened. We wheeled him out at midnight, his eyes glowing at the surprise of finding himself alive.

'We've kept a tiny tube inserted to drain the blood over the next few days, and once that stops, we'll send him home,' I told the family. They were thrilled and thanked me for being so prompt, enamoured by how the whole thing had gone off without a glitch. Their gratitude was a tangible thing, a warmth that filled the room, a stark contrast to the cold steel of the operating table.

The next morning, Aspi Uncle had a seizure. His eyes rolled up, his mouth started frothing and his hands and legs jerked uncontrollably against the crisp white sheets of his bed. We controlled it with medication, but he was knocked out and not waking up. The CT scan looked clean. The family was shaken, as was I. *Did I take the past history of his epilepsy too lightly?* I wondered. Should we have given him some prophylactic medicines?

'Never meet your heroes. If you meet your heroes, you're always going to be disappointed,' the old adage echoed. They saw a saviour, a celestial figure, but I was a mere mortal.

Thankfully, there was nothing to worry about, as Aspi Uncle soon regained consciousness and was back to his normal self. He was discharged a few days later, walking with perfect balance, alert and coherent, able to recount several articles of mine he'd read.

When he returned two weeks later, he was beaming. 'He's been walking seven-to-eight km a day!' his son said. The scars of surgery had disappeared into oblivion, both literally and metaphorically.

'I want to show you something about the work we do with Tata Institute of Social Sciences,' he told me, pulling out two mirrors. One was perfect, the other shattered. 'Look into the good mirror and tell me three positive attributes about yourself,' he suggested. I paused, shrugging my shoulders even though I wanted to say 'competent', 'funny' and 'compassionate'. 'Most people are unable to say anything good about themselves,' he told me. 'Look into the cracked mirror – what do you see?'

'The same person,' I told him, 'But slightly fractured.'

'It's not you who's fractured; it's just the image of you that's broken,' he clarified. 'Most people are unable to identify the difference, and that's why we conduct workshops with cancer patients at Tata Memorial Hospital and in schools and colleges to assist people with mental health issues and help them rebuild themselves.'

'I'm going to keep these,' I told him.

'We got them for you!' they thanked me profusely, as the wife gave me a handmade painting and a whole lot of other paraphernalia.

Every time I feel like I'm not good enough, I look into the broken mirror and remind myself it's just an image. Not the real thing. That I'm whole inside. That I'm more than enough.

There is something to learn from everyone. Thank you, Aspi Uncle and family, for allowing us to treat you. It is I who is your fan.

The Peculiar Hypochondriac

'If you operate on me, I'm sure I will get 100 per cent better,' said Percy, a middle-aged, mid-sized, mild-mannered gentleman. He was single and lived with his mother, a status that is quite common and widely comfortable among Parsis. 'My back is on fire,' he exclaimed animatedly, as he pulled out a cargo of blood tests and MRIs done every single year and religiously organized in colour-coded folders.

'Your lab values are fine. The images look perfect. Your spine looks better than mine!' I said candidly after a detailed examination.

'I've tried yoga, physiotherapy, medications, injections, acupressure and acupuncture, cupping and even black magic,' he continued. I was curious to find out what the last one entailed but figured it would be best to move ahead; the voice in my seasoned brain whispered to me that this was going to be a long consultation.

'Anything else bothering you?' I asked, trying to get a more holistic perspective. Surgeons are often blamed for their single-pronged 'you need surgery now' approach, the kind where 'when all you have is a hammer, everything looks like a nail'.

'My mouth is always dry. I'm extremely agitated and irritated all the time. I keep forgetting stuff. I'm perpetually tired and can't multitask. There is a constant feeling of doom. I keep burping and the 'gas' in my tummy never seems to subside; I'm not sure if it's because I wear my pants right over my belly button. My eyebrows hurt a lot – not my head, my eyebrows;

there is a difference. People think I'm crazy when I tell them this, but it happens mostly after sunset, and when it does, my nose itches. I'm constantly losing hair – I can't be bald at this age!' My interest arose: finally, we had a symptom in common that I thought concluded the description, but after a brief pause, he continued.

'There's always something itching in my throat and I have to drink tons of water with a teaspoon of glycerol to clear it, but nothing seems to work. And if I cough to get rid of the itchiness, I go red in the face. I'm not sure if being constipated has anything to do with this constant feeling that something's stuck in my throat.' I started sinking in my chair.

'I passed a stone in my urine recently. It was as painful as delivering a baby!' He placed the stone on my desk, neatly preserved in its original form in a plastic container.

'Wow,' I said, my eyes widening to the size of the earth. I wanted to ask how he had retrieved it, but pretended to contain my intrigue and let him proceed.

'The space between my ribs hurts and my knees are always crackling. I have this tingling sensation in my little toes all the time and my skin is so sensitive; it doesn't tolerate temperatures above 32 and below 19 degrees. I've seen over 200 doctors and no one can help me,' he concluded, carefully placing the plastic container back in a zip lock. 'Please operate on me,' he pleaded one more time.

I told him that I was a surgeon, and that if there was one thing I was confident of, it was that he didn't need surgery. I recommended guided physiotherapy, a change in medication and a psychiatrist. I explained that a lot of his problems were psychosomatic and could be addressed by a detailed assessment and personalized therapy. This was a prognosis he had probably heard earlier, as evidenced by his melancholic exit.

A few weeks later, Percy sent me an email stating that another surgeon had finally understood his problems correctly and operated on him, and that his back pain had disappeared. *How does one identify a patient who doesn't need surgery but benefits from one?* I wondered to myself. This kind of placebo effect is often short-lived, but in this case, someone had delivered it: he had bolstered the patient's confidence and provided a solution, leaving me perplexed about what had actually been done.

Thankfully, Percy's case is not the norm. On some occasions, when I've told patients they didn't need surgery and they eventually got an operation elsewhere, they returned solemnly stating that the surgery didn't help.

In a slightly different context, I remember another lady who had severe back and leg pain; her MRI showed a grotesque compression in the lumbar spine. These symptoms disappeared remarkably after surgery but, three days later, just before discharge, she developed excruciating abdominal pain. Clinically, the abdomen was soft: the ultrasound and CT scan were clean and an endoscopy from both ends was clear. She insisted that something needed to be 'removed from the stomach'. An experienced general surgeon, a gastroenterologist, an internist, a gynaecologist and a urologist conducted every test there was and gave varying combinations of medications, all of them confirming that there was no need for surgery. She was in immense pain for two weeks, and every time we told her we were giving her a pain injection (but gave her sterile water instead), she said her pain had temporarily vanished, only to return when the injection bottle hanging on the IV pole tethered to her arm was almost empty. Frustrated, her family got her discharged and admitted to another hospital that removed her gall bladder the next day. Miraculously, her pain then evanesced forever.

There is more to disease pattern than we understand. Patients don't read medical textbooks. There is an alchemy to discerning the functional component of an organic illness. Sometimes, patients invent symptoms to claim compensation or exaggerate them to prolong leave. Others genuinely believe that there is something wrong that can only be fixed by surgery, even when the surgeon feels otherwise. Can one ever justify performing an operation that is scientifically unwarranted, but which ends up completely curing the patient for some unforeseeable reason?

It takes a surgeon about five years to learn how to operate. But it takes us 10 years to learn when to and when not to operate, and perhaps 15 years to adjudge on whom to and whom not to operate.

Here's hoping that you never need surgery or even have to pretend to need one.

The Husband with a Phataka in the Throat

Mrs Pednekar walked into the clinic with her husband. They looked like they were both in their sixties. Simple, warm people dressed in pastel shades, they joined their hands in a namaste with bowed heads as they took their seats. 'My husband has been in severe pain for the past 10 years,' she told me, her eyes flooding almost instantly. We often see patients break down in the doctor's clinic within a few seconds of their arrival, even with little being said or done. I imagine the office seems like a portal where they feel they can release that pent-up angst, anxiety or energy.

I allowed for her to feel soothed and then continued. 'Where is the pain?' I inquired.

'In the left side of the throat,' he said, his entire face clenching in a tumultuous spasm simply with the utterance of those three words.

'He cannot talk, eat, chew or swallow when he gets these random bouts of pain multiple times a day – and it's been several years now,' his wife continued, allowing for his electric shock-like sensation to settle. 'But in the past three months, it's become unimaginably unbearable. He's lost 12 kg because he fears eating will trigger a spasm,' she concluded.

'It feels like I have an entire loom of firecrackers bursting in my throat randomly,' he explained once the episode settled.

'Well, with Diwali around the corner, you'll be able to have an internal celebration!' I quipped, wanting to ease the situation and trying to be my usual self, which they understood, but they also wanted me to fathom the magnitude of the problem.

'Doctor *Saab*, it's not funny,' he cautioned with one hand, ready to grasp his own throat if a cracker burst inside. 'Imagine you're fast asleep and someone stabs you in the throat,' he paused, trying to provide another analogy. 'Several times over,' he continued. 'Every night, many times a night,' he stressed. 'You'd rather wish you were dead, but you wake up like a ghost wondering how come you're still alive,' he stopped with a precise description of what he was feeling. I was now confused if it was Diwali we were celebrating or Halloween.

'We've been to so many doctors and taken so many medications and injections that our pain specialist finally referred us to you to try surgery, as they've run out of options,' she said as she handed over the MRI films to me.

Like I had expected from my clinical assessment, it showed an artery at the back of the brain pressing against the glossopharyngeal nerve, the nerve responsible for sensations in the throat, or what is technically called the pharynx. Sometimes, an elongated piece of the mastoid bone called the styloid process can also cause the same sensations, but he didn't have that. 'When this artery pulsates, it's pressing against the nerve and causing this lancinating pain,' I explained to them, adding that as they had tried everything, surgery would be a good idea.

'We're prepared to get admitted today,' the wife said, clearly unable to see her husband suffer any longer.

I adjusted my surgical schedule to accommodate him so that they could check in the next day. Unfortunately, in a pre-operative workup for surgery, his echocardiogram showed very poor heart function. 'Do you get breathless while walking?' I asked when I saw him on rounds the next day.

'Very,' he said.

'He'll need an angiogram of the heart before we can proceed with surgery,' the cardiologist opined, performing it the same evening.

We sat down again with the family to explain the situation to them. 'He has three very severe blockages in the heart,' the cardiologist said, 'and needs three stents or a bypass surgery, but if we do that, he'll have to be on blood thinners and we'll have to defer the brain surgery by at least three months,' he opined.

'If we go ahead with the surgery without the heart procedure ...?' the wife asked.

'Then there is a very high chance of having a heart attack during surgery,' he completed the sentence for her.

'Plus, during this operation, one can have sudden changes in heart rate and blood pressure because we are very close to the brainstem,' I added for them to fully understand the risks of going ahead with surgery in this state.

'I'm willing to die, but I can't live with this pain,' he said with a certain degree of authority.

'You'll have to sign a consent form that you're aware of and accept the possibility of there being a death on the operating table,' I said to sheepishly safeguard myself, but knowing there is a higher force that understood that we were all working in the best interest of the patient. He signed on the paper and his wife countersigned it. They say that when your intentions are pure, nothing horrible will happen. Unfortunately, I have lived and worked enough to know that this is not true.

The next day, we took him into the operating room. His wife stood outside with hands folded. 'Everything will be okay,' I reassured her, as I do with every relative before walking into the operating room.

We positioned him sideways to make an incision behind the left ear and made a coin-sized opening into the back of the skull to get to the artery that had ensconced the nerve so intently. It looked like a boa constrictor that wraps around its prey before killing it. As we separated the artery from the nerve, gently untethering the silvery strands attaching the two together, the heart rate suddenly dropped to 50, then 40, then 30, as the alarms went off. 'Stop whatever you're doing!' the anaesthesiologist alerted.

The moment I released my instrument from the tug it was creating on the brain stem, the heart rate bounced back up. We tried again to gently release the artery but the heart rate crashed once again.

'This could strain his heart,' the anaesthesiologist warned.

'We have to release this completely,' I said, 'or we won't do him justice,' I requested them to hold fort. After multiple attempts and a few heart attacks myself, I was able to free the artery completely from the nerve. We inserted a piece of Teflon padding to keep the two apart. Thankfully for him, he survived the operation and was delighted to realize he was pain-free within a few minutes of waking up.

'I wish someone had told me that surgery was an option 10 years ago, I wouldn't have suffered so much,' he said with relief and regret at the same time, when I went to see him the next morning. I explained to him that it was unfortunate that people are still unaware of conditions like trigeminal and glossopharyngeal neuralgia, as it is quite rare, but awareness is gradually increasing. I told him he should thank his pain doctor for setting him on the right track.

Three days later, the cardiologist inserted the same number

of stents in his heart, giving him a complete overhaul and getting him ready to be discharged.

'Now that your pain is gone, you'll have to burst real crackers,' I took the liberty of joking again.

'I'm not going to burst any crackers, Doctor *Saab*,' he said with folded hands, 'but every night for the rest of my life, I'll light a diya for you and your family,' his eyes glassed over.

'Happy Diwali,' we uttered in simultaneity as we hugged each other goodbye.

The Uncle Who Couldn't Smell

A family of four entered and positioned themselves strategically in my consultation room. The middle-aged parents took the two seats in front of me, the teenage daughter plonked herself on the examination bed and the son chose to stand. This was swift. Often, when there are two chairs and more people, the first five minutes are spent deciding who is going to sit where and, most often, one chair remains vacant because people opt to stand out of courtesy. Every culture is different, and every family has a distinct dynamic.

'He can't smell anything,' the wife started off after pleasantries were exchanged, and then looked at her husband for him to continue.

'My head hurts like hell,' he said clasping it with both his palms. He sat there like a stack of circular Russian dolls. His head was perfectly round. His torso was also thoroughly spherical, a voluminously larger version of his head. And the tumour inside his head was the size and shape of a cricket ball, a glowing third eye. It stood there like a road roller, compacting the nerves responsible for smell into the base of the skull.

The olfactory nerves are microscopic versions of spaghetti that line the insides of one's nose and then enter the skull through a sieve in the bone, forming a bundle that resembles a thick flat noodle, one on each side. Now, thanks to the tumour, his nerves were thin flat noodles. The complex connections of the nerves with various parts of the brain via sophisticated networks allow smell to become integrated with emotion, memory and taste.

'He's also becoming very emotional lately,' the wife interjected. 'We've been married for two decades, and he's told me he loves me twice in 20 years. In the past one month, he's said it a dozen times!' she said with the glimmer of a smile, one tinged with surprise but also concern. The teenage daughter had a bit of a twinkle in her eyes, probably drawing parallels to the affection her dad had also been showering on her. I plugged in the MRI films to show them that the downward pressure of the tumour on the olfactory nerves was causing the dysfunction of smell, and that the swelling of the surrounding frontal lobes was responsible for his emotional effusiveness.

They had all the answers but didn't know what question to ask next. 'We have to remove this with an operation,' I helped. 'Surgery will relieve the headaches, restore his sentiments and he will hopefully regain his smell, at least in one nostril,' I elucidated.

'We'll go ahead with surgery,' the son finally spoke as we discussed some more technical nuances related to the surgery and its outcome.

A few days later, I walked into the operation theatre at 7.00 a.m. for his surgery. An early morning OT has a profound and piercing smell you can feel in your bones. It's ethereal. It is sweet and tangy, zesty and fresh. It has the aroma of mopped floors, buttery walls, sterile packs, warm-pressed linen and gleaming nurses – the intense tenderness of whom you can feel even behind the veneer of their triple-layered masks. And when you've operated hard and long enough like I have, the OT also has the smell of joy, grief, gladness, remorse and hope, with, above all, a fragrance of resilience and compassion.

After fixing the patient's circular head on a clamp, we made a semicircular incision from ear to ear and reflected the scalp down. We then drilled out a 4x4 cm piece of bone above the right eyebrow. The brain was extremely tense as we opened the dura, requiring us to do away with a small and inconsequential part of the frontal lobe called the frontal pole, to get to the tumour.

'We're sucking away the "I love you" centre of his brain,' I told my assistant in jest.

'He's now going to say "I lobe you" to her!' he retorted, my wit rubbing off on him after the years we'd spent chatting under the radiance of the microscope.

'Finally, he'll do justice to his Bengali lineage,' I quipped, before we moved to a more critical stage of the surgery.

Once we got to the tumour, we cut off its blood supply first and then cored into its centre so that it could fall on itself. Then, I gently peeled it off the right olfactory nerve followed by the left one, hoping it wouldn't snap at its thinnest point, where it was almost transparent. I often whisper into patients' brains when I operate. 'Hang in there,' I implored to the cranial nerves, and they did so with tenacity. A few days later, he was discharged with a smile on his face that met the incision on his head.

Six months later, the entire Das family was back in my consultation room. They positioned themselves in exactly the same fashion, as if it were home. A fresh MRI showed no tumour and spotless frontal lobes. He was delighted that his sense of smell was back. 'I've had to add more spice in his food, though,' his wife interjected.

'And how is he emotionally?' I asked.

'Absolutely fine,' she smiled. 'In fact, he's become kinder, softer, and still keeps saying he loves me, but I'm not complaining!' she said as they looked into each other's eyes, happy faces all around.

'I'll readily take credit for that, if you don't mind,' I signed off with an equally happy face.

The Gland That Makes Goliath of David

'My wedding ring doesn't fit anymore, Doctor!' said David, 47, a prosperous banker.

Before he could complete his story, his chatty wife downplayed the symptoms: 'I think it's his excuse to want to appear single again!'

I smiled.

'Every few months, he says his shoes don't fit. He gets jazzier pairs, and also says he can't see clearly. So, he goes and buys a new set of glasses. His jaw is now prominent and he walks around like John Travolta. He speaks in this hoarse voice, trying to sound hot and all,' she concluded, placing her palms on the table to give me her final diagnosis. Just when I thought she was done, she added, 'Please ask him to lose weight.'

'Let me know if you remember anything else you're missing,' I said, turning my attention to the patient.

'My head hurts and I get tired quickly,' David said, 'and my vision is a bit blurry. I've suddenly grown all over and look like a giant in the mirror.' I held his hands as he outstretched them to gesticulate what he was describing.

The wife pulled out a picture of their wedding day from 15 years ago. He looked like another man. The difference was like that between David and Goliath, but they were the same person.

'You've got acromegaly,' I said, going straight to the point after an examination. The hormonal disorder develops when the pituitary gland produces excessive amounts of the growth hormone during adulthood. The bones and soft tissues increase in size, leading to the symptoms David described.

The pituitary or hormone-producing gland is the size of a pea and receives messages from the hypothalamus to stimulate all other hormone-producing glands. It, for instance, controls the thyroid, and tells the kidneys how much water to conserve by producing the vasopressin hormone.

I asked for an MRI of the brain, an eye check-up, and a battery of blood tests to see if any other hormone was affected. As he rose, David asked calmly, 'What do I do about the headache?'

'Stay away from her for a while!' I wanted to say as I scribbled a prescription.

They returned with the reports in a few days, hand-in-hand. As expected, the scan revealed a 3 cm tumour in the pituitary gland, pressing on his optic nerves, causing the diminution in vision. 'This tumour is producing all of the excess growth hormone,' I pointed out on the MRI, 'and we have to remove it with an operation because it is also pressing on your optic nerves.' The good bit was that we didn't need to open his head like neurosurgeons would've done a few decades ago. We could remove it from the nose using a specialized endoscope. Multiple questions later, they agreed to the surgery.

Medical experts believe that Goliath, the Philistine giant mentioned in the biblical *Book of Samuel*, also had pituitary adenoma, leading to his size.

The endoscope, when manoeuvred through the small structures of the nose that clean and humidify air, allows you to reach the base of the skull, where in a small depression of the bone resides the pituitary gland, smack between the carotid arteries, the main arteries supplying blood to the entire brain. Through the nostrils, we got a panoramic view as we took out multiple pieces of the tumour, removing it completely, making sure we preserved the normal gland, which looked a little firmer and more pinkish.

Every time I perform this operation, I think of my mentor Dr Ari Chacko who taught me this surgery, and sharing his exuberant enthusiasm on seeing the normal pituitary gland after removing a tumour aways makes me. I secretly wish someday I can operate like him.

We reconstructed the base of the skull and, within a few hours of the surgery, David confirmed that his vision appeared brighter. Three months later, he had lost the weight and his wife was delighted that the ring fit again. His growth hormone levels came back to normal. I told him he was cured but had to continue following up with me for the rest of his life.

'My headache is gone,' he said.

I looked at the wife, wondering if she had anything to say. 'I'm happy he's my David again, not Goliath.'

The Movers and Shakers

'I have a tremor in my hands,' Meenaben Shah explained as she stretched out both her arms in front of me and showed me her fingers gently and rhythmically twitching away as if she were playing a piano badly. She was a middle-aged Jain homemaker in her late fifties. 'When I have a cup of tea, my hands shake; when I'm stitching, I have a problem,' she continued in Gujarati. 'When I'm cooking and cleaning, it's alright,' she added, 'but when my husband gives me stress, it increases,' she said, looking at him with a hint of a smile.

I examined the tone in her limbs to ensure it wasn't rigid. Her hands were supple. There was no arthritis. Her grip was strong. She had impeccable sensations.

'This is called an essential tremor,' I explained, 'and it's not Parkinson's, which is what most people fear when they start shaking a little. Oftentimes, it's seen in the family, but this is nothing to worry about,' I comforted her. 'Do you drink?' I asked her straightforwardly, but she responded as though I had committed blasphemy. She crisscrossed her palms over her cheeks and pulled her tongue out and said '*Tauba, tauba!* [Good Heavens]' as if I had invoked the devil. 'I'm asking not because alcohol causes your hands to shake, but a small amount of *daaru* [alcohol] is the prescribed treatment for this tremor,' I shocked her with a broad smile.

'Give her problem to me, I will solve it,' her husband suggested. To justify his stance, he added, 'Just because we're vegetarian doesn't mean we cannot drink!'

I prescribed her some medication and asked her to see me in a month. 'If this doesn't work, we have a few other modalities we can try,' I told them as they left.

Surprisingly, around the same time, I saw another lady, an architect and designer, with the exact same problem – but it only affected her right side. 'My hand has this weird tremor; it's as if I don't have control over my movements. It's jerky and unsteady.' I got her to stretch out her arms and the right one drifted away with the hand curling up with some abnormal writhing. 'I was told that this is an essential tremor and nothing needs to be done, but that I should see you just in case,' she clarified.

I looked at her and said, 'I'm glad you took the "just in case" option because this is not an essential tremor.' We got an urgent MRI of the brain done to find a tumour sitting in her left thalamus and the areas around it responsible for movement. The next day, under general anaesthesia and using computer navigation to guide us, we made a hole in her head and took a biopsy of the tumour. It turned out to be a lymphoma that melted with a few cycles of chemotherapy, and her abnormal movements vanished. She was back to drawing straight lines without the aid of a ruler, moulding clay and making buildings.

I couldn't help recalling the vintage classic by John Napier simply titled, *Hands*. Originally published in 1980, Napier blends science and storytelling in the book, observing keenly that 'The hand at rest is beautiful in its tranquillity, but is infinitely more appealing in the flow of action.' As a surgeon, nothing makes more sense than this.

'I have severe pain in the left hand that I just feel like shaking off all the time,' another lady came to me. She was a stenographer. 'The pain zaps up and down the wrist and I've begun to notice numbness in my thumb and three fingers.'

'Do you have any pain in the neck going down your arm?' I asked, because sometimes this pain can be caused by a pinched nerve in the neck.

'No,' she replied.

'Then, in all likelihood, you have carpal tunnel syndrome,' I announced.

'I know. I've tried medication, wearing a splint, stopping my work – but nothing's helped. I need a new hand,' she begged.

We confirmed the diagnosis with a nerve conduction test. We ensured that she didn't have diabetes because diabetic neuropathy can also cause pain and burning in the hands, but often it's in both hands and the feet. We imaged her cervical spine to confirm there was no compression. A few days later, we took her to the operating room and made a small cut over her wrist, slicing the fascia that had entrapped the nerve and freeing it up completely. I wrapped up the hand in a roller bandage and tied a red ribbon round it, as if it was a gift and I was presenting her new hand to her. Afterwards, she was completely pain-free. It was the best present she had ever received, she said.

In that bizarre week, I saw another man who came to me with a wrist drop. One morning when he awoke, he could simply not extend his wrist, something as simple as what bikers do to rev the accelerator of their vehicle. He was a high-functioning lawyer, unable to come to terms with the idea that something so strange could happen to him. The look on his face was just as numb as his hand.

'Either you slept wrongly or there may be a mild viral infection of the nerve causing this. Or, you have diabetes,' I tried to explain. In all honesty, no one quite understands why this happens. On closely examining him, I realized he had a powerless grip, and while his elbow extension was faint as well, the rest of his arm had good strength. An MRI of the brain ruled out a stroke. 'You have a radial nerve palsy,' I told him. 'We'll give you a one-week course of steroids and you'll be fine,' I pronounced, having learnt about that magic potion from my neurologist. This is exactly what happened, and the next time I saw him, he was beaming. It reminded me of Napier again who, in his captivating edification, writes, 'When the hand is at rest, the face is at rest, but a lively hand is the product of a lively mind.'

The human hand is one of the most complex and fascinating anatomical structures we possess. Its dysfunction can result from myriad conditions affecting the brain and spine or the nerves that emanate from it. It can also be a local problem of the bones, joints, muscles and ligaments. It requires astute judgement to identify the problems that nature alone will heal and the ones we need to aggressively implement a cure for. Each hand has 27 bones and 30 muscles. Hands have the largest area dedicated to them within the brain compared to other body parts.

Our hands are an important part of who we are and how we see ourselves. What we do with them gives us our identity. Holding someone's hand eases pain, provides comfort and establishes connection. According to Tiffany Field, director of the Touch Research Institute, 'holding hands stimulates the vagus nerve, which decreases blood pressure and heart rate and puts people in a more relaxed state.'* Hands have a profound power to heal.

Meenaben came back a month later with her husband. 'My tremor is almost gone,' she told me happily. 'I can do everything

*Tiffany Field, 'Touch for Socioemotional and Physical Well-Being: A Review', Developmental Review, 30(4), 2010, pp. 367–383. https://doi.org/10.1016/j.dr.2011.01.001

I want to without being bothered by it!' she confirmed. We exchanged pleasantries, and just as they left, she peeked back into my office and shyly confessed, 'I did try the *daaru* [alcohol] you suggested, and I think it worked more than the medicines.' She tiptoed away.

The Grown-Up Soulmates

Homi, a plump Parsi *bawaji*, was the sole proprietor and owner of a printing press on Mohammad Ali Road. He carried out jobs for a retinue of steadfast clients he had built over decades. In the early 1970s, he befriended a lanky but like-minded bawaji, Firoze (fondly called Filly) who ran a similar business at Fountain. After they started working together, Homi (to Filly he was always bawaji) would visit Filly at his press every day to discuss the jobs on hand and chat in general about various topics under the sun. In the late 1970s, Homi sold his press and joined forces with Filly in Fountain. They trusted each other's judgement and respected the other's decisions implicitly.

Over the years, as happens with most good friendships, families got involved. They started visiting each other's homes for lunches and dinners. Although Homi stayed in town and Filly stayed in Vile Parle (out of town, for the uninitiated), home visits on Sundays became sojourns and picnics for their families. Filly's wife was an excellent cook and treated Homi's family to some mouth-watering dishes, the signature item being boiled eggs garnished with homemade spices. Both the buddies could gobble up a couple of eggs at any time of the day; Parsi, thy name is *eedu* [egg]. Filly also fancied a fruit salad dessert made by Homi's wife. So, every time the boys met, boiled eggs and fruit salad was always on the menu – such was their care and fondness for each other.

Homi's wife turned critically ill in 1992. Filly would come home daily and uplift their spirits. Just before she passed, she urged Filly to take care of Homi, and not only keep him company but also keep the press running so they would have something to be preoccupied with. Unfortunately, soon after, in the event of labour trouble for all presses around South Mumbai, they decided to stop their own printing operations and started contracting their work to presses around Worli and Parel. They also sold their premises and moved into a smaller office at Fountain, as there were no machines or labour to house. Filly would open the office by 11.00 a.m. and then sit there until around 4.00 p.m., when he would leave to beat the local train evening crowd. Homi would reach by around 1.00 p.m. and close the office around 6.00 p.m. That's how they shared responsibility and enjoyed their time with each other. They amplified each other's goodness through a boundless generosity of spirit.

In 2014, the landlord sent them a notice for a massive increase in rent, which made it impossible for them to continue their business. They shut shop. Their ink faded but the friendship blossomed. Filly visited Homi every alternate day at home at 2.00 p.m., and in case he missed a day, he would make up for it with an extra visit the next day, taking the train from Vile Parle to Grant Road well into his late eighties. They spoke about cricket, politics, TV serials, enlarged prostates and bowel movements. Both of them underwent surgeries over 2017–18 but their visits never ceased. Being a daily *agiari* [fire temple] goer, Filly would source out special prayers that would heal them sooner. Not only did they meet thrice a week, they also spoke to each other over the phone thrice a day, which they slowly scaled down due to fading auditory faculties to a daily call at 8.30 p.m. sharp. You could set the time on your watch hearing the phone ring in Homi's home. They were two antique pieces polishing each other's gold.

Is it rare in today's day and age for two perfectly heterosexual men in their nineties to arrive at the centre of a deep friendship? They may not be the 3.00 a.m. friends our generation boasts about, but they were 8.30 p.m. friends – for five decades. They were committed to each other just by being there for one another. It was no earth-shattering friendship, no hero's journey, no gallant acts of sacrifice. Just simple friends. Kind, selfless, committed ones. Their relationship was filled with love, connectedness and a mutual joy that was both wondrous and unbelievable. A touching serenade to the little things that add up to the largeness of love, harmony and devotion.

While most of us focus on committing to a vocation, marriage, faith or philosophy, few commit to deep friendships. We tend to get so tangled in mundane musings, Monday after Monday, that we don't invest in friends because of family, work and the routine prosaicness of life. But we should, because a great friendship is indeed one of life's crowning glories. 'For in the dew of little things,' says Kahlil Gibran on friendship, 'the heart finds its morning and is refreshed.'*

A few days before his ninety-third birthday, Homi's health started deteriorating. On 12 October, Filly had a fall. That day, the 8.30 p.m. phone call was longer than usual, detailing the events that led to it and questions to ask the doctor the next day. Medical notes were exchanged, and they ended the phone call wishing each other well. The next morning, Filly passed away unexpectedly. As Homi wasn't keeping too well himself, the family decided to withhold the news from him until they returned from the funeral. The main concern discussed was what to tell Homi when the phone didn't ring at 8.30 p.m. that day.

---

*Gibran, K. (1923). *The prophet*. Alfred A. Knopf.

He would be devastated. They decided to break the news to him gently, but when Homi's son returned home from the funeral that evening, he discovered that his father too had passed – into the sunset and onto the clouds, somewhere over the rainbow, to be with his best friend, without putting the family in a dilmma regarding how to break the news to him, because he already knew. No more local trains. No more phone calls. No more boiled eggs and fruit salad. Just an everlasting togetherness beyond time and space.

Acknowledgments

This book exists because one day, Tinaz Nooshian, the former editor-in-chief of *Mid-Day*, suggested I write a column for them. In doing so, they lit a match and enabled a dormant volcano to burst forth. I had no idea there were so many stories within me that I wanted to tell. I felt like I had truly arrived as an author when one of my articles in the paper went on to become the base on which my friend was served his bhelpuri, and he sent me a picture of it. *Mid-Day* allowed me to wander freely and creatively between burr holes and blurbs, and I am deeply grateful to them for allowing me to publish these essays. Chiki Sarkar and her team at Juggernaut were kind enough to accept my proposal, structure and edit this book, and print it at a brisk pace. If I had an agent, a manager or a secretary, I would thank them here too.

I first started writing – and still do – for the *Jam-e-Jamshed*, a Parsi newspaper whose editor, Shernaaz Engineer, had encouraged me to share my stories at a time when my travels and family were my only material. I hope that my daughters, who are currently 9 and 11 years old – neither of whom want to become doctors (because surgery is 'eww') – will read this book someday. To my entire family, both immediate and extended – thank you for being in my corner.

To the readers – the kind ones, the critical ones, the ones who stop me at airports, the ones I meet at weddings, parties, in hospital corridors, and occasionally at funerals – thank you. You have read stories about tumours and trauma over your morning chai and still chosen not to switch to the sports page. That is loyalty of the highest order.

Now to the real authors of this book: my patients, most of whom I believe I've helped and some of whom I've inadvertently hurt. Every story here begins with someone who walked into my clinic carrying fear, hope, denial, courage, Google or ChatGPT printouts and, occasionally a disgruntled mother-in-law. You trusted me with your head and heart, which are, objectively, the most dangerous organs to outsource. You allowed me into the most vulnerable corners of your lives. You taught me that science explains anatomy, but humanity explains everything else. These essays are inspired by you. They are not about you; they are because of you.

And then there is Dalzeen, because every writer needs an editor who can say, 'This paragraph is brilliant but unnecessary.' Dalzeen read every single one of these pieces, trimming redundant adjectives, calming dramatic flourishes and gently reminding me that not every sentence requires the word 'existential'. She has been my literary anaesthetist, putting to sleep any excess and appropriately awakening the clarity.

If at any point you feel overwhelmed while reading this book, pause and take a breath. Remember not to take life too seriously; no one's getting out of it alive. It's only bheja fry or brain stew. And I promise, no actual brains were harmed in the making of this book. Well. Almost none.